Theatre/Performance Historiography

Theatre/Performance Historiography

Time, Space, Matter

Edited by
Rosemarie K. Bank and Michal Kobialka

THEATRE/PERFORMANCE HISTORIOGRAPHY
Copyright © Rosemarie K. Bank and Michal Kobialka, 2015.
Softcover reprint of the hardcover 1st edition 2015 978-1-137-39729-4
All rights reserved.

First published in 2015 by
PALGRAVE MACMILLAN®
in the United States—a division of St. Martin's Press LLC,
175 Fifth Avenue, New York, NY 10010.

Where this book is distributed in the UK, Europe and the rest of the world, this is by Palgrave Macmillan, a division of Macmillan Publishers Limited, registered in England, company number 785998, of Houndmills, Basingstoke, Hampshire RG21 6XS.

Palgrave Macmillan is the global academic imprint of the above companies and has companies and representatives throughout the world.

Palgrave® and Macmillan® are registered trademarks in the United States, the United Kingdom, Europe and other countries.

ISBN 978-1-349-48488-1   ISBN 978-1-137-39730-0 (eBook)
DOI 10.1057/9781137397300

Library of Congress Cataloging-in-Publication Data

   Theatre-performance historiography : time, space, matter /
[edited by] Rosemarie K. Bank and Michal Kobialka.
   pages cm
Includes bibliographical references and index.

   1. Theater—Historiography. I. Bank, Rosemarie K., editor.
II. Kobialka, Michal, editor.

PN2115.T46 2015
792.09—dc23   2014038084

A catalogue record of the book is available from the British Library.

Design by Newgen Knowledge Works (P) Ltd., Chennai, India.

First edition: April 2015

10 9 8 7 6 5 4 3 2 1

Contents

List of Illustrations — vii

Introduction — 1
Rosemarie K. Bank and Michal Kobialka

Part I The Space of Formations

1 Performing Speciation: The Nature/Culture Divide at the Creation Museum — 17
   Angenette Spalink and Scott Magelssen

2 A Ridiculous Space: Considering the Historiography of the Theatre of the Ridiculous — 41
   Kelly Aliano

3 The Evolving Process of an Historical View: Aleks Sierz and British Theatre in the 1990s — 55
   Yael Zarhy-Levo

4 Latino/a Dramaturgy as Historiography — 75
   Patricia Ybarra

Part II Temporal Matter

5 The Design of Theatrical Wonder in Roy Mitchell's *The Chester Mysteries* — 95
   Patricia Badir

6 Performing *Ruhe*: Police, Prevention, and the Archive — 123
   Jan Lazardzig

7 The Materiality of Memory: Touching, Seeing, and Being the Past in Patricio Guzmán's *Chile, Memoria Obstinada* — 153
   Kaitlin M. Murphy

Part III Material Spaces

8 Adorno, Baroque, Gardens, Ruzzante: Rearranging Theatre Historiography 177
   Will Daddario

9 A Critique of Historio-scenography: Space and Time in Joseph-François-Louis Grobert's *De l'Exécution dramatique* 199
   Pannill Camp

10 The Ground of (Im)Potential: Historiography and the Earthquake 219
   Gwyneth Shanks

11 Thinking the Space(s) of Historiography: Latina/o Ethnicity Theatre 237
   Jon D. Rossini

Notes on Contributors 253

Index 259

Illustrations

1.1	Lucy at the Creation Museum	18
1.2	Man vs. Ape	23
1.3	Adam and Eve in the Garden of Eden	24
1.4	The first sacrifice	25
1.5	Lucy at the Cleveland Museum of Natural History	26
1.6	Primate phylogeny	28
1.7	Phylogeny depicting evolutionary relationship between *Homo sapiens* and Lucy	29
5.1	Title page of *The Chester Mysteries* printed and published by Egmont H. Arens for the Washington Square Bookshop, New York (1917)	103
5.2	*The Adoration of the Magi.* Typescript (f. 13)	105
5.3	Hart House production of *The Chester Mysteries* (1919)	109
5.4	J. E. H. MacDonald, *Untitled Drawing from Stage Set "The Chester Mysteries of the Nativity and Adoration"* (1919)	112
5.5	Christmas card designed and printed for Vincent and Alice Massey, 1922	114

Introduction

Rosemarie K. Bank and Michal Kobialka

In 1989, Thomas Postlewait and Bruce McConachie introduced their anthology *Interpreting the Theatrical Past: Essays in the Historiography of Performance* without defining "historiography." Forms of the word appear eight times in their introduction: once as "historiographic" (in the context of "historiographic problems and issues"); once as "historiographical" (in the context of "historiographical issues" the collection might raise); and six times as "historiography" (that "scholarship in historiography crosses many disciplines," that there is "a select bibliography that lists not only current studies in theatre historiography but also representative scholarship in cultural studies and general history," that R. W. Vince's essay "summarizes the history of theatre historiography," that Robert Sarlós offers a "methodological essay" in "a series that he has published on theatre historiography," that the contributors "were selected because of their current writing on theatre historiography," and that further "discussion on theatre historiography" and the application of "ideas on methodology and interpretation" by readers will, hopefully, follow). Of the bibliography referenced in the volume's introduction, the first section is headed "Theatre History: Methodology, Terminology, and Theory," the second "Art, Literary, and Cultural History: Methodology, Criticism, and Theory," and the third is headed "General Historiography: Methodology, Criticism, and Theory." No theatre historiographical scholarship is included in this last section (theatre scholarship appears in the first section—Sarlós's and Vince's works are here, and drama—where literary—is in the second bibliographic section). In 1989, then, theatre historiography could be perceived as apart from theatre history, cross-disciplinary (if not interdisciplinary), and synonymous with "methodology," "interpretation" (criticism), and "theory" (and, so, with "terminology" per se), given such statements in the introduction as "no single methodology or theory dominates this collection," that there are "various approaches to the study—that is, the historical interpretation [...] of the past," and that the essays "aim primarily to explore theoretical and methodologicalis sues."[1]

Interpreting the Theatrical Past captured an historical moment in which theatre studies were expanding to include under or unstudied subjects within theatre and without, in the United States and the world, through performance at its broadest parameters. At the same time, analytical strategies brought forward by a range of scholars and disciplines had suggested different ways to look at all these universes of study, some reflected in the 1989 collection, as in the present volume. Simultaneously, however, events were overtaking this expansion even as *Interpreting the Theatrical Past* was published. Joseph Donohue's essay registered the technological developments poised to swamp the archive as we knew it, while the fall of the Berlin Wall in November of 1989 drew a curtain across many of the materialist assumptions reflected in the volume and ushered in an age of geopolitics and global economics that would change theatre, scholarship, and the world. Most tellingly of all, these developments would underscore the problems created in theatre and performance scholarship by the absence of a "historiography" that is not conflated with "methodology," "interpretation," and/or "theory."

In the 26 years since 1989, of course, scholars have not failed to sustain an interest in historiography, recently Postlewait himself in *The Cambridge Introduction to Theatre Historiography* (2009) and *Representing the Past: Essays in Performance Historiography* (with Charlotte Canning; 2010), both discussed by contributors to this volume. We want to recoup a definition of historiography as the arrangement of the historical record. To that end, we called for essays that addressed theatre and performance history in terms of the historiography of time, space, and matter. We were motivated by the idea of materialism one finds, for example, in Walter Benjamin, who, writing about avant-garde performance in the 1920s, drew attention to objects in a state of unrest, that is, to objects that revealed dominant cultural formations in such a way that their forms and contents became readable.[2] We wanted essays to start with the materiality of an historical practice that, when examined, reveals the historiography of which it is made. Like Benjamin, we see historical materialism as an antidote to the "historicism" Benjamin discerned in von Ranke, Hegel, and others who placed objects in a narrative that freezes them in an interpretative matrix.³ Instead of applying historiography *to* historical subjects (rather than deriving historiography *from* them), we sought out work that saw the materiality of history as a state of unrest, of continuous change, a history that was not subject to methodology, that did not receive interpretation, that did not reflect or represent a theory applied to it, but exposed the presence of these in history (and historians). In short, we sought work that generated historiography, that saw history both as the thing studied and the way to study it. This quest reflects interests we articulated in 1991 in exploring spatial historiography for the *Journal of Dramatic Theory and Criticism*, finding in relativity and quantum mechanics both a vocabulary of concepts—for example, "discontinuity, indeterminacy, the limitations of traditional logic and language, elastic and multidirectional temporality"—and a way of thinking that helped articulate the instability of history.⁴

At the same time we sought a more direct examination of historical time and space and how these have been thought by our subjects and ourselves, we seemed to see the materiality of history in theatre historical investigations slide away and Benjamin's sense of "historicism" supply its place. Aware of Karl Marx's and Alfred Sohn-Rethel's exposure of capitalism's culture of abstraction,⁵ events since 1989 have highlighted capitalism's "fellow travelers" in methodologies, theories, and interpretations that fail to force into sight (or that forcefully obscure) the processes through which power and ideology work, indeed, a "new materialism" has emerged in an attempt to confront these "companions" and their usurpation of historical dialectics. It is not our task here to detail either classical or new materialism, but to make use of three (old and new) assumptions that bear upon how time, space, and matter may be understood in the context of this collection of essays. The first is the recognition that, while Newtonian mechanics was important for older version of materialism, today's materialism is shaped not only by Einstein's quantum mechanics and Heisenberg's uncertainty principle, but by the Higgs boson.⁶ Second, the technological advances spurred by new scientific models of matter, human and nonhuman, propel ethical and political questions to the fore, questions ranging from the genomic to surveillance to the distribution of drugs to facial profiling and the like. Third, new materialism testifies to a critical and nondogmatic reengagement with political economy—that is, with the relationship between the material details of everyday life and broader geopolitical and socioeconomic structures and their multitude of interconnected networks, through which social actors move.⁷ Let us take up the implications of these assumptions to the present context.

Time

The 2012 issue of *History and Theory* takes up the new metaphysics of time in the context of time within historical theory. Two trends are brought forth: the awareness of multiple temporalities (by Reinhart Koselleck) and a consideration of "presence" (by Eelco Runia). Koselleck understands early modernity as marking a shift from one experience of time and history to another, from history as a homogenous, unchanging space to history as an indefinite and unstoppable movement to which every historical object, every action, and every intention is subjected. "What is taking place," he writes, "is the temporalization of history, leading to the special kind of acceleration that characterizes our modern world."[8] At the threshold of modernity, history changes into a temporal process constantly moving from the past through the present and into the future. According to Koselleck, restless movement and the progress of modernity altered the idea of history for centuries to come. Koselleck draws attention to three modes of temporal experience: the irreversibility of events, the repeatability of events, and what he terms "the simultaneity of the non-simultaneous," suggesting through these three modes of time that historical events in the same space may have the same natural chronology, but totally different temporal organizations. Koselleck's theory of multiple temporalities, organized in the form of temporal layers that have different origins and duration and move at different speeds, is an alternative to the notion of time as empty, linear, and homogenous. Further, it suggests the futility of periodization.

Space

Eelco Runia's essay pursues "presence" by examining memorials and commemorations, which he sees as attempts to "be in touch"—either literally or figuratively—with people, things, events, and feelings that made you into the person you are. As in history, a transfer of "presence" occurs in these spaces deriving from such phenomena as the incorporation of original material (soil, wreckage, dust) or from naming. So viewed, Runia argues, it is not meaning a space transfers, but presence. Runia's argument for "presence" is derived from his thesis that "what is pursued in the Vietnam Veterans Memorial, in having a diamond made 'from the carbon of your loved one as a memorial to their [*sic*] unique life,' in the reading of names on the anniversary of the attack on the World Trade Center, in the craze for reunions, and in the host of comparable phenomena, is *not* 'meaning' but what for the lack of a better word [he] will call 'presence.'"[9]

Located outside of the philosophy of history, Runia's "presence" relates to Pierre Nora's "places of memory" project in its emphasis on the mechanics of discontinuity and the presence of absence that illuminate our capacity to "surprise ourselves." According to Runia, "Coming to grips with discontinuity requires an adjustment many philosophers of history will hesitate to make: to focus not on the past but on the present, not on history *as what is irremediably gone*, but on history *as ongoing process*" (8). Such a proposition suggests that both present-day reality and the discipline of history—the assemblage of texts, methods, codes, habits, topics, trends, fashion, and the like—offer themselves as *surfaces* that consist of different historical depths. These surfaces may be compared to a city:

> There are "structures" of all sizes and functions, some very old, some relatively new, some still under construction. Some parts of the city are booming, others lie fallow. Some parts are carefully restored, others are dilapidated. There are areas that once were destroyed by war (of which traces may or may not remain), areas that have been completely transformed by public works, areas in which "time has stood still." [...] I would not call such a city a palimpsest: a city is not *uniformly* written over, but locally, irregularly, opportunistically, erratically written over.[10]

Thus, to understand continuity and discontinuity or present-day reality and the discipline of history requires being able to walk around events. The trope of walking around the events, or of spatializing both events and time, gives new prominence to the distinction between a metaphor and metonymy. "Whereas premodern, metaphorical monuments are primarily engaged in a transfer of *meaning*, modern metonymical monuments concentrate on a transfer of *presence*."[11]

Matter

A framing of materiality in terms of new physics, biopolitical/bioethical concerns, and of current socioeconomic structures reconceptualizes time and space as nonsynchronic and noncontemporaneous. We would like to go further than that and suggest a theatre/performance historiography based neither in intracultural introspection nor in a science that is seen as a matter of categories or representations, but, rather, a theatre historiography of values. Instead of espousing a historiography fixed upon ideal historical narratives that "represent the past," we would like to target a historiography that occupies and produces time, space, and matter, that is, a historiography that *is* the time, the space, and the matter it takes. What would a historiography produced by history in this way look and sound like? It could not be the history of "what really happened," the goal of Zola's objective cultural scientist, today fused with more introspective, self-reflexive research perspectives. Rather, this theatre/performance historiography focuses upon the materiality of an historical event as it takes place in time and space. Were we to explore Harriet Beecher Stowe's 1852 novel *Uncle Tom's Cabin*, for example, we would take in the initial conditions of production and reception and the historiography of the event, how the understanding of the novel's appearance has been arranged, not only in the past, but down to our own times. The historiographic question in this would be what has been the mode of thinking produced by *Uncle Tom's Cabin*—and, clearly, this is not a matter of what the historical event represented, what cultures have thought of it, how *Uncle Tom's Cabin* represents the past, or what really happened in 1852, though all these are part of the materiality (or matter) of the subject. Rather, the historiography, the arrangement of the historical record that is "*Uncle Tom's Cabin*," becomes the focus of the investigation, the mode of thinking that allows us to take in apprehensions of the work as diverse as those that make Uncle Tom a hero and those that make him servile and cowardly.

In keeping with this view of historiography, we are interested in addressing the following topics in *Theatre/Performance Historiography: Time, Space, Matter*:

- How do theatre/performance historians analyze the historiographical methodologies that have been used to write theatrical and performance histories?
- How do they resituate theorizations of the archive, of periodization, and of the past within theatre/performance research such that they are historiographical (infrastructural), rather than signs of previously identified categories?
- How are the ethical implications of writing theatrical histories complicated in our current sociopolitical context, and what historiographical strategies are used to confront ethical issues?

In posing these questions, we were guided by a sentiment expressed by Giorgio Agamben in *Infancy and History* (1978; English version,

1993) that every conception of history is invariably accompanied by a certain experience of time (and we would add, space and matter), which is implicit in it, conditions it, and thereby needs to be elucidated.[12] As Albert Einstein put it, "Time and space are modes by which we think and not conditions in which we live."[13]

A historical practice that exhibits its mediality—space, time, and matter—will ask different questions than those being asked in 1989. Accordingly, this volume, almost 25 years after our opening gambit on spatial historiography, considers a historiography whose function is to *be* a mode of thinking, to explore how time, space, and matter mediate historical subjects. This exploration aims to expose the contradictions in the social and ideological organizations of historical subjects by establishing a different way of thinking about historiography, one that concerns how the historical record has been arranged and that challenges current social organizations of and ontologies about historical subjects. Agamben observed that the materiality and "situatedness" of thought in time and space accompanies every conception of history. As a mode of thinking, a material historiography offers a set of criticisms designed to reveal what the sources of those values have been, how they have come into being, what the relationships are that they have constituted, and to expose the powers they have secured.

* * *

The essays in this volume are divided into three parts: (1) the space of formations, (2) temporal matter, and (3) material spaces.

Part I, "The Space of Formations," focuses on historical narratives shaped by the concepts of space, time, and matter and how the space these formations occupy can be challenged by focusing upon how they "arrange the record." The essays explore the effects of power, of conservative Christianity, of biographically oriented "movement" formations, of critic-historians, and of economic politics and neoliberal ideology to shape our perceptions of performative subjects. The authors of these essays see multiple cultural forces at work in their subjects that create relations rather than "states of being" (such as, e.g., a single authority to mandate a view of creation, or of artists, or of a border).

In "Performing Speciation: The Nature/Culture Divide at the Creation Museum," Angenette Spalink and Scott Magelssen examine how the Creation Museum in Petersburg, Kentucky, and the website Answers in Genesis mobilize visitors' bodies to "bring to life" creationist ideologies. Spalink and Magelssen's historiographic approach looks to a Deluzio-Guattarian notion of the relationship between human and nonhuman animals not as a divinely ordained binary opposition, but as an affective state of human-becoming-animal and vice versa. They suggest that, rather than inhabiting a nature-culture binary, human and animal are discursive constructs grounded in their own particular historicities, even as they share a plane of immanence with each other. The museum's performances of the origins of time, space, matter, life, and biodiversity, they argue, relieve humans of accountability for treating other living creatures as equals and for solving the world's ecological problems.

In "A Ridiculous Space: Considering the Historiography of the Theatre of the Ridiculous," Kelly Aliano asks: how do we write about work that has been elided from theatre history? Do we simply insert it into the narrative of how drama developed? Is it necessary to carve out a specific location for the work, reconstructing the historical landscape in which it was once performed? This essay, grounded in Michel Foucault's notion of "heterotopic space," frames the Theatre of the Ridiculous as a literal and figurative movement (rather than as the product of specific artists working independently), a movement that took place in a specific space of representation (Greenwich Village, New York). By drawing attention to Foucault's heterotopia, Aliano contends that the history of and contradictory expressions about the Ridiculous can be recontextualized through a different understanding of the concept of space.

In "The Evolving Process of an Historical View: Aleks Sierz and British Theatre in the 1990s," Yael Zarhy-Levo examines how the critic and historian Aleks Sierz constructed a theatrical trend called *In-Yer-Face Theatre* to characterize British theatre in the 1990s. In subsequent related publications, Sierz seized the opportunity to maintain, reassess, modify, and transform his earlier perceptions and to secure the theatrical trend he had constructed. Sierz's subordination of theatre in the 1990s to his "in-yer-face" construct, Zarhy-Levo argues, serves a historiography of categories that affects how we perceive the time, the space, and the "matter" of that decade, and transforms a historical view into a dominant historical narrative.

Patricia Ybarra's "Latino/a Dramaturgy as Historiography" argues that playwright Victor Cazares's *Ramses Contra los Monstruos* (2011) writes a cultural historiography of neoliberalism in the United States and Mexico. Ybarra explores how *Ramses* stages the geopolitics of narcotrafficking and state violence in El Paso/Ciudad Juarez, from the

1980s to the present, as a queer history of the area, revealing transnational violence as temporally recursive and spatially deterritorialized. By avoiding writing this history as a series of clearly bounded sequential events, Ybarra demonstrates that Cazares opts for eschatology as a way to evade replicating neoliberal structures. Ybarra takes up the challenge of thinking of historiography as a strategy within contemporary Latino/a dramaturgy that, by collapsing time, space, and matter, brings to the fore discrete oppressions rather than neoliberalism's reparative history.

Part II, "Temporal Matter," explores the polychronic and multitemporal construction of archival matter, and how it becomes a source of aesthetic memory. The archive is a place of presence and absence. Material memory and memory matter studied together reveal a historiography that exposes when systems fail. Because the difference between describing a state of affairs (e.g., a state of terror, a state of policing) and experiencing it is so great, aesthetics are put in motion that produce memories in spectators that actually change them. It is a new materiality that abandons critical categories for practices in such a way that the historian and the archive step into the place of the historical subject.

In "The Design of Theatrical Wonder in Roy Mitchell's *The Chester Mysteries*," Patricia Badir unmoors our understanding of the Chester play by placing it in conversation with an archive that documents a revival staged in the early twentieth century. Badir suggests that the archive poses the interplay between motion and stillness as a modality for revitalizing our understanding of theatrical wonder in the medieval play. Likewise, the medieval text provides appropriate material for a theatrical modernism seeking to explore alternative spiritualities by releasing the iconic materialities of religious plays from the restraints of late-nineteenth-century antiquarianism. Badir concludes that the medieval play and the archive of its revival, when placed in proximity with each other, lose their affiliations with a particular time and place and become multitemporal entities that stage an encounter between different materialities, chronologies, and spatialities.

Using Jacques Derrida's theory of the archive, Jan Lazardzig's "Performing *Ruhe*: Police, Prevention, and the Archive" focuses upon the creation of police censorship archives in Vienna and Berlin at the beginning of the nineteenth century. Different practices of audience control and pastoral surveillance become visible against the backdrop of the German eighteenth-century theatre reform movement, which, in endeavoring to redefine theatre as the performance of a literary text, made it accessible to theatre censorship. Lazardzig argues that a regime of *Ruhe* (peace, calm) mediated between the effectiveness of the stage and the state's desire to preserve peace, order, and security in the public sphere. This regime can be seen as the "nomological principle" of police censorship archives.

In "The Materiality of Memory: Touching, Seeing, and Being the Past in Patricio Guzmán's *Chile, Memoria Obstinada*," Kaitlin M. Murphy analyzes Chilean filmmaker Patricio Guzmán's 1996 film, *Chile, Memoria Obstinada*, arguing that the film uses diverse visual and performative historiographic strategies to make targeted interventions into Chile's postdictatorship memory. Through an exploration of how the film navigates and maps memory, and the tactics the filmmaker employs to engage with national consciousness and cultural memory, Murphy considers how the very *matter*—the materiality—of memory functions as a historiographical strategy and turns the film into a strategic historiographical project that engages with individual and collective memory *through* embodied and visual memory matter, challenging and transforming the role of the past in the present.

Part III, "Material Spaces," draws attention to how theatre historical space, constructed from an encounter with fragments and displaced matter, exposes a historiography that unsettles (rather than confirms) the notion of historical fixity. Approached in a dialectical materialist way, historical subjects yield up their contradictions and "unintentional realities," their contingencies and (im)potential, indeed, they demonstrate the futility of reducing materiality to representation at the same time they show the power of the material spaces historical subjects occupy.

Will Daddario's "Adorno, Baroque, Gardens, Ruzzante: Rearranging Theatre Historiography" mobilizes a historiographical practice that embraces the materiality of the encounter with historical events and the act of thinking those events. Framed by the philosophy of Theodor W. Adorno, Daddario develops a practice capable of tuning in to the scraps and shards of historical material that linger at the fringes of discourses surrounding the Baroque and the theatre practice of Angelo Beolco, known as Ruzzante (*ca.* 1502–1542). In Daddario's investigation, Ruzzante becomes an artist who "baroques," one who reveals the contradictions active within the spaces of his performances and provokes his audiences with an off-kilter attack on reigning ideologies. Daddario ponders the possibility of creating a theatre historiography that "baroques" static modes of thinking about the archive, temporal periodization, and theatrical space.

In "A Critique of Historio-Scenography: Space and Time in Joseph-François-Louis Grobert's *De l'exécution dramatique*," Pannill Camp argues that that theatre, by synthesizing particular experiences of space, promotes historically contingent understandings of space and its relationship to time. These understandings, in turn, generate ideas about space and time that hold sway in extratheatrical domains. Historians adopt these conceptions and render them into premises for statements about historical theatre space. The result is historical writing about theatre that treats its objects of inquiry affirmatively without attention to the way those objects have surreptitiously informed the writers' own understanding of space. Camp elaborates a critique of this tendency with particular attention to Jacques-François-Louis Grobert's rationalized theory of theatre space in the early nineteenth century and proposes a means to overcome the resulting parallax by applying Adorno's concept of nonidentity in historical cognition.

In "The Ground of (Im)Potential: Historiography and the Earthquake," Gwyneth Shanks theorizes the temporal and material stakes of historiography through the analytic of the earthquake. Grounding the essay in the 1906 San Francisco earthquake, Shanks interweaves her family's archive of the event and municipal and national narratives about the earthquake with Giorgio Agamben's notion of (im)potentiality, to propose the idea of historiography-as-earthquake. Historiography-as-earthquake disrupts the notion of historical fixity and grapples with a mode of reality making that plays between the space of potential and (im)potential, the still ground and the shaking earth.

In "Thinking the Space(s) of Historiography: Latina/o Ethnicity Theatre," Jon D. Rossini argues for a rethinking of the practice of theatre historiography that does not figure a representation of the past as its logical endpoint. He suggests that this focus on representation emerges from a desire to fix things in place, and replicates problematic conceptions of identity, reducing concepts such as ethnicity to forms of representation, rather than modes of thinking or engaging with the world. Using Kristoffer Diaz's *Welcome to Arroyo's*, Rossini demonstrates the possibility to think otherwise about historiography by developing a historiography that, rather than moving us toward representation and provisional fixity, makes us consider ethnicity not as a category or condition of identity formation, but as potential emerging from the possibilities of an historical space and its material content.

* * *

It has been our intention to offer readers historical work that varies in how, historiographically, it approaches its subject. To this end, we recruited contributors across the academic spectrum of theatre historians, graduate students through full professors, whose interest in theatre historiography was reflected in a scholarship that uses historiography to illuminate a theatre historical subject. Our purpose was not to engage the ageing dispute between modernists and postmodernists (what else would we be but reflections of our times and spaces?), but to demonstrate the range of contemporary historiographies theatre historians now illuminate. Accordingly, rather than striving to include subjects and milieus because they demonstrate a desire to be done with Eurocentric thought and historiography, the essays in this collection work against centrism by understanding historiography as the encounter with a material "Other" that forces the historiographer to acknowledge his/her own temporal and spatial materiality. Superficial gestures of "inclusiveness," Timothy Brennan reminds us, can become "a simple way of conveying the reality of the other realm in a milieu of oppressive universality while employing alien terms and strategies of verbal circumnavigation to evoke what lies outside the vision of the dominant."[14]

The essays in this collection focus on disclosing how particular modes of thinking have been embedded in our perceptions of time, space, and matter and how those modes have been shaped to serve political, cultural, and ideological agendas. We hope they will provide a much needed corrective to a theatre/performance historiography that dislodged its own presence in favor of the pursuit of "methods," "theories," "interpretations," and "representations," a presence that has always been IN the matter of history itself. As Michel de Certeau observes:

> To think [...] is to pass through; it is to question that order, to marvel that it exists, to wonder what made it possible, to seek in passing over its landscape traces of the movement that formed it, to discover in these histories supposedly laid to rest "how and to what extent it would be possible to think otherwise."[15]

Notes

1. *Interpreting the Theatrical Past: Essays in the Historiography of Performance*, eds. Thomas Postlewait and Bruce McConachie (Iowa City: University of Iowa Press, 1989). The quotations in this paragraph will be found in this volume on pp.ix–xi.
2. See, for example, Benjamin's extensive writings on the production, reproduction, and reception of the work of art; on image and script-image; on paintings

and graphics; on photography; on film; or on the publishing industry and radio published in a collection *The Work of Art in the Age of its Technological Reproducibility and Other Writings on Media*, eds. Michael W. Jennings, Brigid Doherty, and Thomas Y. Levin (Cambridge, MA: Harvard University Press, 2008).
3. For Benjamin's distinction between historicism of von Ranke and Hegel and historical materialism, see Walter Benjamin, "Eduard Fuchs: Collector and Historian," *The Essential Frankfurt School Reader*, eds. Andrew Arato and Eike Gebhardt (New York: Continuum, 2002), 225–53.
4. See Rosemarie Bank, "Time, Space, Timespace, Spacetime: Theatre History in Simultaneous Universes," and Michal Kobialka, "Inbetweeness: Spatial Folds in Theatre Historiography," *Journal of Dramatic Theory and Criticism* 5:2 (Spring 1991): 65–84; 85–100.
5. Karl Marx, *A Contribution to the Critique of Political Economy* (New York: International Publishers, 1970), 206; and Alfred Sohn-Rethel, *Intellectual and Manual Labour: A Critique of Epistemology*, trans. Martin Sohn-Rethel (London: Macmillan, 1978).
6. There exist different models in physics that describe the material world—from the world made of atoms to the world made of protons, neutrons, and electrons, and finally quantum quarks and leptons. However, the universe, and the material world in which we exist, according to the standard model developed in the 1970s, does not only contain matter, but also forces that act upon that matter. In this model, our entire universe is made of 12 different matter particles and 4 forces. Among those 12 particles, there are: 6 quarks, which make up protons and neutrons, and 6 leptons, which include the electron and the electron neutrino, its neutrally charged counterpart. Among those four forces, there are: gravitational force, electromagnetic force, strong force, and weak force. The scientists think each one of those four fundamental forces has a corresponding carrier particle, or boson (known as the Higgs boson), which acts upon matter. The Higgs boson is described as weights anchored to the matter particles that generate them. In the standard model, matter does not inherently have mass without the Higgs boson. All particles gain mass by passing through a field. This field, known as a Higgs field, affects different particles in different ways: photons slide through unaffected, while W and Z bosons get bogged down with mass. In fact, assuming the Higgs boson exists, everything that has mass gets it by interacting with the all-powerful Higgs field, which occupies the entire universe. Consequently, "matter" is generated only by interacting with the field—the Higgs field—which affects matter in different ways. Thus, the property of matter is not stable, but its properties are both acquired and altered when matter interacts with the field. For more information see, for example, Robert Oerter, *The Theory of Almost Everything: The Standard Model, the Unsung Triumph of Modern Physics* (New York: Plume, 2006); Ian and James Randerson, "What Is the Higgs boson?" *The Guardian*, December 13, 2011: http://www.guardian.co.uk/science/2011/dec/13/higgs-boson-lhc-explained.
7. *New Materialisms: Ontology, Agency, and Politics*, eds. Diana Coole and Samantha Frost (Durham, NC: Duke University, 2010), 7–24.

8. Reinhart Koselleck, quoted in Helge Jordheim, "Against Periodization: Koselleck's Theory of Multiple Temporalities," *History and Theory* 51 (May 2012):158.
9. Eelco Runia, "Presence," *History and Theory* 45 (February 2006): 5. Subsequent references in this paragraph will be noted as page numbers in the text.
10. Ibid., 9; emphasis in the original.
11. Ibid., 17; emphasis in the original.
12. Giorgio Agamben in *Infancy and History*, trans. Lize Heron (London: Verso, 1993),91.
13. A. Forsee, *Albert Einstein: Theoretical Physicist* (New York: Macmillan, 1963), 81. For discussion of these theories and experiments, see, e.g., Max Jammer, *Concepts of Space* (Cambridge, MA: Harvard University Press, 1969); Milič Čapek, *The Philosophical Impact of Contemporary Physics* (New York: Van Nostrand Reinhold Company, 1961); Stephen Kern, *The Culture of Time and Space* (Cambridge, MA: Harvard University Press, 1983).
14. Timothy Brennan, *Borrowed Light: Vico, Hegel, and the Colonies* (Redwood City: Stanford University Press, 2014), 12.
15. Michel de Certeau, *Heterologies: Discourse on the Other*, trans. Brian Massumi, foreword by Wlad Godzich (Minneapolis: University of Minnesota Press,1986), 194 .

I

The Space of Formations

1

Performing Speciation: The Nature/Culture Divide at the Creation Museum

Angenette Spalink and Scott Magelssen

This essay concerns the historiographic constructions of time, space, and matter as produced and performed by Answers in Genesis, a nonprofit Christian apologetics ministry, in its Creation Museum, "[a] state-of-the-art 70,000 square foot museum" in Petersburg, Kentucky. The museum "brings the pages of the Bible to life"[1] by steering its visitors through slick displays and interactive exhibits, effectively mobilizing visitors' bodies to "bring to life" the story of young-earth creationism, a literal interpretation of Judeo-Christian scriptures that maintains the earth is only a little over six thousand years old. Creation Museum visitors find not only biblical simulations with animatronic dinosaurs sharing the garden of Eden with Adam and Eve, they also encounter a reconstruction of "Lucy," the hominid fossil scientists identify as an early ancestor of contemporary humans (figure 1.1). Rather than standing upright like an early human, however, the Creation Museum's figure hunches in a simian pose, knuckles dragging, spine parallel to the ground. Through exhibits like Lucy, the museum, while recognizing the existence of fossils as evidence of life forms that no longer inhabit the earth, positions itself against science's view of the earth as billions of years old, and of the earth's life forms—especially human beings—as the current state of millions of years of evolutionaryc hange.

The Lucy exhibit is an example of the Creation Museum's view of a divinely ordained separation between humans and animals, both a cause and a symptom of an entrenched discursive divide between nature and

Figure 1.1 Lucy at the Creation Museum. Photo by Scott Magelssen.

culture, traceable to the time of the composition of Genesis. Lest anyone believe that human and nonhuman animals exist on a continuum or share a genealogy, the Lucy exhibit, along with depictions of the Fall and Noah's Ark, reifies the biblical mandate that Man shall have dominion over the earth. The anthropocentric striation of humans and animals into hierarchical tiers across time relieves humans of accountability for not treating other living creatures as equals, and, by extension, for not addressing the world's ecological problems. Given current threats to the earth and its atmosphere, such a position is anathema to a more progressive position, which recognizes the potential for the Creation Museum's cosmology to sanction irreparable damage to the earth. The purpose of this essay is not, however, to advocate for more progressive conceptions of time, space, and matter that seek to erase such discursive constructions, but, rather, to discuss the ways in which these conceptions—and, indeed, counterpositions—are maintained, performed, and policed by particular institutions or languages of intelligibility. To engage this discussion is to recognize that the historiographic systems put into practice by the Creation Museum not only perpetuate damaging perceptions of the cosmos, they serve corporate, political, and religious agendas.

Theatre and performance scholars have established a fruitful academic foundation from which to launch an analysis of the performance practices of the Creation Museum. John Fletcher's *Preaching to Convert: Evangelical Outreach and Performance Activism in a Secular Age* places the practices of the Creation Museum (which he describes as a blend of *Jurassic Park* and the Smithsonian) in the category of activist performance—an evangelical strategy to win over and convert the hearts and minds of audience members in a global theological war. An even larger function of these performances, however, is to reify the beliefs of many Creation Museum visitors, namely, that God's unalterable word is the more fundamental truth. Fletcher identifies this logic as "preaching to the converted."[2] In *Sensational Devotion: Evangelical Performance in Twenty-First Century America*, Jill Stevenson posits that the Creation Museum, and other performative enterprises that share the museum's political and religious agendas, engage in what she calls "evangelical dramaturgy," a set of practices "designed to foster embodied beliefs that respond to specific devotional needs and priorities." These practices, contends Stevenson, "constitute a worldview even as they reinforce it."[3] In addition to the discussions offered by Fletcher and Stevenson, we maintain that an analysis of the historiographic constructions of time, space, and matter is fundamental to understanding the performances of the Creation Museum, thus we interrogate here the Creation Museum's performative exhibition practices by engaging conceptions of time, space, and matter as informed by the philosophy of immanence advanced by Gilles Deleuze and Felix Guattari. We then use these conceptions to expose and critique the systems by which the Creation Museum understands and presents the world.

With the editors and other contributors to this volume, we recognize that time, space, and matter are not only produced by historiography, but that the historiographic project occupies and *is* the time, space, and matter it produces. We understand time to be the mode of thinking by which we assimilate and structure events into narrative order. We take matter (in the present context) to refer to the materiality of the cosmos, and the ways in which that materiality is categorized and policed vis-à-vis time and space by institutional practices. In this regard, we offer a couple of different conceptions of space. One is the way we understand the abstraction of time as occupying a spatial trajectory (a line, a plane, an intersection or fold, etc.). The other is the arena in which discursive constructions are performed and activated in an institutional "place" (here, the Creation Museum). The popular paradigmatic apprehension of time is structured by a Cartesian and Hegelian linearity in which events occur along a linear continuum of precise and homogenous instants, and the accumulation of these instants over elapsed time gives a forward pitch to past, present, and future.[4] Deleuze and Guattari focus upon the constructedness of these conceptions and position our understanding of the past not as a line of development, as it is apprehended in the Cartesian/Hegelian model, but as a field or plane that contains all possibilities. History and time, that is, the past and present, are all part of the same plane. Events do not happen as the culmination of chains of cause-and-effect, but emerge at spatial "junctures" within the field. In these spatial terms, the event and the state of affairs meet and intersect as two vectors: the vector of the multiplicity of possibilities of events and the vector of the multiplicity of states of affairs. The states of affairs actualize the event at the juncture between the two vectors, and the event, in turn, absorbs the states of affairs. Neither the event nor the state of affairs can be reduced to itself, as if apart from its other term in the relation, because "a state of affairs cannot be separated from the potential through which it takes effect and without which it would have no activity or development."[5] The event, in other words, is the actualization of a multiplicity of possibilities within a state of affairs.

In this philosophy, to conceive of distinct and autonomous categories of plants, animals, humans, and other organisms appearing in sequential order through a kind of linear process of causality is untenable. Rather, plants, animals, humans, and other organisms are perceived as sharing a plane of immanence and as existing in various and continued states of becoming. Using a historiographic approach to the past informed by the Deluzio-Guattarian notion of "human-becoming-animal," we suggest that, rather than inhabiting a nature-culture binary, human and animal are discursive constructs grounded in their own particular historicities. "Affects are precisely these non-human becomings of man," write Deleuze and Guattari in *What Is Philosophy?*[6] Philosophy, they continue, is an exploration of the virtual possibilities of what things are capable of *becoming* and the ways in which they are capable of transforming, and science is that which is concerned with the actualization of the virtual, exploring the "states of affairs" and the means by which these actual concrete bodies relate to other material objects.

"States of affairs" actualize an event or concept, concretizing a virtual possibility or *becoming* that resided in the plane of immanence. Deleuze and Guattari describe states of affairs as "actualities, even though they may not yet be bodies or even things, units, or sets. They are masses of independent variables, particles-trajectories or signs-speeds."[7] In the case at hand, these variables might include the range of biological taxa diffused across a geographical landscape at a specific temporal snapshot, the spatial and temporal relationships between these taxa, and the conditions that shape the materiality of biological forms and enable them to shift and change. It follows that, in a philosophy of immanence, we apprehend both humans and animals as concepts on the plane of immanence that have become/are becoming actualized through intersections with these "states of affairs," thus moving from the realm of the virtual and philosophical to the scientific. Scientists understand the materialization of these events through the theory of evolution.

Conceiving of time, space, and matter through a philosophy of immanence discloses not only the ways in which the Creation Museum hews to conceptions of time, space, and matter informed by a literalist interpretation of the Bible, but also discloses how this view has been forced through the lens of the linear, forward-moving chronology dominant in Western thought since the nineteenth century. In this vein, Ken Ham, the founder of Answers in Genesis, maps the Hebrew Scriptures onto a linear, progressive timeline, beginning with Creation and proceeding to the second coming of Christ, which will initiate a new Heaven and Earth. This process involves forcing often stylistically disparate and contradictory scriptural passages into discrete sequential events in order to function as a literal chronology of Creation. Ham can, thereby, write on the Answers in Genesis website that "the Bible—the 'history book of the universe'—provides a reliable, eye-witness account of the beginning of all things, and can be trusted to tell the truth in all areas it touches on. Therefore, we are able to use it to help us make sense of this present world."[8]

"Making sense," in Ham's case, hinges on a reification of the nature-culture divide. A material practice that draws a bold line between human and nonhuman animals and plants[9] allows the Creation Museum to extricate humans from nature, relegating the latter to beyond "nature-culture borderlands."[10] Man, in the museum's epistemology, is separate and distinct in the world in which he lives. He has been given dominion to rule over the Earth and every living organism therein. This epistemology is traced back to the creation account in the book of Genesis:

> So God created man in his *own* image, in the image of God created he him; male and female created he them. And God blessed them, and God

said unto them, Be fruitful and multiply, and replenish the earth, and subdue it: and have dominion over the fish of the sea and the fowl of the air, and over every living thing that moveth upon the earth. And God said, Behold, I have given you every herb bearing seed, which *is* upon the face of all the earth, and every tree, in the which *is* the fruit of a tree yielding seed; to you it shall be for meat.[11]

Historian Lynn White, Jr., posits that the "roots" of the human-caused ecological crises in the West can be tracked to the cosmology laid out in this and other passages in Genesis. "What people do about their ecology," he writes, in his groundbreaking 1967 essay in *Science* magazine, "depends on what they think about themselves in relation to things around them. Human ecology is deeply conditioned by beliefs about nature and destiny—that is, by religion."[12] According to White, the status given to Man in the Genesis creation account ordains him to oversee nature from a position of authority (as God's designee), furthering his dominion through a process of divinely extended nomination: "Man named all the animals," White writes, "thus establishing his dominance over them. God planned all of this explicitly for man's benefit and rule: no item in the physical creation had any purpose save to serve man's purposes. And, although man's body is made from clay, he is not simply part of nature; he is made in God's image."[13] The concept of the nature-culture divide, unsurprisingly, has likewise shaped historiography. As Dipash Chakrabarty points out, the very notion that humans and the rest of the natural world could share a role as the object of a historical account has largely been inconceivable. "Philosophers and students of history," writes Chakrabarty, "have often displayed a conscious tendency to separate human history—or the story of human affairs, as R. G. Collingwood put it—from natural history, sometimes proceeding even to deny that nature could ever have history quite in the same way humans have it."[14]

The material divide between human and nature is announced and reinforced in the Creation Museum's Walk through History and its sequential displays and dioramas, a linear trajectory that strategically and calculatingly barrages the visitor with a creationist apologetics. This is by no means a new strategy. "History exhibitions," writes museum critic Timothy W. Luke, drawing on the work of Michel Foucault, "formalize norms of how to see without being seen."[15] An early exhibit visitors encounter upon entering the museum is a glass display case housing the articulated skeletons of a human and a chimpanzee. The human skeleton is arranged in a slight contrapposto, appearing to be absorbed in a Bible held in its upstage hand. The chimpanzee skeleton hunches at the human's feet, its bestial, fanged skull barely higher than its shoulder blades, its gaze fixed vaguely off set (figure 1.2). A placard on the display's backdrop proclaims in large lettering, "Man vs. Ape," and underneath it reads:

> What is the most striking difference you see between the human and chimpanzee in this display? Only humans are made in the image of God and are able to communicate with Him. God communicates with man through His Word, and we communicate with God through our prayers. Animals were not given such ability. In contrast, the anatomy of humans and chimps...is basically similar. Nearly every bone in this human skeleton can be found in a similar form and position in the chimpanzee skeleton...Such a similarity in parts between different kinds of creatures is called *homology*. Evolutionists attribute homology to common ancestry, but creationists attribute homology to a common Creator, reflecting common design principles to meet common needs.[16]

Figure 1.2 Man vs. Ape. Photo by Scott Magelssen.

With the signage, props, and deliberate positioning of the skeletal specimens mediating the visitor's reception of the display, the Creation Museum immediately establishes that the ability of humans to communicate with God distinguishes them from animals, and that they are (and have always been) superior to all other animals, despite physical andanatom icals imilarities.

Visitors continue through the permanent exhibition to the Walk through History exhibit, followed by a series of animated tableaux featuring the events of Genesis. Here, they encounter Adam and Eve in paradise, at Creation's outset, living side by side with the gentle dinosaurs and other animals (all of whom at this stage eat only plants), free from pain or danger (figure 1.3). Poison, carnivorism, suffering, and death have not yet been created and, therefore, are all outside the realm of cognition.[17] The dioramas take a marked turn after Eve seduces her companion with the forbidden fruit. Indeed, the very next exhibit depicts the haggard and aged figures of a clothed Adam and Eve standing over two grisly lambs they have sacrificed and skinned (figure 1.4). The placard accompanying the diorama states: "God killed animals to provide skins to cover Adam and Eve. This was the

Figure 1.3 Adam and Eve in the Garden of Eden. Photo by Scott Magelssen.

Performing Speciation   25

Figure 1.4   The first sacrifice. Photo by Angenette Spalink.

first sacrifice to cover their sin. For centuries, animals would continue to be sacrificed for sin. But because humans are not related to animals, animal sacrifices cannot take away sin. They can only cover it temporarily."[18] In *The Anatomy of Disgust*, William Ian Miller asserts that clothing "marks us off from savage and beast and from one another by rank or status, gender and age. Without clothing, man and woman were unaccommodated, unfit, unlocatable in the cultural order."[19] The animal skins in the display mark Adam's and Eve's bodies as hierarchically above animals and other organisms, clothing Adam's and Eve's bodies with the new order that reminds humans that they are separate from nonhuman animals. The lambs function as literal scapegoats in the exhibit, providing penance for human sin, but deferring forgiveness until the sacrifice of Jesus Christ, some four thousand years(downthe lin e)inthe futur e.

Every aspect of the Creation Museum reifies the human-nature divide, on either side of which it accords humans and animals their respective realms. To accomplish this, the museum must account for evidence of hominids early in the fossil record. It does so by adroitly taking advantage of debate within the paleontological community.

The Creation Museum's Lucy exhibit depicts her as "ape-like," positioned on all fours and covered with hair from head to toe (figure 1.5). Pictures and renderings of other Lucy reconstructions are scattered beneath her body, however, encouraging visitors to regard Lucy's claim to human ancestry as a matter of doubt. The museum's own position is reinforced by such tactics as an illustration depicting Lucy dangling from a branch, marking her as an ape-like animal, while a placard at Lucy's feet affirms that "biblical Creationists believe that humans and apes were never related, so we naturally conclude that [Lucy] was not on her way to becoming human."

In an article posted on the Answers in Genesis website, Dr. Elizabeth Mitchell, author of the site's weekly News of Note feature, and Dr. David Menton, a frequent contributor of web-posts and speaker at the Creation Museum, challenge the idea of Lucy "becoming human" or what they consider a linear "molecules to man" evolution. They cite disagreements about Lucy's fossil record, challenges to carbon dating procedures, and the ways in which paleontologists have arranged and

Figure 1.5 Lucy at the Cleveland Museum of Natural History. Photo by Angenette Spalink.

rearranged the construction of her skeletal parts to arrive at a picture of an early bipedal hominid that eventually evolved into *Homo sapiens*.[20] Mitchell and Menton provide interpretations of Lucy's fossil remains by paleontologists who configure the hips and pelvis to the legs and spine to resemble those of a contemporary ape (like that shown in the Lucy exhibit in the Creation Museum). For the Creationists Mitchell and Menton, nothing in the Lucy fossils or other recent paleontological discoveries in sub-Saharan Africa testify to anything other than "some long ago deaths." Given these disagreements about Lucy's fossil remains, to them, Lucy does not present any threat to the conviction that God created Adam and Eve and the animals on the same day, without using evolution. Instead, they assert that

> faith should be grounded in a correct understanding of Scripture and a discernment of the difference between *observations* of the fossils and *interpretations* about them. Lucy's anatomy may suggest a gait that differed somewhat from that of the chimp, but on its best day it was not actually bipedal. In fact, her anatomy is quite consistent with that of a knuckle-walker. But even if Lucy and her cousins had a more versatile anatomy than some other apes, tiptoeing through the jungle didn't make anything ape-like turn into a person. Nothing could.[21]

For Mitchell and Menton, and the Creation Museum, the fossil evidence demonstrates that Lucy is an animal and not a human ancestor, and attempts to make her anything else are exercises in human error.

While the Creation Museum demonstrates its particular classification of what it constitutes as human and as animal in several displays located throughout the museum, the divide is most blatantly presented in the placard displayed with the Lucy exhibit. It is here that the Creation Museum shows the discursive slip in its conceptions of time, space, and matter. Without a literal mention of early hominids in Genesis to fall back upon, the museum must resort to contesting science's claim that Lucy was a human relative and catalog her, instead, with other animals. To do so, the museum misrepresents "Man's Word" (i.e., science) as holding to the same Cartesian-Hegelian notion of time as a causal linear trajectory to which the museum subscribes. The phrase "becoming human" on the placard suggests evolutionary processes are a linear, progressive, unidirectional movement, while the placard also insinuates that human evolution is progressing toward a highly advanced, completed state, that is, the top of the ladder.[22] Ladder-thinking is in concord with Hegelian empiricism, in which monological instants can be mapped onto a Cartesian timeline that moves from simple to complex, where complex represents Progress. It is a fallacious and unhelpful paradigm that results in regarding evolutionary relationships as hierarchical, with nonhuman animals and plants occupying lower tiers on the march toward evolutionary perfection.

Evolutionary biologists do not understand evolutionary relationships between species as a linear progression, rather, they conceive of the continual process of evolution in a manner closer to the Deleuzio-Guattarian philosophy of immanence. Science is concerned with those spatial junctures at which concepts become actualized in states of affairs. Thus, evolutionary biologists represent evolutionary relationships over time with divaricating and branch-like visual diagrams called phylogenies. Phylogenies or "tree-thinking" images depict evolutionary relationships united by common ancestors, wherein any taxon can be linked to any other solely on the basis of common ancestry. The degree of relatedness is determined by molecular and morphological evidence (figure 1.6). In a simple phylogeny, Lucy and a human would be connected to a third taxon, but not directly to each other, depicting a common descent consistent with evolutionary theory (figure 1.7). The University of California Museum of Paleontology explains evolutionary descent as follows:

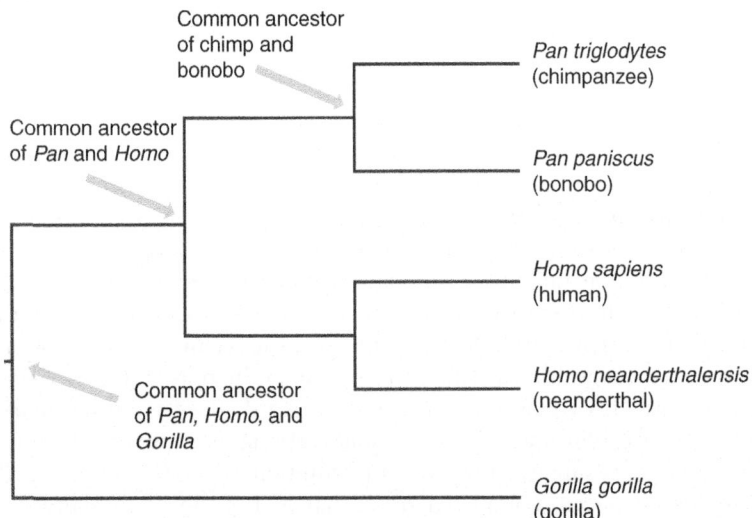

Figure 1.6 Primate phylogeny. Image by Daniel Spalink.

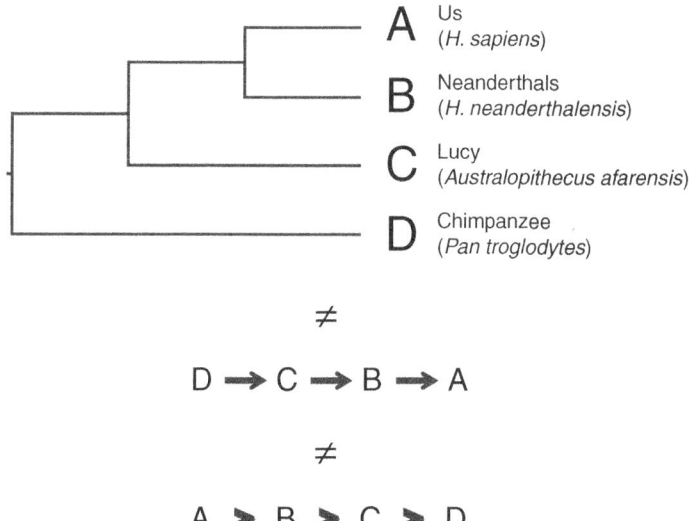

Figure 1.7 Phylogeny depicting evolutionary relationship between *Homo sapiens* and Lucy. Image by Daniel Spalink.

> The central idea of biological evolution is that all life on Earth shares a common ancestor…Through the process of descent with modification, the common ancestor of life on Earth gave rise to the fantastic diversity that we see documented in the fossil record and around us today. Evolution means that we're all distant cousins: humans and oak trees, hummingbirds and whales.[23]

Using a tree model instead of a ladder to depict evolution is critical to comprehending the ancestral relations between humans, animals, and plants, because it demonstrates that rather than humans evolving from chimpanzees, they both share a common ancestor from which they each have diverged. "Humans and chimpanzees are evolutionary cousins and share a recent common ancestor that was neither chimpanzee nor human." As a result, paleontologists do not regard humans as "'higher' or 'more evolved' than other living lineages. Since our lineages split, humans and chimpanzees have each evolved traits unique to their own lineages."[24] Above and beyond correcting simple misconceptions of scientific theories of evolution, tree-thinking reveals that every becoming iteration of human, plant, animal, and all other life forms, including hominids like Lucy, are materially connected to one anotherthr oughr elationshipsac rosstim eands pace.

When we brought up the question of what makes humans separate from other animals with Dr. Menton, following a talk he gave at the Creation Museum entitled "Body of Evidence," he reiterated the arguments presented in the "Man vs. Ape" display (the text of which Menton wrote). "What makes humans *unique*," he answered, "is our innate ability to communicate with God and each other. Through language." While animals like bees may be able to communicate, the "last we checked, bees weren't having any philosophical thoughts." On our question of whether humans and animals had the same materiality, the same kinds of tissues (Menton is a physiologist), and even the same organs, Menton replied that this is the case but that this testifies not to a common ancestor, but to a common Creator.[25]

The Creation Museum's language of intelligibility dictates that humans and the rest of nature are fundamentally separate from one another on temporal, spatial, and material levels, that this separation is divinely mandated, and that the museum's duty is to reify and police this separation in the exhibition space of the Creation Museum, no matter the cost in distorting scientific conceptions of evolution. It is not difficult, then, to move from this language of intelligibility, from the nature-culture divide as produced and practiced at the Creation Museum, to a resistance to the idea of human-caused global climate change, and an endorsement of laissez-faire exploitation of the earth's natural resources. We propose to demonstrate such a move and to show its complicity with conservative corporate and political agendas. Indeed, an investigation of Answers in Genesis's position on ecological issues reveals that their responses to questions about humans' relationship with other animals is supported by the conceptions of time, space, and matter upheld in its exhibits.

When Scott contacted representatives of Answers in Genesis, he asked, "I'm wondering what God and Genesis say about whether human beings are 'part' of nature, or rather 'separate' from it. In other words, what is the answer to those who say that Man would treat earth better if nature and animals were seen more as equals?"[26] We received a response from Correspondence Representative Troy Lacey, titled "Stewardship," within a week: "We have a few excellent articles on biblical stewardship of earth, and the first one below, really hits the core of your question, as do the other two to a lesser extent."[27] Lacey included links to articles on the Answers-in-Genesis website, which spoke to the question of Man's commitment to the care of earth. In each of these articles, the past, present, and future of the universe were laid out in a linear, chronological trajectory, with Creation at the outset and the Last Judgment at the end. In this trajectory, Man is given dominion over the earth, but, because of his sin, the earth is corrupt and cannot be fixed, except through its consummation with God in its final days. Throughout this narrative, ecological problems are presented as manifestations of Man's broken relationship with God. As such, these problems can never be redressed through human action. One of the articles Lacey recommended, cynically titled "Can an Environmentalist Celebrate Earth Day?," states:

> The Bible makes it very clear that this Earth is a temporary, fallen domicile (2 Peter 3:10, 12)—with environmental problems a specific curse that came as a result of the Fall (Genesis 3:17–19, Romans 8:20)—that will ultimately be destroyed through God's actions, and, thus, none of our actions will "heal" the Earth (Isaiah 51:6, 65:17; Romans 8:21; Hebrews 1:10–12; 2 Peter 3:13; Revelation 21:1).

The article concludes that while we cannot solve the earth's problems, and ought to responsibly steward its resources, we "have the responsibility to bear the burden of the Fall's environmental consequences, which fall not only on us, but on all of creation (Romans 8:22)." It is therefore our duty, "our Christian duty," to be passionate about this planet and "to show a greater, truer devotion (a *justifiable* devotion) for protecting the Earth than do non-Christians—most of whom show devotion in contradiction to their worldview."[28]

This argument for stewardship over nature until Judgment Day is in line with the tenets laid out by Answers in Genesis founder Ken Ham, who argues, in his essay "Creation and Conservation," that our environmental ethic needs to be based not on an atheist scientific paradigm, but rather on the Bible. "We need to take dominion, ruling over the earth and subduing it, gaining fruit for our labour, all the while understanding that our own sinful nature may blind us, and we must reject wanton and needless exploitation of the creation for selfish gain." No answer to environmental crisis is to be found in human action, he writes. "There will be no better solution to the environmental crisis until God makes a new heaven and a new earth in which 'righteousnessdwe lls.'"[29]

The second and third articles recommended by Lacey look to biblical evidence, first, to contest scientific claims that current, drastic global climate changes are the result of human behavior, and, second, to reject any idea that we should enact legislation or take other human action to rectify it. "While some of the evidence suggests that the earth has warmed recently," writes John Upchurch in "Go Truly Green by Starting with Genesis,"

> many scientists build their conclusions upon a faulty view of earth's history. If we start with the Bible, we know how old the earth truly is, what happened in history (e.g., the global Flood, the one Ice Age), and what will happen in the future (Revelation 21–22). God is in control and reminds us in His Word not to be afraid of what tomorrow will bring (Matthew 6:34).[30]

In a similar move, Ken Ham, in "Earth Day: A Creationist's Perspective," tells readers that environmental shifts on a global scale are nothing new if one looks at the Bible as a history book of the universe. Humans, he writes, have witnessed an "unsettled earth in its sin-cursed state" since Genesis, when "the Flood of Noah's time, "about 4,400 years ago," was ordained by God to punish mankind for turning from his covenants. "Whether humans have contributed significantly in a detrimental way," argues Ham, "is just not suggested by the evidence we have at hand." This does not mean we should be purposefully bad to the earth, as he argues in "Creation and Conservation," rather that we should care for it for "man's good and God's glory."[31]

Does such care include concerted efforts to mitigate damage to the atmosphere by, for instance, enacting legislation to control pollution? A recent article by Wayne Spencer, posted on the Answers in Genesis website, cites Isaiah 45:18, which says God created the earth "to be inhabited." God designed the atmosphere with a "series of 'checks and balances' which prevent climate from getting out of control," Spencer writes. To put emission caps on businesses, he argues, is not helpful for humanity and is harmful in the long run. The atmosphere will take care of itself, with God's help.[32]

Ecological problems, as the Creation Museum sees it, are not new nor were they created by Man. They have existed since the time of Genesis, as a result of human sinfulness. Only by salvation through Jesus Christ can the sinful world be redeemed, at which point this present and corrupt earth will pass, and a new heaven and earth will be established. In the meantime, we are off the hook. As long as our souls are being cared for, we are free, in fact commanded, to extract and process the earth's resources through deforestation, factory farming, hydraulic fracturing, bioengineering, animal testing, strip mining, oil drilling, and unfettered industrial dumping and emissions without fear that we are negatively affecting our homes and our lives.[33] Indeed, the most recent book edited by Ham argues that drastic environmental changes to the earth have benefited humankind. Take the creation of fossil fuels: "It is humbling to remember that when God was judging the earth with a global flood that He was creating inexpensive fuel sources for future generations."[34]

While the Creation Museum may seem like a boutique tourist attraction for a niche audience, it is, on the contrary, a multimillion dollar operation whose brand of biblical literalism and young earth creationism may be gaining ground.[35] Personal cosmological beliefs have extended into the realms of education and political policy. Answers in Genesis's insistence that scientific observations of global climate change are fraudulent and ought to be ignored are part of a larger agenda that allies the religious and corporate right. In 2012, for example, the Tennessee Senate approved a bill that allows "'alternate' scientific theories, essentially allowing anti-evolutionists and climate change deniers a voice in the science classroom."[36] In 2013, antievolution and anticlimate change bills were introduced in Arizona, Colorado, and Kansas.[37] Antievolution activists sit on Texas state textbook review boards and insist that "intelligent design" be taught as an alternative to evolution in public schools. Because Texas represents such a proportionately large percentage of the United States textbook market, major academic publishers (Pearson, Houghton Mifflin Harcourt, McGraw Hill, etc.) may simply make these changes to textbooks across the board.[38] In the not-too-distant past, former President George H. W. Bush quipped that "he was going to fight the greenhouse effect with the 'White House effect.'"[39]

We have committed this essay to mapping the historiographic procedures, spatial layout, and narratives of the Creation Museum, and the complementary rhetorical structures perpetuated in the Answers in Genesis website. These organizations allow no other analytical approach to evolutionary processes and ecological problems than an evangelical one that maintains humans are irreconcilably divorced from the rest of nature. The Creation Museum visitor is performatively manipulated to reject any notion that humans, nonhuman animals, and plants are related through his or her encounter and exchange with the exhibits, completing a circuit of meaning-making Jill Stevenson calls "evangelical dramaturgy." By extension, everything else in the picture (whether mentioned in Genesis or not) is reified as authentic. That means dinosaurs in the Garden of Eden, Adam and Eve performing animal sacrifices, and the narrative that Original Sin initiated the eating of meat, the presence of poison, animal predators, death and procreation, but also, most dangerously, that it marked a separation between the realms of human and animal, nature and culture. Outside of the museum's language of intelligibility it is clear that its own constructed relationship is informed by particular historical knowledges that have been generated and reified by dominant and interlocking systems of power. Our email exchanges with Answers in Genesis reveal not just systems of museological performance or of biblical literalism, but much larger political and social systems, systems that serve reactionary corporate and political, not just religious agendas. While explicit commentary on ecological issues is absent from the exhibit space of the Creation Museum, the underlying language of intelligibility that informs it is clearly articulated by its spokesmen and women at Answers in Genesis. All these strategies—religious, political, and corporate—rely upon a reading of time, space, and matter that reflects a historiography in which past and present can never coexist and events can, therefore, have only one possible outcome, a state of affairs at once limited and ahistorical, and dire in its implications for the natural world.

Notes

1. Answers in Genesis, "Creation Museum," *Creation Museum.*, http://creationmuseum.org/.
2. John Fletcher, *Preaching to Convert: Evangelical Outreach and Performance Activism in a Secular Age* (Ann Arbor: University of Michigan Press, 2013).
3. Jill Stevenson *Sensational Devotion: Evangelical Performance in the Twenty-First Century America* (Ann Arbor: University of Michigan Press, 2013) 4.
4. Giorgio Agamben, "Time and History: Critique of the Instant and the Continuum," *Infancy and History: Essays in the Destruction of Experience*, trans. Liz Heron (London: Verso, 1993), 91.
5. Deleuze and Guattari, *What Is Philosophy?*, trans. Hugh Tomlinson and Graham Burchell (New York: Columbia University Press, 1994), 153.
6. Ibid.,169
7. Ibid.,153 .
8. Ken Ham, Answers in Genesis website, http://www.answersingenesis.org/about (accessed March 18, 2014).
9. The Creation Museum also distinguishes between animals and plants in order to explain why, although eaten by animals, plants did not experience death before the Fall. In "Was There Death before Adam Sinned?", Ken Ham states "it is very clear that the death of a plant (tree) is categorically different from the death of a man. So when animals and people ate plants in the world before sin, it did not involve death, because plants do not 'die' in the sense that man and animals do" (http://www.answersingenesis.org/articles/nab3/death-before-adam-sinned, April 25, 2014 [accessed April 29, 2014]).

10. Una Chaudhuri, "Animal Geographies: Zooësis and the Space of Modern Drama," *Modern Drama* 46:4 (Winter 2003): 647.
11. Genesis 1:27–29, The Holy Bible, *King James Version* (Nashville: Thomas Nelson Publishers, 1976); emphasis in the original.
12. Lynn White, Jr., "The Historical Roots of Our Ecologic Crisis," *Readings in Biology and Man*, ed. Miguel A. Santos (New York: MSS Information Corporation, 1973), 270. Originally appearing in *Science* 155 (1967): 1203–207.
13. Ibid.,271.
14. Dipash Chakrabarty, "The Climate of History: Four Theses," *Critical Inquiry* 35 (Winter 2009): 201. Citing R. G. Collingwood's 1913 translation of Benedetto Croce's *The Philosophy of Giambattista Vico* (New Brunswick, NJ: Transaction, 2002), 5.
15. Timothy W. Luke, *Museum Politics: Power Plays at the Exhibition* (Minneapolis: University of Minnesota Press, 2002), 3.
16. Creation Museum, "Man Vs. Ape" sign, emphasis in original.
17. In "Why Are There 'Green Crises?'", Ken Ham writes that all living things were in perfect harmony, until the Fall detailed in Genesis 3 led to "all living things and all world systems decaying and dying" as well as thorns and thistles, and human toil to grow and harvest crops. "Romans 5:12 explains that man's actions (disobedience to God's command not to eat of the forbidden fruit) led to sin, which resulted in God's cursing the world with death," Ham continues, and "the whole of creation is now running down and wearing out. 'The earth shall wax old like a garment' (Isaiah 51:6), and man's sinful nature has disrupted the relationship with the environment" (http://www.answersingenesis.org/articles/cm/v17/n4/conservation, September 1, 1995 [accessed July 19, 2013]).
18. Creation Museum, "God Killed Animals" sign.
19. William Ian Miller, *The Anatomy of Disgust* (Cambridge: Harvard University Press, 1997), 53.
20. http://www.answersingenesis.org/home/area/bios/e_mitchell.asp (accessed July 19, 2013).
21. Elizabeth Mitchell and David Menton, "A Look at Lucy's Legacy," Answers in Genesis website, June 6, 2012 (accessed July 19, 2013), http://www.answersingenesis.org/articles/aid/v7/n1/lucy-legacy (emphases in the original).
22. This misconception is perhaps most famously depicted in the "primate to man" cartoon, where various phases between the hairy quadruped and the upright hairless man with a spear are shown.
23. "An Introduction to Evolution," Understanding Evolution, University of California Museum of Paleontology, October 25, 2013, http://evolution.berkeley.edu/evolibrary/article/0_0_0/evo_02 (accessed December 9, 2013).
24. "Trees, Not ladders," Understanding Evolution. University of California Museum of Paleontology, October 25, 2013, http://evolution.berkeley.edu/evolibrary/article/0_0_0/evo_07.
25. David Menton, question and answer session following "Body of Evidence," Lecture, Creation Museum, May 31, 2013.
26. Scott Magelssen, inquiry electronically submitted to AiG, July 3, 2013. Scott agreed to allow his name and question to be posted on the website if it prompted an eventual article.

27. Troy Lacey, Answers in Genesis, personal email correspondence, July 8, 2013.
28. Edd Starr, "Can an Evolutionist Celebrate Earth Day?" Answers in Genesis website, April 22, 2006, http://www.answersingenesis.org/articles/2006/04/22/evolutionist-celebrate-earth-day (accessed July 8, 2013) (emphasis in the original).
29. Ken Ham, "Creation and Conservation," *Creation* 17:4 (1995): 20–23.
30. Far from being an excuse to abuse the world, this is the real justification to take care of it—without resorting to scare tactics and exaggerations of the data" (John UpChurch, "Go Truly Green by Starting with Genesis," April 22, 2009, http://www.answersingenesis.org/articles/2009/04/22/go-truly-green-by-starting-with-genesis (accessed July 8, 2013).
31. Ken Ham, "Earth Day: A Creationist's Perspective," Answers in Genesis website, http://www.answersingenesis.org/articles/2010/04/22/earth-day-creationist-perspective (accessed July 8, 2013).
32. Wayne Spencer, "Global Warming and Earth's Design," June 16, 2010, http://www.answersingenesis.org/articles/aid/v5/n1/global-warming-and-earth-design (accessed July 3, 2013). Such a position is not distinctly Christian, but is associated with the conservative brand of ideology found in some evangelical branches of Christianity. There are a number of Christian environmental groups, such as Earth Ministry, which is "committed to engaging the Christian community in environmental stewardship" and partners with "individuals and congregations to respond to this great moral challenge through education, individual and congregational lifestyle choices, and organizing for social change through environmental advocacy" (Earth Ministry Website, http://earthministry.org/ [accessed September 19, 2013]), ecumenical groups such as Faith Action Network (FAN), and even evangelical environmental groups such as the Evangelical Climate Initiative (ECI), which recognizes the threats of "Human-Induced Climate Change" (ECI statement, http://christiansandclimate.org/statement/ [accessed November 24, 2013]).
33. "Much of the emphasis of the modern conservation movement," writes Ham in "Creation and Conservation," "is evolutionary and pantheistic, worshipping the creature rather than the Creator (Romans 1). This ignores the biblical mandate to rule over the earth and subdue it. The development of energy sources (coal, natural gas, petroleum, atomic power, etc.), the mining of mineral resources, the cutting of timber for building, etc., is not wrong. Ecclesiastes 3:1–8 states that there is a time to plant and a time to uproot, a time to kill and a time to heal, a time to tear down and a time to build, a time to keep and a time to throw away, a time for war and a time for peace. It is the abuse of these resources — the exploitation, the waste, the greed and the haste — that is wrong" in the same way as "Deuteronomy 25:4 states: 'Thou shalt not muzzle the ox when he treadeth out the corn'" and "Proverbs 12:10 says, 'A righteous man regardeth the life of his beast: but the tender mercies of the wicked are cruel.'" http://www.answersingenesis.org/articles/cm/v17/n4/conservation, September 1, 1995 (accessed July 19, 2013).
34. Alan White, "Should We Be Concerned about Climate Change?" *The New Answers Book 4: Over 25 Questions on Creation/Evolution and the Bible*, ed. Ken Ham (Green Forest, AR: New Leaf Publishing Group, 2013), 198.

35. According to a 2013 analyses conducted by the Pew Research Center, 33 percent of Americans believe "humans and other living things have existed in their present form since the beginning of time." On the other hand, 60 percent believe that "humans and other living things have evolved over time." According to this survey, however, those who believe that living organisms have evolved over time understand these processes in various ways, with 24 percent stating, "God or a supreme being played a role in the process of evolution" (Pew Research, "Public's Views on Human Evolution." *Religion and Public Life Project*, http://www.pewforum.org/2013/12/30/publics-views-on-human-evolution/, December 30, 2013 [accessed March 17, 2014]).
36. Cara Santa Maria, "Scopes Monkey Trial Revisited: Tennessee Is Still Officially Anti-evolution as Science Education Bill Passes," *The Huffington Post*, http://www.huffingtonpost.com/2012/03/20/tennessee-evolution-scopes-education_n_1368636.html, March 21, 2012 (accessed March 17, 2014).
37. National Center for Science Education, "Anti-evolution and Anti-climate Science Legislation Scorecard: 2013," http://ncse.com/evolution/anti-evolution-anti-climate-science-legislation-scorecard-2013, May 20, 2013 (accessed March 17, 2014).
38. Motoko Rich, "Creationists on Texas Panel for Biology Textbooks," *New York Times*, September 29, 2013, http://www.nytimes.com/2013/09/29/education/creationists-on-texas-panel-for-biology-textbooks.html?nl=todaysheadlines&emc=edit_th_20130929&_r=0 (accessed September 29, 2013).
39. Chakrabarty, "The Climate of History," 199, citing Bush's quote in Mark Bowen, *Censoring Science: Inside the Political Attack on Dr. James Hansen and the Truth of Global Warming* (New York: Dutton, 2008), 228.

Bibliography

Arons, Wendy. "Beyond the Nature/Culture Divide: Challenges from Ecocriticism and Evolutionary Biology for Theater Historiography." In *Theater Historiography: Critical Interventions*. Edited by Henry Bial and Scott Magelssen. Ann Arbor: University of Michigan Press, 2010.
Chakrabarty, Dipash. "The Climate of History: Four Theses." *Critical Inquiry* 35 (Winter 2009).
Chaudhuri, Una. "Animal Geographies: Zooësis and the Space of Modern Drama." *Modern Drama* 46, no. 4 (Winter 2003).
———. "Animal Rites: Performing beyond the Human." In *Critical Theory and Performance*. Edited by Janelle G. Reinelt and Joseph R. Roach. Ann Arbor: The University of Michigan Press, 2006.
Creation Museum website. Answers in Genesis. http://creationmuseum.org/. Accessed September 17, 2013.
de Certeau, Michel. "The Laugh of Michel Foucault." In *Heterologies: Discourse on the Other*. Translated by Brian Massumi. Minneapolis: University of Minnesota Press, 1986.
Deleuze, Gilles. *Difference and Repetition*. Translated by Paul Patton. New York: Columbia University Press, 1994.

Deleuze, Gilles, and Felix Guattari. *What Is Philosophy?* Translated by Hugh Tomlinson and Graham Burchell. New York: Columbia University Press, 1994.

Dolan, Jill. "Performance, Utopia, and the 'Utopian Performative.'" *Theatre Journal* 53, no. 3 (October 2001).

Dox, Donalee. "The Willing Sustenance of Belief: Religiosity and Mode of Performance." *Journal of Religion and Theatre* 8, no. 1 (2009).

Elizabeth Mitchell biography. Answers in Genesis website. http://www.answersingenesis.org/home/area/bios/e_mitchell.asp. Accessed July 19, 2013.

Fletcher, John. "Prepare to Believe: Performing the Evangelical Worldview at the Creation Museum." Unpublished manuscript shared with the authors.

———. "Tasteless as Hell: Community Performance, Distinction, and Countertaste in Hell House." *Theatre Survey* 48, no. 2 (November 2007).

Genesis 1.27–29, *The Holy Bible, King James Version*. New York: Oxford Edition, 1769.

Gould, Stephen J. "Nonoverlapping Magisteria." In *Philosophy of Religion: An Anthology*. Edited by Louis P. Pojman and Michael Cannon Rea. Stamford, CT: Cengage Learning, 2008.

———. *Rock of Ages: Science and Religion in the Fullness of Life*. New York: Ballantine, 1999.

Ham, Ken. "Creation and Conservation." *Creation* 17, no. 4 (1995), 20–23.

———. "Earth Day: A Creationist's Perspective." Answers in Genesis website, April 22, 2010. http://www.answersingenesis.org/articles/2010/04/22/earth-day-creationist-perspective. Accessed July 8, 2013.

———. *The New Answers Book 4: Over 25 Questions on Creation/Evolution and the Bible*. Green Forest, AR:New Leaf Publishing Group, 2013.

———. "Why Are There 'Green' Crises?" Creation Museum website, September 1, 1995. http://www.answersingenesis.org/articles/cm/v17/n4/conservation. Accessed July 19, 2013.

Hodge, Bodie. "Feedback: Why Do You Take the Bible Literally." AIG website, January 13, 2006. http://www.answersingenesis.org/articles/2006/01/13/feedback-why-take-bible-literally. Accessed December 6, 2013.

Hutcheon, Linda. "Historicizing the Postmodern: The Problematizing of History." In *A Poetics of Postmodernism: History, Theory, Fiction*. New York:Routledge, 2004.

Ian Miller, William. *The Anatomy of Disgust*. Cambridge: Harvard University Press, 1997.

"An Introduction to Evolution." Understanding Evolution. University of California Museum of Paleontology. October 25, 2013. http://evolution.berkeley.edu/evolibrary/article/0_0_0/evo_02. Accessed December 9, 2013.

Kershaw, Baz. *The Politics of Performance: Radical Theatre as Cultural Intervention*. New York: Routledge, 1992.

Lacey, Troy. Answers in Genesis, personal email correspondence, July 8, 2013.

Luke, Timothy W. *Museum Pieces: Power Plays at the Exhibition*. Minneapolis: University of Minnesota Press, 2002.

Lyotard, Jean-François. *The Differend: Phrases in Dispute*. Minneapolis: University of Minnesota Press, 1991.

Magelssen, Scott. Inquiry electronically submitted to AiG, July 3, 2013.
Marion, Jean-Luc. *Being Given: Toward a Phenomenology of Giveness*. Translated by Jeffrey L. Kosky. Stanford: Stanford University Press, 2002.
May, Theresa J. "Beyond Bambi: Toward a Dangerous Ecocriticism in Theatre Studies." *Theatre Topics* 17, no. 2 (2007).
McCarthy, Colmon. "James Watt & the Puritan Ethic." *The Washington Post*. May 24, 1981.
Menton, David. Question and answer session following "Body of Evidence." Lecture. Creation Museum. May 31, 2013.
Mitchell, Elizabeth, and David Menton. "A Look at Lucy's Legacy." Answers in Genesis website, June 6, 2012. http://www.answersingenesis.org/articles/aid/v7/n1/lucy-legacy. Accessed July 19, 2013.
Muñoz, José Esteban. *Cruising Utopia: The Then and There of Queer Futurity*. New York: New York University Press, 2009.
National Center for Science Education. "Anti-evolution and Anti-climate Science Legislation Scorecard: 2013," May 20, 2013. Website. http://ncse.com/evolution/anti-evolution-anti-climate-science-legislation-scorecard-2013. Accessed March 17, 2014.
Rich, Mokoto. "Creationists on Texas Panel for Biology Textbooks." *New York Times*, September 29, 2013. http://www.nytimes.com/2013/09/29/education/creationists-on-texas-panel-for-biology-textbooks.html?nl=todaysheadlines&emc=edit_th_20130929&_r=0. Accessed September 29, 2013.
Santa Maria, Cara. "Scopes Monkey Trial Revisited: Tennessee Is Still Officially Anti-evolution as Science Education Bill Passes." *The Huffington Post*, March 21, 2012. http://www.huffingtonpost.com/2012/03/20/tennessee-evolution-scopes-education_n_1368636.html. Accessed March 17, 2014.
Spencer, Wayne. "Global Warming and Earth's Design." Answers in Genesis website. June 16, 2010, http://www.answersingenesis.org/articles/aid/v5/n1/global-warming-and-earth-design. Accessed July 3, 2013.
Starr, Edd. "Can an Evolutionist Celebrate Earth Day?" Answers in Genesis website. April 22, 2006, http://www.answersingenesis.org/articles/2006/04/22/evolutionist-celebrate-earth-day. Accessed July 8, 2013.
Stevenson, Jill. "Embodying Sacred History: Performing Creationism for Believers." *TDR: The Drama Review* 56, no. 1 [T213] (Spring 2012).
———. *Sensational Devotion: Evangelical Performance in the Twenty-First Century*. Ann Arbor: University of Michigan Press, 2013.
"Understanding Evolution." University of California, Berkeley. http://evolution.berkeley.edu/evolibrary/article/evo_07. Accessed September 19, 2013.
UpChurch, John. "Go Truly Green by Starting with Genesis." April 22, 2009. http://www.answersingenesis.org/articles/2009/04/22/go-truly-green-by-starting-with-genesis. Accessed July 8, 2013.
Watt, James G. Testimony before the House Committee on Interior and Insular Affairs, February 5, 1981.
White, Alan. "Should We Be Concerned about Climate Change?" In *The New Answers Book 4: Over 25 Questions on Creation/Evolution and the Bible*. Edited by Ken Ham. Green Forest, AR: New Leaf Publishing Group, 2013.

White, Lynn, Jr. "The Historical Roots of our Ecologic Crisis." In *Readings in Biology and Man*. Edited by Miguel A. Santos. New York: MSS Information Corporation, 1973.

Wolfe, Cary. *Animal Rites: American Culture, the Discourse of Species, and Posthumanist Theory*. Chicago, IL: The University of Chicago Press, 2003.

2
A Ridiculous Space: Considering the Historiography of the Theatre of the Ridiculous

Kelly Aliano

How do we write the history of work that has consistently been elided from the writing of history? Can we simply reinsert it into the progressive narrative of the development of drama or is it necessary to carve out a specific location in which this work may reside, reconstructing the historical landscape in which it was once performed? How can we create a theoretical framework for studying these productions, and how can that operate as a "space" in which these theatre pieces can finally live?

Answering these questions in terms of the Theatre of the Ridiculous is difficult. The movement (if indeed we can call it one) is so fluid that its traces seem both hard to uncover and to be present everywhere. Because of this, rather than simply pinpointing starting and ending dates for the movement and including all its artists within that time frame, it makes more sense to "map" the movement, both literally and figuratively, as it traveled across and throughout Greenwich Village, New York, and shaped the theoretical contours of its boundaries. What the Ridiculous *is* was always shaped by *where* it was, by the hands crafting it, by the spaces in which an artist found him- or herself, and by the larger socioeconomic setting in which the Ridiculous was being performed.

Even this literal mapping, however, would not go far enough in encapsulating what Ridiculous Theatre was. Yes, it was defined by the literal spaces in which it was performed and presented, but it also demands a specific sort of theoretical space, one in which its unique aesthetic elements make sense. What, then, would such a theoretical map—a space built not of physical geography but of a "form of relations among sites,"[1] as Michel Foucault puts it—look like? Would it continue to privilege Charles Ludlam as the sole or key practitioner of Ridiculous Theatre? It might, since Ludlam is the best remembered and most famous of the artists labeled "Ridiculous," and his work is the most commonly produced as Ridiculous Theatre. Yet, Ludlam himself might have built a Ridiculous space differently, placing experimental filmmaker and artist Jack Smith at the center, since, Ludlam claimed, "Jack was the daddy of us all."[2] Even that progressive historical narrative might prove problematic, since Smith's work was heavily indebted to his interest, bordering on obsession, with B-movie starlet Maria Montez, who offers a different central point for a Ridiculous map, as do other artists and subjects. The complexity of the interconnected threads of influence and inspiration that surround the Ridiculous suggests that any sort of literal mapmaking or drawing of specific historical trajectories is disingenuous, with respect to the nature of the development of the Ridiculous. This is a different sort of space, one whose history demands to be told through a different understanding of the progression of time.

The threads of this complex theatrical movement are hard to trace because of seemingly infinite loops of influence, collaboration, stealing, and sharing among the artists that I discuss in this essay. Their landscape was one of relational bonds, though those connections were often fraught with tension and jealousy. A Ridiculous space is consistently shifting, constantly in flux, depending upon whose hands applied and manipulated the term. The trajectory of the Ridiculous is always relative, an example of a "world [that] is less that of a long life developing through time than that of a network that connects points and intersects with its own skein."[3]

I will discuss Ridiculous space in this essay by using Michel Foucault's "Of Other Spaces: Utopias and Heterotopias" as my theoretical base, highlighting some specific locations in the downtown scene, while, at the same time, providing a theoretical investigation of space as a way to understand theatre. The development of the Ridiculous—its entire history, its many expansions and contractions in terms of content and form—can be traced entirely through an understanding of the concept of space. An emphasis on literal locations matters here; an actual map of these theatres would help to expose their interactions with one another. Closeness in proximity not only allowed, but also, in some cases, forced these disparate artists to work together and share ideas. Yet, more significant is a figurative construction of space, which allows the formation of a theoretical framework that facilitates the discussion of works in the same Ridiculous conversation. Building such a theoretical space gives the Ridiculous a clearer shape, making it easier to define and discuss. In this essay, then, I draw a map of the Theatre of the Ridiculous, linking such artists as Charles Ludlam, Jack Smith, and Ethyl Eichelberger via their aesthetic techniques, in order to argue that the Ridiculous was, in fact, an important *movement*, not just a style.

The larger significance of the work that I do here is its application beyond discussions of Ridiculous Theatre in offering theory as a space, suggesting that a theoretical lens or framework can operate in the same way as other "heterotopias," becoming a place that is both there and not there, one in which some things belong and others do not. In this way, theory, as space, becomes a new tool for understanding how to define theatrical movements and periodization.

Mappingthe Space

On the one hand, Ridiculous Theatre can be defined by physical geography: it was born of a particular set of artists who all had at least a peripheral connection with one another in the same literal location, downtown New York City. In this way, the Ridiculous might be fraught with the same issues as any other theatre movement: a style of work that, as it expanded from company to company, would have to struggle to find actual spaces in which to be performed. Indeed, as Foucault reminds us, "Our epoch is one in which space takes for us the form of relations among sites."[4] Used as the backbone for a study of the Ridiculous as a theatrical movement, however, space becomes a relationship that facilitates seeing the connections between various spaces, aesthetic as well as physical, as the theatre style adapted and shifted from company to company and from theatre to theatre.

In order to frame the Ridiculous as a movement, instead of as the product of specific artists working independently, it is useful first to look at space *literally*. In this respect, all of the artists share something in common. Performance makers, such as John Vaccaro, Jack Smith, and Ethyl Eichelberger, all worked principally in and around the Greenwich Village section of New York City, from the 1960s through the mid-1990s. During this time, Ridiculous performances could be found in such traditional theatres and recognized performance spaces as One Sheridan Square and P.S. 122, in downtown clubs like 8 B.C., and in artists' apartments. Space—the site of performance—is key to recognizing a work as Ridiculous and unpacking what is meant by that term. Jack Smith, for example, often performed his works in his home, a loft he converted into his own performance space. Most of his performances had a ritualistic quality, one that was conflated with his obsession with screen siren Maria Montez. Ridiculous playwright and Smith's friend Ronald Travel contends:

> [Montez's] ultimate influence on him [Smith], and his ultimate tribute to her was the rebuilding of Baghdad/Babylonia into his apartments, a city, a world, a wall, a building. He had duplex lofts in Soho and removed the floor between them to construct, virtually by himself, and ostensibly for a projected picture called *Sinbad*, a cathedralling set that reminds [one] of Fairbanks, Sr.'s silent, *Thief of Bagdad*: but which got its seed from Maria's *Raiders of the Desert*, *Arabian Nights*, *Ali Baba and the Forty Thieves*, and *Tangier*.[5]

The setting of Smith's loft suggested the exotic settings of Montez's films, and his performances were deeply engaged with attempting to evoke her presence on stage. Smith would don costumes and makeup suggestive of her exotic style and would often reference her film work in his plays. In *What's Underground about Marshmallows*,[6] for example, he listed some of her film titles as part of the dramatic proceeding. Smith's rituals and theatrical settings were all about Montez and, for him, the site of his performance was, itself, an integral part of the ritual. Smith's plays took a nontraditional approach to theatrical time as well as theatrical space. Stefan Brecht describes the lack of structure to Smith's performances, which meander into the wee hours of the morning: "The show as a whole is slow—the same thing is done for a long, long while each time, [and] there are long waits."[7]

By contrast, Charles Ludlam performed many of his best-known works in a theatre (One Sheridan Square) and his tightly scripted farces mixed references from highbrow art—plays by Molière or Shakespeare, for example—with lines from advertisements and B-movies, and Ludlam's own quips and witticisms. As performative as many of his plays were—and, indeed, his cross-dressed Camille was all about performance—Ludlam's works were literary in nature, written plays that could be read as easily as they could be seen. There is not much, on the other hand, to make of a Smith production on paper. For him, the playing space defined the nature of his personal and ritualistic work, performances born of Smith's own esoteric thoughts and dreams, and unfettered by textual constraints.

Looking at space literally reveals how spaces impart a particular meaning to a production. In Smith's case, the audience entered a theatrical fantasyland, built into an individual's living quarters. This unique theatrical setting brought its own set of rules for audience engagement. In his narrative about this theatrical setting, Stefan Brecht describes being led up to the loft by some acquaintances of Smith's. He writes that people were milling about and Smith offered them the option to "just listen to some records."[8] The formality that usually accompanies attending a theatrical performance in a traditional theatre is absent here; there are other procedures to follow, indeed, the new guidelines included expectations for what the role of the spectators would be. Brecht describes entering into a performance as a participant who moves the night's entertainment along, but also receives instructions from Smith on how to perform his role: "Smith corrects our acting often. We are doing it too fast. Finally I am processioning so slow[ly] Smith has to ask me to speed my steps up a little."[9]

Smith's informal theatrical space allows for direct audience participation in the art of theatre making itself, a mirroring effect between the nontraditional theatrical space and the type of nontraditional theatrical practices he employed. Ludlam's plays, on the other hand, particularly those from the latter part of his career when his company was comfortably situated at One Sheridan Square, have no room in their dramaturgy for Smith's sort of audience interaction. They are polished, scripted farces meant to be enjoyed by an audience in a conventional way, in a conventional space bearing little resemblance to Smith's. What is Ridiculous, then, is crucially affected by the place of performance, the major factor in both the cause and execution of Ridiculous differences.

The works of Ethyl Eichelberger offer a third example of the impact of space upon how a movement becomes defined. Eichelberger often performed in downtown clubs, where setting forced a different sort of performance than one might execute either in a home or in a traditional theatre. During this period, downtown clubs and bars were a mainstay of the performance landscape, "the downtown scene." These spaces, Roselee Goldberg suggests, demanded "larger-than-life performers such as Ethyl Eichelberger"[10] because performers not only had to compete with the loud social atmosphere of the clubs, they could take advantage of the opportunity to interact with the audiences within them. According to Joe E. Jeffreys, "A style developed in conjunction with his [Eichelberger's] Ridiculous experiences and, in reaction to the rowdy club environment in which he found himself performing, it strove to steal focus away from the noisy, drunken chatter of late night bar patrons."[11] Eichelberger took what he knew of performance from his Ridiculous forebears and adapted those ideas to the setting in which he performed. Space made his performance technique, as it did with both Smith and Ludlam. Eichelberger's broad performances, such as his iconic *Minnie the Maid*, could stand up against the raucousness of an interactive setting.

These examples make clear that the nature of the Ridiculous aesthetic consistently shifted and redefined itself depending upon the site in which Theatre of the Ridiculous was performed. Those sites, in turn, allowed the Ridiculous to include many different types of performance. Linking artists together merely by geography or by place of performance, of course, is not reason enough to see Ridiculous Theatre as a cohesive theatrical movement. There were other downtown performances that would not fit under the umbrella of the Ridiculous. Rather, space has to be understood more abstractly, if it is going to be used as a way to delineate the boundaries of Theatre of the Ridiculous as a movement.

Spacea s Theory

"Heterotopias," Foucault contends, "are most often linked to slices in time—which is to say that they open onto what might be termed, for the sake of symmetry, heterochronies."[12] Theatre of the Ridiculous constitutes a heterotopia, a particular space that existed in a particular historical moment, positioned outside of mainstream cultural reality. Of heterotopias, Foucault writes:

> There are also, probably in every culture, in every civilization, real places—places that do exist and that are formed in the very founding of society—which are something like counter-sites, a kind of effectively enacted utopia in which the real sites, all the other real sites that can be found within the culture, are simultaneously represented, contested, and inverted. Places of this kind are outside of all places, even though it may be possible to indicate their location in reality.[13]

The Ridiculous occurred in "real places" that actual people could experience and witness. Yet, as Foucault suggests of heterotopias, it also offered a kind of "utopic space" in which people could live in a way that was outside of mainstream heteronormative culture. Stefan Brecht contends of Ridiculous Theatre, "I think this theatre proposes a certain ideal life-style or attitude, doing theatre as part of living that way, which it conveys by its style on stage and which it defends in its plays by ridiculing its opposite."[14] Ridiculous Theatre created a space that allowed its practitioners to make art and to practice a lifestyle as they saw fit. In Brecht's view, "The theatre of the ridiculous is produced by a family or families of approximately free persons as part of their family life. Its members adopt and act roles as the f.p. [free person] playfully assumes his identity—without identifying and only for the sake of playing them."[15] The Ridiculous became a site in which the individual could put on a character, whether for a play or for the world around him or her, and could then dismiss that character at will, inasmuch as all selves were performative. The heterotopia of Ridiculous Theatre allowed its participants to imagine new ways to make art and new ways to live.

In a sense, then, the Ridiculous Theatre space could be the sort of heterotopia that Foucault saw as supplanting the transitional sites of ancient cultures. Foucault labels these sites "heterotopias of deviation," defining these as spaces "in which individuals whose behavior is deviant in relation to the required mean or norm are placed."[16] Although Foucault suggests these heterotopias as sites into which people are coerced or even forced—such as correctional facilities—the Ridiculous could function as an optional heterotopia, one into which an individual might choose to escape, in order to live in a way separate from, even in defiance of, mainstream society.

Foucault's construction of heterotopia suggests a kind of cultural blending at work to create the boundaries of a space in which "all the other real sites that can be found within the culture, are simultaneously represented, contested, and inverted."[17] In this way, the particular middlebrow position of the Ridiculous, if we understand middlebrow as David Savran constructs it ("the unapologetic consumer and cultural middleman"[18]), is also heterotopic. The dramaturgy of Ridiculous plays is always built from a series of references and allusions from all strata of culture. In a sense, a Ridiculous play is a kind of archive or library, a potential heterotopia in its own right, of other cultural material. What defines these sites as sites is not, therefore, their literal positioning on a map, but, rather, the theory they present, within which we can situate Ridiculous work and the aesthetic elements that this work contains. These, in turn, come to define the shape of the Ridiculous as a movement. Ridiculous space, then, is not defined by the literal connections between theatre spaces and performers. This sort of mapping only grounds the notion that Ridiculous Theatre might be worth studying. Rather, it is the interplay of significant theoretical and aesthetic concerns that make the Ridiculous a significant "site" in theatre history.

Notably, the Ridiculous site is one of accumulated cultural knowledge, based on the Ridiculous artists' middlebrow positionality, a positionality with a particularly queer valence. I am building here on Robert Mills's idea that "queer-history exhibitions will adopt a style of presentation partly modeled on scrapbooks and collage; in place of the representative 'object,' they will appropriate fragments, snippets of gossip, speculations, irreverent half-truths."[19] The Ridiculous space is this sort of queer archive because Ridiculous artists collected ideas, characters, lines of text, and anything else one could imagine from anywhere in the cultural spectrum. They would then use this collection of sometimes extremely mismatched material to create their plays. Given these appropriations, the Ridiculous functions as its own kind of heterotopic space, a space similar to Foucault's discussion of libraries and museums: "First of all, there are heterotopias of indefinitely accumulating time, for example museums and libraries. Museums and libraries have become heterotopias in which time never stops building up and topping its own summit."[20] In these spaces, a never-ending process of accumulating information occurs. Time is infinite, because there is always something new to archive. In a sense, Theatre of the Ridiculous operated like an archive, collecting all the cultural data for which its artists felt an affinity. They then used this archive to construct their plays (Charles Ludlam's 1967 *Big Hotel*, e.g., is nothing more than a series of references to various films and plays that Ludlam admired).[21]

Theatre of the Ridiculous took a modern approach toward its own archival project, one much in line with Foucault's understanding of heterotopias:

> The idea of accumulating everything, of establishing a sort of general archive, the will to enclose in one place all times, all epochs, all forms, all tastes, the idea of constituting a place of all times that is itself outside of time and inaccessible to its ravages, the project of organizing in this way a sort of perpetual and indefinite accumulation of time in an immobile place, this whole idea belongs to our modernity.[22]

Ridiculous plays often operated as this sort of cultural repository, taking stock of all of the material that the artists involved deemed worthy of reverence. Ridiculous Theatre, then, is both a collection of works of drama and of a particular historical space, one that archives material relevant to a specific group of insiders who were aware of these plays happening in spaces not easily found on a map of New York theatre.

In place of a clear explanation of the term "Ridiculous," Charles Ludlam once quipped, "The Ridiculous is a convenient name. Each time you do a play, it expands the definition of Ridiculous."[23] In addition to being a "ridiculous" way to contend with this query, Ludlam's comment also suggests that the Ridiculous is something that defies easy definition. Nonetheless, he spent much of his career explaining what he meant by Ridiculous Theatre. In an interview with Gautam Dasgupta, Ludlam makes a useful (if lengthy) assessment of what this style actually is:

> It has to do with humor and unhinging the pretensions of serious art. It comes out of the dichotomy between academic and expressive art, and the idea of a theatre that re-values things. It takes what is considered worthless and transforms it into high art. The Ridiculous theatre was always a concept of high art that came out of an aesthetic which was so advanced it really couldn't be appreciated. It draws its authority from popular art, an art that doesn't need any justification beyond its power to provide pleasure. Sympathetic response is part of its audience. Basically for me, and for twentieth-century art, it's always been a problem of uncovering sources; it proceeds by discoveries…It's really an exercise to try to go beyond limitations and taste, which is a very aural, subjective and not a very profound concept for art. And to admit the world in a way that hasn't been pre-censored…Ridiculous theatre is in color; it's hedonistic. Different artists define it their own way, but basically it's alchemy, it's the transformation of what is in low esteem into the highest form of expression.[24]

In Ludlam's view, Ridiculous performance has a strong cultural imperative: to engage the world as it is, using all aspects of culture as its source material. In this way, Ridiculous Theatre undoes the hierarchies in place at its time of construction.

Foucault notes that "each heterotopia has a precise and determined function within a society."[25] Cultural shifting is the function of the heterotopia that is Ridiculous Theatre. In her introduction to *Theatre of the Ridiculous*, Bonnie Marranca specifically ascribes this role to the Ridiculous:

> What is the Ridiculous? Here's one way to describe it: an anarchic undermining of political, sexual, psychological, and cultural categories, frequently in dramatic structures that parody classical literary forms or re-function American popular entertainments, and always allude to themselves as "performances." A highly self-conscious style, the Ridiculous tends toward camp, kitsch, transvestism, the grotesque, flamboyant visuals, and literary dandyism. It is comedy beyond the absurd because it is less intellectual, more earthy, primal, liberated. Not

tragi-comedy [sic] but metaphysical burlesque, the Ridiculous offers a new version of the "clown." Its dependency on the icons, artifacts, and entertainments of mass culture in America—the "stars," old movies, popular songs, television and advertising—makes the Ridiculous a truly indigenous American approach to making theatre.[26]

Marranca's list of elements suggests that there can be several contesting cultural products operating simultaneously within Ridiculous plays, a position similar to Foucault's view of heterotopias as "capable of juxtaposing in a single real place several spaces, several sites that are in themselves incompatible."[27]

Theatre of the Ridiculous, then, is not something that exists in theatre history; it is an eventless event, often elided or overlooked. At the same time, Theatre of the Ridiculous is present, as an heterochrony, in the theatre practices that both preceded and followed the putative date of its inception "at the Coda Galleries, on June 29, 1965," when playwright Ronald Tavel and director John Vaccaro met.[28] This space, on East 10th Street, near 4th Avenue,[29] was the site of the first production to which the term "Ridiculous" was applied, yet the threads that came together there can be traced back much further than 1965. Neither in time nor in space, it seems, can Theatre of the Ridiculous be confined to a single site or absolute moment of birth, indeed, we might say that the Ridiculous movement was not singularly born and thus never truly died.

A Ridiculous Theatre that has no specific past or future, only a continuous present, cannot be a satisfactory way to define a historical movement, however much it may satisfy to suggest Ridiculous Theatre is an abiding style. Rehistoricizing the subject requires situating Ridiculous Theatre outside the dichotomy between culture and counterculture. Stephen J. Bottoms contends that work from the downtown scene during this period is interested in altering conceptions of how to make art, not in promoting or condemning particular political agendas, platforms, or ideas. Thus Ridiculous Theatre possesses a "relative disregard of 'agendas,' whether political or aesthetic,"[30] and displays an "'underground' disregard for conventional wisdoms and categories, and...a playful blurring of borders between artistic 'isms.'"[31] The historical meaning of the Ridiculous, then, lies in difference, in the space between what it borrows from popular culture and what it eschews of the status quo, a difference that can be specifically delimited.

The Ridiculous Theatre's emphasis on cultural references—and a positionality outside of mainstream culture and counterculture alike—creates an art that, like a heterotopia, is "not freely accessible like a public place."[32] Ridiculous plays are riddled with references to particular cultural icons, which, like Maria Montez, are not considered among the most significant. (Filmmaker Nick Zedd says of Montez, e.g., "She seemed to be a mediocre actress, at best...I think it was some kind of a [sic] inside joke to gay people. They seem to find her an object of adoration."[33]) Ridiculous Theatre can function as a kind of "inside joke," filled with references that make the most sense if one were to share its creators' interests and senses of humor. Heterotopias, Foucault writes, can be similarly exclusive and excluding: "Everyone can enter into the heterotopic sites, but in fact that is only an illusion—we think we can enter where we are, by the very fact that we enter, excluded."[34] Just because one enters into the space does not mean that one either belongs in or comprehends that location. In the same way, Ridiculous Theatre would make perfect sense to those who shared its cultural opinions, but to others, these preoccupations might have seemed entirely preposterous.

In this "insider" space, artists were able to revere their own cultural icons and to imagine another way of being. In Stefan Brecht's view, Theatre of the Ridiculous suggests a lifestyle that exists entirely outside of mainstream culture. This queer place is one of the most progressive aspects of Ridiculous space. As José Muñoz writes:

> Queerness is not yet here. Queerness is an ideality...Queerness is a longing that propels us onward, beyond romances of the negative and toiling in the present. Queerness is the thing that lets us feel that this world is not enough, that indeed something is missing. Often we can glimpse the worlds proposed and promised by queerness in the realm of the aesthetic.[35]

In a queer space, like that of the Theatre of the Ridiculous, those involved can imagine a future that is better than the present. Like a heterotopia, Ridiculous Theatre is able "to create a space that is other, another real space, as perfect, as meticulous, as well arranged as ours is messy, ill constructed, and jumbled."[36] The Theatre of the Ridiculous imagines a queer space in which the boundaries of traditional lifestyles are no longer relevant: "Queer temporalities...are points of resistance to this temporal order that, in turn, propose other possibilities for living in relation to indeterminately past, present, and future others: that is, of living historically."[37] Freeman's notion that a refiguring of time can be a "point of resistance" suggests that a queer space might be possible, a site where theoretical boundaries allow for a new understanding of what space is and how it might operate. The queerness of the Ridiculous marks it as having a geography all its own, while serving as a theoretical map for others, itself both a literal and a figurative space.

What is learned, then, from studying Theatre of the Ridiculous is not limited to information about the Ridiculous itself. Rather, the complexity of this theatre movement reminds researchers to consider other ways to understand the writing of history. Previous studies of American drama have considered periodization and historical lineage as tools for the telling of history, yet these approaches have often led to the elision of Ridiculous Theatre. Looking critically at physical space, or geography, is valuable in constructing an understanding of what a movement was and who participated in it, but conceiving space theoretically gives shape to how we might discuss a theatrical practice, as opposed to merely pinpointing that theatre practice's exact location on a temporal map.

Testing various theatrical practices via theoretical lenses and seeing if those practices match or, perhaps more importantly, diverge from the proposed model(s) allows for a more nuanced history of theatre, one that provides space, both literally and figuratively, for unique, underappreciated, and even niche types of performance that often cannot find a place in the grand historical narratives of world drama. This approach suggests that the space of theatre history, and any theoretical space within it, is always in flux, always shifting its borders, and is always being reimagined in the present. This queer impulse, in and outside Ridiculous studies, allows theatre to continue to be a tool for change, not only for history as it is happening, but for the writing of historyits elf.

Notes

1. Michel Foucault, "Of Other Spaces: Utopias and Heterotopias," *Architecture/ Mouvement/Continuité* (1984); originally presented in French as "Des Espace Autres" in March 1967, translated by Jay Miskowiec, 2.
2. Charles Ludlam quoted on the back cover of Jack Smith, J. Hoberman, and Edward Leffingwell, eds., *Wait for Me at the Bottom of the Pool: The Writings of Jack Smith* (London and New York: Serpent's Tail Press, 1997).
3. Foucault, "Of Other Spaces," 1.
4. Ibid.,2.
5. Ronald Tavel, "Maria Montez: Anima of an Antediluvian World," in *Flaming Creature: Jack Smith, His Amazing Life and Times*, ed. Edward Leffingwell (New York: Serpent's Tail, 1997), 12.
6. PS 1 Archives, I. A. 2086. The Museum of Modern Art, New York.

7. Stefan Brecht, *Queer Theatre* (Germany: Suhrkampf, 1978), 17.
8. Ibid.,13.
9. Ibid.
10. Roselee Goldberg, "Art after Hours: Downtown Performance," in *The Downtown Book: The New York Art Scene, 1974–1984*, ed. Marvin J. Taylor (New York: Grey Art Gallery and Study Center, Fales Library, 2006), 114.
11. Joe E. Jeffreys, "An Outre Entrée into the Para-Ridiculous Histrionics of Drag Diva Ethyl Eichelberger" (PhD diss., New York University, 1996), 243–44.
12. Foucault, "Of Other Spaces," 6.
13. Ibid.,3–4.
14. Brecht, *Queer Theatre*, 30, emphasis in original.
15. Ibid.,31.
16. Foucault, "Of Other Spaces," 5.
17. Ibid.,3.
18. David Savran, *A Queer Sort of Materialism: Recontextualizing American Theatre* (Ann Arbor: University of Michigan Press, 2003), 6.
19. Robert Mills, "Queer Is Here? Lesbian, Gay, Bisexual, and Transgender Histories and Public Culture," *History Workshop Journal*, no. 62 (Autumn 2006): 253–63, 262.
20. Foucault, "Of Other Spaces," 7.
21. This play was built from a notebook of quotations that Charles Ludlam carried around with him and was produced by John Vaccaro at the Play-House of the Ridiculous.
22. Foucault, "Of Other Spaces," 7.
23. Charles Ludlam, *Ridiculous Theatre: Scourge of Human Folly*, ed. Steven Samuels (New York: Theatre Communications Group, 1992), 131.
24. Charles Ludlam and Gautam Dasgupta, "Interview: Charles Ludlam," *Performing Arts Journal* 3:1 (1978): 69–70.
25. Foucault, "Of Other Spaces," 5.
26. Bonnie Marranca, "Introduction" to *Theatre of the Ridiculous*, ed. Bonnie Marranca and Gautum Dasgupta (New York: Performing Arts Journal, 1979), 6.
27. Foucault, "Of Other Spaces," 6.
28. Dan Isaac, "Ronald Tavel: Ridiculous Playwright," *TDR* 13:1 (Autumn 1968): 108.
29. http://www.warholstars.org/ridiculous.html.
30. Stephen J. Bottoms, *Playing Underground: A Critical History of the 1960s Off-Off-Broadway Movement* (Ann Arbor: University of Michigan Press, 2004),11.
31. Ibid.,14.
32. Foucault, "Other Spaces," 7.
33. *Jack Smith and the Destruction of Atlantis* documentary.
34. Foucault, "Of Other Spaces," 7–8.
35. José Muñoz, *Cruising Utopia: The Then and There of Queer Futurity* (New York: New York University Press, 2009), 1.
36. Foucault, "Of Other Spaces," 8.
37. Elizabeth Freeman, "Preface," in *Time Binds: Queer Temporalities, Queer Histories* (Durham, NC: Duke University Press, 2010), xxii.

Bibliography

Bottoms, Stephen J. *Playing Underground: A Critical History of the 1960s Off-Off-Broadway Movement.* Ann Arbor: University of Michigan Press, 2004.

Brecht, Stefan. *Queer Theatre.* Germany: Suhrkampf, 1978.

Comenas, Gary. "Conquest of the Ridiculous: Ronald Tavel, John Vaccaro and Charles Ludlam." 2008, revised 2009. http://www.warholstars.org/ridiculous.html.

Foucault, Michel. "Of Other Spaces: Utopias and Heterotopias." In *Architecture/Mouvement/Continuité* (1984). Originally presented in French as "Des Espace Autres" in March 1967. Translated by Jay Miskowiec in *Diacritics* 16, no. 1 (Spring, 1986): 22–27.

Freeman, Elizabeth. *Time Binds: Queer Temporalities, Queer Histories.* Durham, NC: Duke University Press, 2010.

Goldberg, Roselee. "Art after Hours: Downtown Performance." In *The Downtown Book: The New York Art Scene, 1974–1984.* Edited by Marvin J. Taylor. New York: Grey Art Gallery and Study Center, Fales Library, 2006.

Halberstam, Jack. *In a Queer Time and Place.* New York: New York University Press, 2005.

———. *The Queer Art of Failure.* Durham, NC: Duke University Press, 2011.

Isaac, Dan. "Ronald Tavel: Ridiculous Playwright." *TDR* 13, no. 1 (Autumn 1968), 106–15.

Jeffreys, Joe E. "An Outre Entrée into the Para-Ridiculous Histrionics of Drag Diva Ethyl Eichelberger." PhD diss., New York University, 1996.

Ludlam, Charles. *Ridiculous Theatre: Scourge of Human Folly.* Edited by Steven Samuels. New York: Theatre Communications Group, 1992.

Marranca, Bonnie. "Introduction." In *Theatre of the Ridiculous.* Edited by Bonnie Marranca and Gautum Dasgupta. New York: Performing Arts Journal, 1979.

Mills, Robert. "Queer Is Here? Lesbian, Gay, Bisexual, and Transgender Histories and Public Culture." *History Workshop Journal*, no. 62 (Autumn 2006): 253–63.

Muñoz, José. *Cruising Utopia: The Then and There of Queer Futurity.* New York: New York University Press, 2009.

PS 1 Archives, I. A. 2086. The Museum of Modern Art, New York.

Tavel, Ronald. *The Life of Lady Godiva.* In *The Theatre of the Ridiculous.* Edited by Bonnie Marranca and Gautum Dasgupta. New York: Performing Arts Journal, 1979.

———. "Maria Montez: Anima of an Antediluvian World." In *Flaming Creature: Jack Smith, His Amazing Life and Times.* Edited by Edward Leffingwell. New York: Serpent's Tail, 1997.

3

The Evolving Process of an Historical View: Aleks Sierz and British Theatre in the 1990s

Yael Zarhy-Levo

How does a prevalent historical view come into being? In tackling this question, I set out here to inquire into the process of forming an historical view, which is then transformed into a dominant historical narrative (a historical materiality).[1] Considering that a number of possible approaches can underlie such an inquiry, it is necessary first to provide a contextual background for the specific approach taken in the present investigation.

When a particular view regarding past theatrical developments emerges from an historical account (complying with what Tom Postlewait terms "an interpretative history"),[2] it can obscure a range of highly intricate historiographical considerations. Such interpretations prompt a variety of questions about their characteristics, the presentation of alternate views, whether the interpretation is consensual or controversial, whether it has remained stable or undergone changes through time, and so on. Although some of these questions echo throughout this essay, I am primarily interested in yet another one: how such views are constructed and how they evolve into prevalent ones.

Elsewhere I have shown that *mediation*—the workings of various individuals or organizations that act as mediators (such as theatre reviewers, journalists, funding bodies, publishers, producers, artistic directors, critics, and academics)—plays a central role in the making of theatrical reputations.[3] Mediating figures "authorize" theatrical works (plays or productions) and theatre creators (playwrights, directors etc.) and influence where they are placed on the cultural map. Mediation has an affinity with the "institutional approach" (manifested, notably, in the sociocultural studies of Pierre Bourdieu), according to which the canonization of literary and theatrical works is attributed to institutional factors.[4] In accordance with my perception of the central role mediation plays in reception, I have also shown that the emergent historical view pertaining to a number of major developments in the history of modern British theatre has been the outcome of specific configurations of mediating factors and agents involved in its shaping process (a notable example is the view of *Look Back in Anger* as the turning point in modern British theatre).[5]

The contributive role of theatre reviewers and critics, among mediating agents, is often highly significant.[6] While theatre *reviewers* can be seen as an important force affecting the careers of individual playwrights, specific theatre *critics* have played a major role in categorizing and defining new theatrical trends, movements, or schools as a means of promoting a new type of drama associated with several playwrights.[7] The grouping of theatrical matter into trends, movements, or schools fills a central function in theatre histories. These groupings serve both to distinguish between theatrical developments, while also connecting them and determining their significance within a perceived theatre "tradition." They denominate influences, continuities, and emphases in different periods, classify theatrical means, forms, and styles, affiliate the works of individual playwrights with these forms and styles, and, importantly, organize historical sequence(s). In defining new groupings, critics have the potential power to influence the views expressed in theatre histories.

Elsewhere, I have discussed two case studies—Martin Esslin's *The Theatre of the Absurd* (1961) and Aleks Sierz's *In-Yer-Face Theatre* (2001)—illustrating the specific strategies employed in *constructing* a new theatrical trend, school, or movement.[8] The enquiry here continues the analysis of the critical moves involved in defining a trend, but it also focuses upon the trajectory of Sierz's perception of British theatre in the 1990s, centering upon how the historical view generated by Sierz's construction of the new theatrical trend of In-Yer-Face Theatre evolved from his 2001 study. Sierz's attempt to capture and classify British theatre in the 1990s, I argue, demonstrates a new materiality in which the critic (Sierz) plays the leading role. In maneuvering to promote and enhance the significance of his constructed trend in the face of obstructive (at times countering) factors, Sierz exemplifies a form of mediation that turns the critical perception (Sierz's) itself into the subject matter. His case also demonstrates how critical views of theatrical developments in a past decade have been maintained in subsequent historical accounts, exemplifying how the mediating agents that preserve and foster these past views contribute to the shaping of histories that follow.

The Forming of a View: Sierz's 2001 Study and Subsequent "Gate-Keeping"

Elsewhere, I have suggested that Sierz's 2001 study followed in the footsteps of Esslin's *The Theatre of the Absurd*.[9] In their studies, both Esslin and Sierz assume the position of authoritative cultural commentators, exploiting their authority to promote their perception of a new theatrical grouping. Notably, in both studies, written four decades apart, none of the dramatists grouped under the particular label (i.e., In-Yer-Face or Absurd) considered themselves to belong to a movement, school, or trend. The new theatrical grouping, then, represents, in itself, an authoritative critical move. Furthermore, both critics employ a specific repertoire of strategic means essential for such a grouping, means that manifest their practice of claiming authority.

In his study, Sierz defines a group of new playwrights (a preliminary requirement in constructing a new theatrical trend) whose works he associates, to varying extents, with a new type of drama, which he labels "In-Yer-Face Theatre" ("name-giving" serves an essential constitutive function).[10] These writers, he claims, have pioneered "a new aesthetic—more blatant, aggressive and confrontational—that opened up new possibilities for British drama."[11] Sierz presents three dramatists—Antony Neilson, Sarah Kane, and Mark Ravenhill—as distinctly associated with the new type of drama because their works, as compared with other playwrights grouped under the label, contain a large number of characteristics distinguishing this new type. By defining a group of playwrights as a new theatrical trend, and positing particular dramatists as its major representatives, Sierz (like Esslin) manifests his authority to include and exclude. The definition of a group of dramatists as comprising a center to and the margins of the new trend also serves as a means of promotion by presenting the new type of drama as a theatrical phenomenon widespread enough to call for recognition.

Though Sierz's study elicited some controversy, it is apparent that the label for the trend, the characteristics and number of its playwrights, and the works Sierz defined as representative of in-yer-face writing have become associated with British theatre of the 1990s.[12] Even had the extent and manifestations of the study's influence remained undetermined during the few years following its 2001 publication, Sierz seems nonetheless to have acquired an authoritative position with respect to British theatre of the 1990s.

Significantly, Sierz himself has played an active role in maintaining his position, reinforcing his authority by publishing essays and reports dealing with the topic of In-Yer-Face Theatre.[13] To this extent his conduct resembles that of his predecessors Martin Esslin and John Russell Taylor, both of whom preserved the authoritative position they had acquired following the publication of *The Theatre of the Absurd* and *Anger and After*.[14] Both Esslin and Russell Taylor have added prefaces and/or elaborations to subsequent editions of their studies, and have maintained their status as "gate-keepers" by serving as editors of and/or writing introductions to various works that engage with "their" major playwrights.[15] In the same vein, Sierz has contributed to studies published in this century that engage the subject of British theatre in the 1990s, particularly the collections *British Theatre of the 1990s: Interviews with Directors, Playwrights, Critics and Academics*, published in 2007, and *Cool Britannia? British Political Drama in the 1990s*, published in 2008.[16] Sierz's contributions to these two studies include an interview that took place in 2003, two years after publication of his study, and a chapter in the 2008 collection that sprang from a conference entitled "In-Yer-Face? British Drama in the 1990s," held in 2002, which Sierz also discussed in a 2003 issue of NTQ.[17] These activities reflect Sierz's mediatory conduct in maintaining his authoritative position as a "gate-keeper."[18]

Maintaining the Perception and Countering Critiques: The 2003 Interview and 2008 Chapter

Both the interview, published in 2007, and Sierz's chapter in the 2008 study mark an in-between phase in the evolving course of the historical view generated from his 2001 book. While, in the interview conducted with him, Sierz primarily defends and clarifies his conception, his chapter sets out to counter the critiques directed at his book. A brief look at a number of his reactions and approaches to major issues in these sources serves, first, to demonstrate the main strategies and emphases he used to support and further advance his perception, and, second, these intermediate defenses can be compared with Sierz's later views, to reveal ongoing changes and modifications in his strategic devices and the ongoing development of the historical view represented by his study.

In his first reply in the interview, Sierz discloses and shares with his interviewer and readers his behind-the-scenes considerations. He explains that his claim regarding a crisis in new writing at the end of the 1980s was essential to presenting a "dramatic" story—a narrative that argues "in favour of the creative outburst of the mid-1990s."[19] Sierz is asked to relate his narrative, which highlights the parallels between the 1950s' New Wave and the 1990s' renaissance in new writing, to the revisionists' rereading of the history of postwar British theatre. He unequivocally declares: "The story that puts *Look Back in Anger* centre stage in British postwar theatre history is the correct one."[20] Sierz clarifies that he rejects the revisionists' attempts to shift the focus from the Royal Court "because it distracts attention from the *main* narrative of British theatre, in which the Royal Court is central to discovering and developing new writers."[21] Sierz's uncompromising preference for the "main" narrative (or story) of the 1950s, which positions the Royal Court "group" at center stage, clearly complies with his narrative of the 1990s, which gives his group of in-yer-face writers a central stand. Implied in this is a continuity between and connecting theatrical developments within the history of British theatre as Sierz perceives it, in which the 1950s' "main" narrative not only facilitates his own argument concerning the 1990s, but also serves to legitimize and promote it. Coexisting alternate views can only threaten dominant narratives (such as his own).

Noteworthy, too, is Sierz's defense of the label "In-Yer-Face Theatre" against such labels as "New Brutalism" or "neo-Jacobeanism." Sierz explains his insistence on this label (which initially appeared in reviews of the new plays), stating that it "describes the relationships between the stage and the audience, between the writer and society."[22] He further declares that this label is "the one that is truly distinctive of the 1990s. It's not the only style that writers used; it's not a movement—it is a *sensibility*."[23] The playwrights of the 1990s classified under the label "in-yer-face" drama, Sierz admits, should have included a number of authors whose works "do not fit comfortably into this in-yer-face sensibility."[24] His reply concerning "the archetypal figure of the 1990s" notes the three playwrights (Kane, Neilson, and Ravenhill) he posited in his study as the major representatives of In-Yer-Face Theatre, plus Martin Crimp, whom Sierz regrets not having added to the "core" playwrights. This omission, Sierz claims, derived from his plan to deal with playwrights who had made their debuts in the 1990s (Crimp, whom Sierz perceives as "in some senses [...] a quintessentially 1990s writer," had started in the 1980s).[25]

In response to the critique concerning the suppression of the role of "other 1990s' women playwrights, besides Sarah Kane," Sierz refers to four women playwrights he discusses in his book, admitting that "the work of older playwrights who succeed in reinventing themselves, such as Caryl Churchill," could also be highlighted. Age matters to Sierz, even though the time frame of the 1990s as a criterion for affiliation with the theatrical trend or school called In-Yer-Face Theatre is of his choosing, as is the classification of Crimp and the exclusion of Churchill. Simultaneously, Sierz often uses time in an indefinite way when he responds to critiques directed at his study, for example, "there are numerous women playwrights that have emerged recently" or when he rejects critiques regarding his study's political shortcomings and comments that in-yer-face writers "were less interested in big public events and more interested in private ones." The connection between the personal and the political in the 1990s is further elided by comparison, for example, "There's definitely a slide away from explicit political material, and definitely a refusal to offer people solutions. Since 9/11, of course, all that is changing."[26]

Both 1990s' women playwrights and the politics of in-yer-face reemerge in Sierz's later writing, as does his connection to the Royal Court, in Sierz's view "the market leader in new writing."[27] Giving the court, "the oldest new writing venue," the lead role in developing new playwrights in the 1990s welds In-Yer-Face to the "main" narrative of postwar British theatre. At the same time, the comparison underscores the incompatibility between a time frame in which In-Yer-Face debuts in the 1990s, yet manifestations of its sensibility appear earlier, in Churchill—"a quintessentially 1990s writer"[28]—and Crimp. These latter playwrights as well as Kane, Ravenhill, and Neilson, Sierz believes, are likely to "pay revisiting" at some later (future) point. In replying to the question whether in-yer-face sensibility has come to an end, Sierz notes Sarah Kane's death in February 1999 as a "convenient endpoint."[29]

Sierz's replies in the 2003 interview demonstrate how adept he is at exploiting his authoritative position (maintained by his gate-keeping) and at preserving and fostering his critical perception regarding the 1990s. Later writing illustrates yet a further step in the maintaining of his views. Sierz's chapter in the 2008 collection is titled "'We All Need Stories': The Politics of In-Yer-Face Theatre."[30] If the title itself suggests a shift in emphasis (i.e., to the politics of in-yer-face), so, too, does the editors' decision to locate Sierz's chapter in the first section of the collection, entitled "In-Yer-Face Theatre: A Reconsideration." So framed, Sierz is well-served to address the controversies elicited by his 2001 study, relating, in particular, to the critique concerning the issue of the politics of In-Yer-Face Theatre. Sierz now pronounces In-Yer-Face Theatre to be political, highlighting its emphasis on "the sense of rupture, a radical break, with the past" and its stress on the new and innovative.[31] He further claims that this "brand" of theatre implies "the existence of an avant-garde: although cultural critics have announced the death of the avant-garde on more than one occasion in the past 50 years, in theatre its re-emergence in the 1990s took a classical form: innovation, scandal and then retrenchment."[32] Recounting the story of the emergence of In-Yer-Face Theatre within the broader political and theatrical context, Sierz now declares that "as a cultural avant-garde, the dissenting new writers of the 1990s produced work that was on the extreme left, being fiercely, sometimes ferociously, critical of consumer capitalism, social inequality, sexual discrimination, violence and war. No social custom was left unturned."[33]

Sierz foregrounds his book as "first and foremost a text," whose "politics are the product of time and place." He then refers to the controversial debuts in the mid-1990s of playwrights such as Kane and Ravenhill. In light of the attacks on these 1990s' new plays, he explains, "it was essential, both politically and artistically, to defend this new theatre sensibility and make a case for its radical credentials."[34] He further adds that his study "was both a report from the front line and an advocacy argument. It also aimed to counter academic hostility to the work of the new playwrights—led by Ravenhill and Kane—who had emerged in the 1990s" (he refers here to two especially vitriolic academic comments). By presenting his study as championing new radical writing that had been faced with a hostile reception (critical and primarily academic), Sierz offers yet another "dramatic" story with a "happy ending" (though this time it concerns his own book). "Gradually," he comments, seemingly in passing, "the work of these playwrights has become accepted, and the relevance of their work more widely appreciated."[35] This latter comment inevitably serves to prove his case for the 1990s' new playwrights (hence, promoting his study), while, in the bargain, striking back at academic critiques.

Sierz's clarifies that, although his study seems ("silently") to suggest a schematic division between "those playwrights who are in-yer-face and those who are not," "the reality was very different."[36] Referring to the metaphor for in-yer-face writing—"an arena" (which he suggests in the conclusion to his 2001 study)—Sierz explains that "this 'arena' is a very complex phenomenon because it is both a sensibility and a fistful of theatre techniques." "As a sensibility," he claims, "it blows through the work not only of young playwrights, but also of older ones, such as Martin Crimp, Caryl Churchill and Harold Pinter," repeating (yet again) that his study includes only those who made their debut in the 1990s, and thereby excludes older playwrights.[37] If "there is not such a thing as a simple 'in-yer-face' playwright,"[38] what does In-Yer-Face delimit? Defending or, rather, supporting his study, Sierz suggests that "at its worst, a concept such as in-yer-face theatre downgrades those writers who have worked in a variety of styles or whose work is only partially touched by this sensibility."[39] In the context of the book's exclusions, he also addresses the issue of 1990s' women writers, remarking (somewhat awkwardly) that "the book prefers women writers—led by Kane—who don't accept being labeled as feminists to those that do."[40] Compared with his replies in the 2003 interview, Sierz's clarifications, most of which address issues raised in critiques of his book, demonstrate anew the tactics he developed in mediating his book, within which he now integrates the controversial issues through which it was critiqued.

Finally, Sierz addresses an additional issue appearing in critiques directed at his 2001 book. "Perhaps the most radical exclusion," he acknowledges, "was theatre outside London." Although he reasons that "to experience live theatre, you have to be there," he also concedes that for those who were living outside London "the story of the 1990s would have been radically different." "Taking the capital as its center," Sierz admits, marginalizes those playwrights who made their careers outside London, "and it leaves the politics of an overcentralized British culture largely unchallenged."[41] Sierz's acknowledgment of his exclusion of theatre outside London, taken with his earlier (2003) reassessing comments on Crimp and Churchill, underscore the importance of time and space where criteria for affiliation to a theatrical trend are concerned.

The conclusion of Sierz's chapter, which draws to some extent on his hindsight, can be read in the main (despite some deviations) as his own high praise of his book. Typically (in this chapter and later on), Sierz promotes his view by combining, seemingly in passing, a major claim with a minor reservation, for example, "It's surely not controversial to say that, although the general narrative of the renaissance of new writing in the mid-1990s is true, several key episodes need a touch of shading" (he refers to the initial hostility to *Blasted* at the Royal Court script meeting as a "key" episode).[42] He begins his conclusion by proclaiming that "as a discourse, *In-Yer-Face Theatre* works like a myth," and goes on to proclaim that "the myth of in-yer-face theatre now lives on independently of the *In-Yer-Face Theatre* book." Assuming a modest pose, Sierz comments that "maybe the time has come to radically reassess in-yer-face theatre,"[43] but matters can't be left there, thus, "the story told by *In-Yer-Face Theatre* is the best general narrative of the 1990s that we have so far, but clearly the fact that it has become so rapidly naturalized could only happen with the exclusion of many other aspects of British theatre."[44]

Undoubtedly, Sierz's 2008 chapter testifies to his highly effective advocacy of his 2001 book in the face of dissenting (and some disdaining) critical and academic voices. I have discussed elsewhere the significance of the diverse channels through which mediation is practiced, all of which are bound to institutional frames or regulations.[45] In Sierz's case, the specific mediating channels include conferences devoted to the theatre of the 1990s (such as those held in 1997 and 2002), the journal *New Theatre Quarterly* (in which he published his reports and essays), and the publishing house of Palgrave Macmillan. (The latter two have come to be seen by many theatre scholars as central and influential publishing channels.) These channels of mediation (and the specific editors involved) have not only contributed to Sierz maintaining his gate-keeping position, but have also provided him, by means of their reputations, with a central stage for advancing his perceptions. Both prepared the ground for Sierz's next mediating channel, the highly reputable publishing house, Methuen.

Presenting an Historical Narrative: The 2012 Account

How do the mediating agents that preserve and foster past critical perceptions contribute to the shaping of the histories that follow? Indeed, where Sierz's strategic devices are concerned, the most intriguing aspect of his ongoing campaign for his 2001 conception is his contribution to the six-volume series *Modern British Playwriting*, published by Methuen Drama in 2012.[46] Sierz served as editor and main author of the fifth volume of the series, which presents an account of the 1990s.[47] This authoritative position implies, on the one hand, that Sierz would provide a broad account of a decade that had witnessed many different theatrical developments, rather than focus on the specific phenomenon of In-Yer-Face Theatre. On the other hand, however, it is reasonable to assume that he would also seek to exert his authority and exploit this opportunity to further propel his perception of the 1990s. Of all Sierz's strategic engagements, tackling these opposing agendas presents a considerable challenge. While, in his 2003 interview, Sierz defended and further clarified his 2001 perception, and, while, in his 2008 chapter, he countered critiques of his book by developing new mediating tactics, in 2012 Sierz had to maneuver between the series' demands and the promotion of his own conception. Now, as a major authority, though, hence, also a main "suspect" holding a preconceived perception of the 1990s, Sierz needed to exploit the influential new stage for promoting his views without jeopardizing his position as editor and main author of the rewritten historical account of the decade. As his 2012 account shows, Sierz embarked upon an overall policy that has enabled him simultaneously to eliminate the potential minefield obstructing his designated path, while radically advancing his desired viewpoint.

The structure of the fifth volume adheres, in the main, to that of the four previous volumes in the series. It begins with a general introduction, "Living in the 1990s," which is subdivided into topics (such as "Background," "Media," "Culture"), most of which appear in the other four volumes. The first chapter deals with the theatre of the decade (the subsections comprising this chapter differ to a large extent in each of the series' volumes, manifesting the differences in outlook of the editors/authors in regard to the particular decade). "Theatre in the 1990s" lists among its subsections "Flagship Theatres: West End, National and RSC," "Off-West End and Companies," "New Writing," "Experimental, Fringe and Live Art," and "Outside London: England, Scotland, Wales and Northern Ireland." In considering these subsections, it appears that, in his 2012 account, as compared with his 2001 study, Sierz attempts to provide a fuller view of the theatre of the decade. Moreover, it is especially noticeable that he neither devotes a particular subsection, nor even a marked section in one of the subsections, to In-Yer-Face Theatre. Although he does include a discussion of his own trend, rather than highlighting it with a subheading he integrates it smoothly into his account of new writing. A brief look at this first chapter's subsections—"New Writing" and "Conclusion"—can serve to demonstrate Sierz's strategies in adapting his 2001 perception to the 2012 modified framework, while concomitantly inserting and promoting his views.

In "New Writing," Sierz primarily focuses on London, listing the state-subsidized theatres that specialized in new writing. He notes, too, the Traverse in Edinburgh and Live Theatre in Newcastle-upon-Tyne as significant new writing theatres outside the metropolis. Sierz also points out several unsubsidized venues in the London fringe and stresses the "vital contribution" of several small touring companies to producing new playwrights.[48] Echoing, yet cautiously rephrasing his earlier claim, he now recounts: "Following cuts in state subsidy during the 1980s, the genre of new writing was widely perceived to be in trouble at the start of the decade."[49] This time he also chooses to refer to others' views as to the state of crisis in new writing, citing the playwright David Edgar and the critic Michael Billington.[50] "But just as the obituaries of new writing were appearing in the media," he states, "a revival was beginning."[51] Significantly, he then marks Philip Ridley's *The Pitchfork Disney*, staged at the Bush in January 1991, as the revival of new writing, highlighting the comment by Dominic Dromgoole (at the time, the new artistic director of the Bush) that the play unexpectedly introduced a new sensibility, and was one of the first "to signal the new direction for new writing."[52] If Sierz presents his familiar narrative, now in a slightly modified and more cautious mode, and relies on others' views, he nonetheless maintains and promotes his 2001 perception that In-Yer-Face saved British theatre.

Sierz traces the new plays, from 1991 to 1994, that had "shocked the audience," relating the debut of Kane's *Blasted* (January 1995) and the media furor that followed, emphasizing that it "put British new writing on the map."[53] In completing his list of the early "new sensibility" voices, Sierz notes Jez Butterworth (1995) and Mark Ravenhill (1996), and, in keeping with his revised policy, Sierz reduces the visibility of his own role in the definition of the new theatrical group and refers to the playwrights, saying: "This loose group of young writers formed something of an avant-garde, sharing a similar sensibility, which has been labeled 'in-yer-face theatre.'"[54] This cautious and somewhat vague description ends, as can be expected, with a reference (albeit in an endnote) to his 2001 study. He calls attention to his own view, however, by pronouncing that "some of the clearest examples" of In-Yer-Face Theatre "came from the keyboards of Ridley, Neilson, Kane and Ravenhill," pointing out that the latter two were especially influenced by the work of Crimp.[55] In his 2012 account, Sierz adds Ridley (whom he had discussed only briefly in his 2001 study) to his three "core" playwrights (those he had posited in his book as major representatives of In-Yer-Face Theatre) and highlights the influence of Crimp—the playwright who had made his debut in the 1980s, but whom he defined in his 2003 interview (and also refers to in his 2008 chapter) as "a quintessentially 1990s writer" (again, the time frame dominates). Sierz's shifting of Ridley and (albeit in a different way) Crimp to the center ties in with other issues in the volume addressed later on.

On the whole, Sierz's volume expands his view of new writing in 1990s London (e.g., referring to an influential playwriting style that came from Ireland).[56] He also briefly discusses several older playwrights who had emerged in the 1980s, highlighting, yet again, Crimp's work, refers to "old veterans" who "broke new ground," such as Churchill and Pinter, and comments on the "renaissance of gay and lesbian dramas" in the early 1990s.[57] Sierz also expands the list of theatres serving as venues for new writing[58] and the factors influencing new writing (American playwrights are included).[59]

In concluding his account of the new writing, Sierz refers to the dominant themes in these works (most of which had appeared in his earlier writings), stressing that "the idea of storytelling [one of the characteristics that Sierz attributes to Ridley's drama] also interested playwrights."[60] "In the final analysis," he claims, "the sheer variety and richness of British playwriting left a lasting impression on both critics and audiences," concluding that "given its richness and its success in many countries abroad [...] it gave British theatre an international boost."[61] The two remarks that emphasize the richness and its affective consequences are in line with Sierz's tendency (apparently responding to the series', or perhaps editors', demand) to widen the scope of the discussion of 1990s' new writing. At the same time, these remarks, written from the perspective of 2012, also seem to provide a justification for the reassessed, expanded account. Moreover, Sierz's claim as to the variety and richness of 1990s' playwriting serves him further in concluding his account of the theatre of the decade.

Sierz begins the "Conclusion" with two statements, the second of which is especially significant. It reads: "In the 1990s, British theatre was not simply in-yer-face, nor flagship dominated nor newly commercialized, nor even a mix of all three."[62] This is a key rhetorical sentence in that, by using a negation, Sierz emphasizes three major components of the 1990s' theatre, the first of which—in-yer-face—is posited as equal in importance to the other two. At the same time, In-Yer-Face is distinguished from the other two by representing the new writing of the decade.

While the expansion of the 2012 account of the theatre of the 1990s in the volume's first chapter suggests a turn in Sierz's view of the decade, the volume in its entirety in fact presents a strategically disguised promotion of the essence of Sierz's 2001 perceptions. The second chapter of the volume, "Playwrights and Plays," betrays Sierz's underlying intentions and his consistency, rather than transformation. This chapter includes a discussion of four playwrights—Ridley, Kane, Neilson, and Ravenhill—who comply with Sierz's reassessed, modified list of in-yer-face "core" writers. As in the previous four volumes of the series, which also highlight four playwrights, with a discussion of each dramatist by a different scholar, in the fifth volume Sierz writes the account of Philip Ridley, Catherine Rees does Sarah Kane, Trish Reid does Antony Neilson, and Graham Saunders discusses Mark Ravenhill. While Rees questions and reassesses Kane's role as an in-yer-face playwright, suggesting other ways of perceiving her work, Sierz presents Ridley as "a pivotal figure in the history of 1990s playwriting,"[63] a perception he interjects and develops throughout the volume. Sierz's decision to add Ridley to his "core" playwrights and to write the discussion of Ridley's work himself suggests Ridley, not Kane, is *the* major representative of in-yer-face writing, an assumption corroborated in the volume's "Afterword." Kane remains as one of the "core" writers, her career (and especially her early plays and their reception) now inseparable from the in-yer-face concept. Sierz's choice of the four playwrights, whom he perceives as distinctly associated with In-Yer-Face Theatre as representative of 1990s British playwriting in general, reflects his intent to highlight the role of the trend he has constructed as descriptive of the theatre of that decade.

The last two chapters of the fifth volume are "Documents" and "Afterword." The first features a piece written by Ridley, an interview with Kane, extracts of writing by Neilson, and a talk delivered by Ravenhill.[64] The "Afterword" declares, "The new young playwrights who emerged in the 1990s found that, by 1995, there was a real buzz about British theatre."[65] Noting the stormy reception of Kane's *Blasted* and the gradual recognition and appreciation of "a whole host of new talents" in the balance of the decade, Sierz points out that "by the new millennium, the moment of in-yer-face theatre was past and a new theatre landscape began to open up."[66] The "new theatre landscape," in Sierz's writing of it, concerns the evolving perception of Kane's work, which is followed by an overview of the development of Ridley's, Neilson's, and Ravenhill's careers.[67]

In the last part of his "Afterword," Sierz states that, whereas his 2001 study was written from the perspective of the dawn of the new millennium, by the second decade of the new age, "it is essential to alter that perspective by looking at the past through a different optic."[68] He then suggests five ways of applying a different focus to the 1990s: "Art schools not theatres"; "Euro-modernism not in-yer-face"; "Older and darker, not younger"; "Scotland not England"; and "the effects of *an unpredictable real-life tragedy*; the murder of toddler Jamie Bulger."[69] Sierz highlights the effect of the massive media coverage of the murder on Kane's initial reception and the impact of the murder on Ravenhill's early writing. "Without this unpredictable event," Sierz suggests, "the theatre history of the 1990s might have been very different."[70]

Sierz's topics and emphases in his "Afterword" demonstrate (directly and indirectly) how he has upgraded his construction of In-Yer-Face Theatre by expanding the borders of time and space. He first follows the careers and/or perception of his four "core" playwrights through the first decade of the twenty-first century, then, in his five proposed ways to alter how we view the 1990s, Sierz points to the emergence of an in-yer-face sensibility in the context of art schools and the wider art scene, thereby integrating this phenomenon into a broader cultural system. He also roots In-Yer-Face Theatre in both British tradition and Continental modernism and broadens its scope by relating In-Yer-Face to influential older writers, particularly Crimp, a view he articulates throughout the volume. Sierz also shifts the beginning of "the new writing boom of the 1990s" to Scotland and links the in-yer-face phenomenon to a real-life event, key to any cultural account of a decade. In expanding the borders of time and space, Sierz updates the criteria for affiliation with the trend he has constructed, presenting the In-Yer-Face sensibility as a much wider phenomenon.

Sierz's overall policy in his 2012 volume can be summarized as follows: in adapting his 2001 conception to the demands of the series (or perhaps its editors), Sierz chose both to downplay his own role as a major commentator on the 1990s and to suppress the label associated with his trend and known book. While doing this, he simultaneously employs a range of strategies to secure the theatrical grouping he has defined. Although it may seem that In-Yer-Face Theatre, either as a label of a theatrical trend and/or as a book title, is not brought directly to the fore (no marked section or subsection headings), the writers associated with Sierz's brand are not only highlighted throughout the volume, but effectively star in the expanded account (numerous references to these playwrights and their plays in the volume's index also makes their dominance clear). By 2012, Sierz had the authority to upgrade his "core" playwrights, positing them as the distinct representatives of new playwriting in the 1990s, indeed, using newness and the innovative as criteria distinguishing one decade from another helps Sierz's writers to emerge as *the* representatives of the theatre of the 1990s.

If, like Martin Esslin, Aleks Sierz constructed a new theatrical grouping in his 2001 study and maintained his authority over the first decade of the twenty-first century by securing a "gate-keeping" position (even while clarifying his perception and countering critiques), in the 2012 volume, like Russell Taylor, Sierz presents his narrative on playwriting in the 1990s, a narrative to which he attributes a pivotal role in the construction of that decade's cultural history. Notably, however, Sierz's mediation distinguishes him from his two predecessors, since it is apparent that his maneuvers to enhance the significance of the trend he has constructed exhibit a form of mediation unlike that previously practiced (by Esslin, for example), namely, the positing of the critical perception (the in-yer-face grouping) itself as the subject matter.

The unique two-phase process, with its in-between mediation, through which Aleks Sierz plays the lead, demonstrates not only the evolving course of an historical view, but also how the critical perception of a theatrical development in a past decade is subsequently fostered so as to transform that perception into a dominant historical narrative. The case of Aleks Sierz likely represents a new, twenty-first century, take on mediation and the shaping of an historical view that works to replace the thing historicized with the critic/historian's perception.

Notes

1. This essay draws on a paper presented at the meeting of the Theatre Historiography Working Group at the IFTR conference in Barcelona (July 2013). I thank the participants for their helpful comments.
2. Thomas Postlewait, *The Cambridge Introduction to Theatre Historiography* (Cambridge:Cambridge University Press, 2009), 3.
3. For elaboration on the various figures who act as mediators in the theatre and the principles underlying their practice of mediation, see Yael Zarhy-Levo, *The Making of Theatrical Reputations: Studies from the Modern London Theatre* (Iowa City: University of Iowa Press, 2008), 1–14.
4. See, for example, Pierre Bourdieu, "Mais Qui a Créé les Créateurs," *Questions de Sociologie* (Paris: Minuit, 1980), 207–21; Pierre Bourdieu and Richard Nice, "The Production of Belief: Contribution to an Economy of Symbolic Goods," *Media, Culture & Society* 2:3 (1980): 261–93; Pierre Bourdieu,

"The Market of Symbolic Goods," *Poetics* 14:1 (1985): 13–44. Also see C. J. Van Rees, "How a Literacy Work Becomes a Masterpiece: On the Threefold Selection Practised by Literary Criticism," *Poetics* 12: 4 (1983): 397–417. Van Rees's essay is also a distinct representation of the institutional approach.
5. Zarhy-Levo, *The Making of Theatrical Reputations*, 15–62.
6. Ibid., in particular, see 161–208.
7. Yael Zarhy-Levo, "Dramatists under a Label: Martin Esslin's *Theatre of the Absurd* and Aleks Sierz' *In-Yer-Face Theatre*," *Studies in Theatre and Performance* 31:3 (2011): 315–26. See also Zarhy-Levo, *The Theatrical Critic as Cultural Agent: Constructing Pinter, Orton and Stoppard as Absurdist Playwrights* (New York: Peter Lang, 2001).
8. Ibid. Martin Esslin, *The Theatre of the Absurd* (New York: Anchor Books, 1961); Aleks Sierz, *In-Yer-Face Theatre: British Drama Today* (London: Faber and Faber, 2001).
9. Zarhy-Levo, "Dramatists under a Label," 315–26.
10. Bourdieu, "The Production of Belief," 289. Also see Bourdieu, "The Social Space and the Genesis of Groups," *Theory and Society* 14:6 (1985): 729.
11. Sierz, *In-Yer-Face Theatre*, xii.
12. See, for example, Liz Tomlin, "English Theatre in the 1990s and Beyond," *The Cambridge History of British Theatre*, vol. 3 (Cambridge: Cambridge University Press, 2004), 504.
13. See, for example, Aleks Sierz, "Still In-Yer-Face? Towards a Critique and a Summation," *New Theatre Quarterly* 18:1 (2002): 17–24. Also see Aleks Sierz, "'In-Yer-Face' Theatre Conference," *New Theatre Quarterly* 19:1 (2003): 90.
14. John Russell Taylor, *Anger and After: A Guide to the New Drama* (London: Methuen, 1962). It is noteworthy that both studies, Esslin's and Russell Taylor's, are noted by Sierz as those that inspired his own study (see Alex Sierz, "'We All Need Stories': The Politics of In-Yer-Face Theatre," *Cool Britannia? British Political Drama in the 1990s*, eds. Rebecca D'Monté and Graham Saunders [Houndmills: Palgrave Macmillan, 2008], 29). The reference to Esslin and Russell Taylor here, however, primarily relates to their mediatory conduct, which perhaps also inspired Sierz's own conduct.
15. See, for example, Martin Esslin, "Introduction," *Absurd Drama* (Middlesex: Penguin, 1965), 7–23. Also see John Russell Taylor, ed., *John Osborne: Look Back in Anger: A Casebook* (London: Macmillan, 1986).
16. See Mireia Aragay, Hildegard Klein, Enric Monforte, and Pilar Zozaya, eds., *British Theatre of the 1990s: Interviews with Directors, Playwrights, Critics and Academics* (Houndmills: Palgrave Macmillan, 2007); D'Monté and Saunders, eds., *Cool Britannia? British Political Drama in the 1990s* (Houndmills: Palgrave Macmillan, 2008).
17. See Aragay et al., "Aleks Sierz," *British Theatre of the 1990s*, 139–56.
18. Significantly, Sierz's maintenance of his gate-keeping position is clearly reflected in the lead-in paragraph of his 2003 account, referring to an earlier conference "About Now"—the Eighth Birmingham Theatre Conference in 1997—which he describes as "an interim report on the recent renaissance of new writing in British theatre" (Sierz, "'In-Yer-Face' Theatre Conference," 90). It is hardly surprising that he also published the account of this 1997 conference in *New*

Theatre Quarterly (see Aleks Sierz, "'About Now' in Birmingham," *New Theatre Quarterly* 13:1 [1997]: 289–90).
19. Aragay et al., "Aleks Sierz," *British Theatre of the 1990s*, 139.
20. Ibid.,140.
21. Ibid., emphasis in original.
22. Ibid.,143.
23. Ibid., 143–44, emphasis in original.
24. Ibid.,144.
25. Ibid.,145–46.
26. Ibid.,146.
27. Ibid.,150.
28. Ibid.,151.
29. Ibid.
30. Sierz, "'We All Need Stories,'" 23–37. The chapter's title includes a quotation from a major speech (by Robbie) in Mark Ravenhill's play *Shopping and Fucking*. Drawing upon this quote, Sierz presents his 2001 study as responding "to this need for contemporary stories by offering a narrative about new writing [...] in the 1990s" (24).
31. Ibid.,25.
32. Ibid.
33. Ibid.,26.
34. Ibid.,27.
35. Ibid.
36. Ibid.,29.
37. Ibid.,30.
38. Ibid.
39. Ibid.,31.
40. Ibid.
41. Ibid.,32.
42. Ibid.,33.
43. Ibid.,34.
44. Ibid.,35.
45. Zarhy-Levo, *The Making of Theatrical Reputations*, 13–14.
46. Richard Boon and Philips Roberts, series eds., *Modern British Playwriting* (London: Methuen Drama, 2012).
47. Aleks Sierz, *Modern British Playwriting: The 1990s* (London: Methuen Drama,2012).
48. Ibid.,54.
49. Ibid.
50. Ibid.,54–55.
51. Ibid.,55.
52. Ibid.
53. Ibid.
54. Ibid.,57.
55. Ibid.
56. Ibid.,59–61.
57. Ibid.

58. Ibid.,63–64.
59. Ibid.,65–66.
60. Ibid.,67.
61. Ibid.,67–68.
62. Ibid.,85.
63. Ibid.,89.
64. It should be noted that in the fourth and sixth volumes of the series, as in the fifth one, the documents presented concern the "selected" playwrights featured in these volumes (four and five, respectively). Significantly, however, the "selected" playwrights in the fifth volume comply with Sierz's particular perception (2012) of the in-yer-face "core" writers.
65. Sierz, *Modern British Playwriting*, 222.
66. Ibid.
67. Ibid., 222–31. The "Afterword" in the second and fourth volumes of the series also centers on the four "selected" playwrights (in the first volume it centers on three of the four). What distinguishes the fifth volume, however, is that the "Afterword" mainly focuses on the in-yer-face phenomenon (whether playwrights or topics discussed).
68. Ibid.,231.
69. Ibid., 233, emphasis in original.
70. Ibid.,234.

Bibliography

Aragay, Mireia, Hildegard Klein, Enric Monforte, and Pilar Zozaya, eds. *British Theatre of the 1990s: Interviews with Directors, Playwrights, Critics and Academics*. Houndmills: Palgrave Macmillan, 2007.
Boon, Richard, and Philips Roberts, series eds. *Modern British Playwriting*. London: Methuen Drama, 2012.
Bourdieu, Pierre. "Mais Qui a Créé les Créateurs." In *Questions de Sociologie*. Paris: Minuit, 1980, 207–21.
———. "The Market of Symbolic Goods." *Poetics* 14, no. 1 (1985), 13–44.
———. "The Social Space and the Genesis of Groups." *Theory and Society* 14, no. 6 (1985), 723–44.
Bourdieu, Pierre, and Richard Nice. "The Production of Belief: Contribution to an Economy of Symbolic Goods." *Media, Culture & Society* 2, no. 3 (1980), 261–93.
D'Monté, Rebecca, and Graham Saunders, eds. *Cool Britannia? British Political Drama in the 1990s*. Houndmills: Palgrave Macmillan, 2008.
Esslin, Martin. "Introduction." In *Absurd Drama*. Middlesex: Penguin, 1965, 7–23
———. *The Theatre of the Absurd*. New York: Anchor Books, 1961.
Postlewait, Thomas. *The Cambridge Introduction to Theatre Historiography*. Cambridge: Cambridge University Press, 2009.
Sierz, Aleks. "'About Now' in Birmingham." *New Theatre Quarterly* 13, no. 1 (1997), 289–90.
———. *In-Yer-Face Theatre: British Drama Today*. London: Faber and Faber, 2001.

———. "'In-Yer-Face' Theatre Conference," NTQ Reports and Announcements. *New Theatre Quarterly* 19, no. 1 (2003), 90–91.
———. *Modern British Playwriting: The 1990s*. London: Methuen Drama, 2012.
———. "Still In-Yer-Face? Towards a Critique and a Summation." *New Theatre Quarterly* 18, no. 1 (2002), 17–24.
———. "'We All Need Stories': The Politics of In-Yer-Face Theatre." In *Cool Britannia*. Edited by D'Monté and Saunders. 23–37.
Taylor, John Russell. *Anger and After: A Guide to the New Drama*. London: Methuen, 1962.
———. ed. *John Osborne: Look Back in Anger: A Casebook*. London: Macmillan, 1986.
Tomlin, Liz. "English Theatre in the 1990s and Beyond." In *The Cambridge History of British Theatre* 3. Edited by Joseph W. Donohue et al. Cambridge: Cambridge University Press, 2004, 498–513
Van Rees, C. J. "How a Literacy Work Becomes a Masterpiece: On the Threefold Selection Practised by Literary Criticism." *Poetics* 12, no. 4 (1983), 397–417.
Zarhy-Levo, Yael. "Dramatists under a Label: Martin Esslin's *Theatre of the Absurd* and Aleks Sierz' *In-Yer-Face Theatre*." *Studies in Theatre and Performance* 31, no. 3 (2011), 315–26.
———. *The Making of Theatrical Reputations: Studies from the Modern London Theatre*. Iowa City: University of Iowa Press, 2008.
———. *The Theatrical Critic as Cultural Agent: Constructing Pinter, Orton and Stoppard as Absurdist Playwrights*. New York: Peter Lang, 2001.

4

Latino/a Dramaturgy as Historiography

Patricia Ybarra

For José Esteban Muñoz

Poised at the end of the world, and perhaps at the beginning of a new one, Victor Cazares's *Ramses Contra Los Monstruos* (2011) chronicles a love affair between Ramses, a man who makes his living dissolving the bodies of those killed in the business of narcotrafficking, and Tito/Titus, a young, United States–born Mexican who became obsessed with him after a hookup. We enter the action with Ramses in crisis. Cursed by his cousin, who destroys the effectiveness of his recipe, the bodies he is charged with disappearing are no longer dissolving, and his job security and his life are in danger. Tito/Titus takes Ramses to a long-shuttered movie theatre to hide out. There, in the midst of eleventh-hour revelations about HIV status and criminal activity, the couple reencounters the 1980s, whose legacy persists in the stale popcorn and broken glass on the theatre floor. As Tito/Titus explains:

> When I take the pill,
> I feel that I'm swallowing the 80s.
> I learned love from Enrique Iglesias songs.
> The ones that played at the beginning of telenovelas—
> telenovelas made in a Mexico made for export.
> Clear images of love.
> Clean images of blood.
> Neverr eal.
> Never ending without resolution.

Injected us with the televisuals of love and happy endings and sex without
  nudity or penetration.
When I take the pill,
I'm swallowing the 80s hole whole.
The 80s never happened.
It's a decade we only dreamt of.[1]

The pill to which Tito/Titus refers is an antiviral and, for him, taking it performs a simultaneous remembering and forgetting of the violence of the 1980s AIDS crisis and his sentimental televisual education. That Cazares links the rise of telenovelas, made for export throughout the hemisphere, with a health crisis, ignored by the United States in a moment of intense queer intimacy fueled by narcoviolence, transforms Tito/Titus's revelation from a personal disclosure of serostatus to a world-historical depiction of violent transnational commerce in bodies, drugs, and media. In contradistinction to Mexican and Chicano nationalist dramas of unidirectional migration, which concentrate on the singular event of a violent crossing, and to United States–based AIDS dramas that depend on the event of white, gay male monogamous coupling (i.e., *The Normal Heart*), Cazares's play refuses to stop: stop moving, stop crossing, stop killing. The last scene—titled "dose without end"—remixes texts and themes from throughout the play into a gripping anticlimax, in which Tito/Titus reveals that he has known about Ramses's job since the beginning of the relationship and plans to stay with him anyway. Cazares leaves us in the movie theatre hiding out with Ramses and Tito/Titus among the ruins of Juarez, waiting.[2]

In this essay, I wish to think carefully about Cazares's "dose without end" as a dramaturgico-historiographical intervention into the neoliberal history of the Americas. Part monster movie and part crime drama, *Ramses* tells the story of the intensification of neoliberal practice in the Americas. By looking at the period between the 1980s and the present as a continuous, transnational cultural moment, Cazares rethinks nationalist histories that separate United States and Mexican histories of neoliberalism and their attendant violences, forcing his readers to confront the transnational nature of contemporary necropolitics.[3] Cazares's historiography and his dramaturgy are queer, meaning that he depicts time queerly in Elizabeth Freeman's sense—as eschewing chrononormativity (which naturalizes the time of industrial labor and reproductive labor)—and heteronormativity. On a more basic level, the play centers on queer relations as the primary lens through which to view the time period. As Freeman writes: "Queer temporalities...are points of resistance to this temporal order, that in turn propose other possibilities for living in relation to indeterminately past, present and future others: that is, of living historically."[4] For Freeman, this movement is not only a departure from nationalist time that depends on "empty homogenous time," but also from the proper temporality of movements, such as "coming out, consummation, development, domesticity, family, foreplay, genealogy, identity, liberation, modernity, the progress of movements," which all "contribute to a vision of time as seamless, unified and forward moving."[5] The particular location of *Ramses* and its open engagement with United States-Mexican neoliberalism particularizes Freeman's queer temporality. Engaging queer time through cross-generational relationships, Cazares also points out the recursivity of neoliberal time itself. This revelation stands in sharp contrast to the form of progressive time assumed to undergird late capitalist neoliberal development. Thus, unlike many mobilizations of queer or nonlinear time as always being liberating, Cazares reveals that recursive time might be ambivalent in the neoliberal Americas. I perform a close reading of Cazares's play to illustrate this open secret about neoliberal time and to articulate how "post-national" neoliberal spatial practices interact with the era's recursive temporality and movement. By revising 1990s paradigms about the borderlands and recent work on queer temporality, Cazares offers a different mode of negotiating with the neoliberal paradigms naturalized within narco-entrepreneurship: eschatology. Following the work of Iranian American director Reza Abdoh (1963–95), whose *Law of Remains* stages the afterlife of Reagan-era political violence based on the *Egyptian Book of the Dead*, Cazares veers away from the secular queer utopia theorized by José Muñoz. He opts instead for the imagination of end-times where the collapse of the cosmological and material worlds holds the promise of renewal, if not redemption.[6] In proffering the possibility of the end of the world, Cazares models a modality for unthinking the neoliberal, and its temporal and spatial manipulations, through eschatology. I define that modality here as historiographic eschatology, a vision of the end of the world and the fate of humanity at that end.[7]

Neoliberalism in the Americas is, in fact, a history of transnational commerce and laboring. As Lara Nielsen and Claire Fox have pointed out, this process began in 1965 in the United States-Mexico region with the border industrialization program that encouraged the creation of maquiladoras (factories) in northern Mexico.[8] The proliferation of maquiladoras continued throughout the 1970s, through the Mexican oil boom and bust, and the beginning of Mexico's economic debt difficulties in the 1980s. As a result, Ciudad Juarez became a boom town. From 1970 to 2000 its population quadrupled without requisite expansion of infrastructure.[9] The emergence of Juarez as a megacity accompanied the liberalization of the Mexican economy in the 1980s, which entailed the International Monetary Fund coercing Mexican legislators into submitting to structural readjustment programs that privatized the formerly state protected businesses and subjected the economy to shock therapy. Narcobusiness in the 1980s between the United States and Mexico also lived alongside these developments, although it has escalated considerably from the 1990s forward.[10] The upswing in transnational commerce has come with increased violence as Mexican cartels began to provide drugs directly to the United States, as opposed to being middlemen for Colombians. Other forms of cartel revenue generation—a diversification of their market—include human trafficking, kidnapping, and theft from Central American transmigrants, who cross into Mexico on their way to the United States. The murders of women in Juarez in the 1990s were part of the same necropolitical world, exposing the violence exacerbated, if not caused, by economiclibe ralization.[11]

The violent neoliberal period of the past 30 years brackets Tito/ Titus's life and Ramses's life cycle as "Ramses." That life cycle begins one night when Alex meets Ramses on the road home from the maquiladora. After an act of public sex, Ramses and Alex go back to Alex's place to continue. Their pillow talk reveals the relationship between narcotraffic, the flourishing of the AIDS crisis, and a deeply embedded transnational history of violence:

Ramses: Never do heroin.
Alex: Why?
Ramses: It's more dangerous
Alex: Really?
Ramses: Yes. Only do coke.
Alex: In this house, only coke-a-cola. Like in all of Mexico.
Ramses: I'ms erious.
Alex: Do you sell it?
Ramses: Not yet. But soon.
Alex: What's your name?
Ramses: If I tell you, I'll have to kill you.
Alex: Don't tell me then.
Better I tell you.

//
I'll name you Ramses.
Ramses: Just trying to survive, chiquito.
Just trying to live.[12]

The name Ramses recalls the Egyptian pharaoh and the condom brand, linking imperial violence and latex protection (which they don't use) in the era of AIDS. The title of this scene is "the first dose," which refers both to Tito/Titus's ingestion of antiviral drugs earlier in the scene and to Alex's first dose of Ramses and cocaine. The era in which the scene occurs (the early 1980s) also contained the first dose of the effects of neoliberal economic shock therapy in Mexico. This title of the scene is prescient, given that this first dose becomes the "dose without end" by the end of the play, a state one might refer to as a "neoliberal existence": the recursive time of living with HIV, taking antivirals, experiencing financial crises, and making ourselves anew in order to survive the times. In addition to the amount of time spent talking about cocaine and heroin, the scene also sketches out a pharmacological history in which the consumption and sale of illicit and licit drugs determine the contours of the neoliberal era.[13] That Coca Cola is mentioned here places it in the pharmacological world, both because it persists as an overt symbol of United States market saturation and because Coca Cola began its life as a drug (it contained cocaine). This equivalence is all the more telling because the scene traces the emergence of a pharmacological era or, perhaps better said, an era of pharmacological violence that has existed from the 1980s to the present.

Cazares makes it clear that the intensification of neoliberal practices in the United States, such as deregulation, the dismantling of unionized labor, and the AIDS crisis, are linked to the rise of the maquiladora and the emergence of narcotraffic in Mexico. Usually, the AIDS crisis is not thought to be a symptom of the neoliberal, and, certainly, I do not posit causality here. Yet, as Cazares notes, the crisis and its pharmacological supplement (antiviral drugs) are not isolated from networks of violence. The era marks a particular biopolitical moment when the (mis)management of populations articulates a pharmacological rendering of the world. Historically speaking, the denial of AZT to those who could not afford it accords with the rise of narcotrafficking as the capitalist venture par excellence. In this play, it is Amelia's sacrifice of her organs and hair, in addition to her salary from the maquiladora, that allows her daughter Chema to go to school in the United States, a sacrifice that explicates the network of biopolitical maneuvers enacted by those peripheral or external to neoliberal "progress."

Despite its warnings of moral hazard, *Ramses* is not interested in offering a reparative history that would, however inadvertently, give credence to a teleological narrative, with clear demarcations between past and present or cause and effect. To this end, many of the scenes change times within their courses, so that we are confused about where and when we are. The aforementioned scene between Alex and Ramses, for example, follows a scene some 20 years later between Ramses and Tito/Titus where Tito/Titus says for the first time, "When I take the pill, I feel like I'm swallowing the 80s whole." He then asks Ramses, "Ramses, Ramses, What were you doing in the 80s?" Ramses responds with the comment, "I was just a kid, Tito. I was just a kid. Trying to survive in Juaritos. I don't want to talk about it."[14] While the scene's cross-temporal connection depends on each portion's shared line—Ramses's claim that "he was just trying to survive"—that line is not the overlap between two temporal spaces. Instead, it is a line serially uttered, militating against the idea that the movement between the scenes is the result of any one character's flashback. It's a shared imagination and experience. Ramses is always "just trying to survive" in the neoliberal order. He does not "progress" even as he becomes more involved in the cartel and moves up the ranks. No change of place is marked in this scene either. These conjugal connections represent a shared history of the Americas that moves between the past and present. It is for this reason that the reach across time, in which Freeman is so invested in *Time Binds*, is so ambivalent in Cazares's work. Cross-generational relationships do not save one from history's violence: they instantiate it.

The Alex-Ramses scene is emblematic of many others in the play, in that relationships coexist between present and past worlds and between the living and the dead. To this end, many of the early scenes of the play are described as "espantos," which Cazares translates as "haunting," rather than as "ghosts" or "frights," the more popular translations of the word. The term "haunting" describes the coexistence of past and present in spectral visitation. Padre Alonso, the priest who has sex with the Narcoboss La Yuri, Lydia, the laundress who washes the laundry of narco victims and perpetrators, and Chema, a friend of Tito/Titus's who dies in the play, all appear in this way. The implication here is not that the past haunts the present, although the play is invested in exposing connections between the 1980s and contemporary narcopolitics. Instead, Cazares reveals how the past and present coexist so as to remind us that the neoliberal era is a continuous present whose oscillations of violence and pleasure never disappear or submit to a sequential or teleological order. Cazares, unwilling to participate in a narrative of progress or of demise, does not allow us to think that we are either postneoliberal or, alternately, that today's neoliberalism is new or worse than it was in the 1980s. By framing history within a queer sexual relationship, he suggests that even the most pleasurable of encounters is located in a history that cannot be escaped (although this does not make the moments any less pleasurable in the present). No matter how good the new antiviral drugs are, Tito/Titus can't absent himself from the violence of the 1980s AIDS crisis or the transnational network of narcorelations in which he is embedded. He still needs to take his pill everyday. He *remembers* that he forgets the 1980s. Tito/Titus comes to understand his historicity. By the end of the play, his comment "When I swallow the pill, I feel like I am swallowing the 80s whole," becomes "When I take the pill, I'm swallowing the 80s hole whole,"[15] acknowledging the "hole" that is the 1980s with a grim certainty, rather than a tentative speculation.

Cazares exposes the transnational aspects of neoliberal violence and the differential poverty and violence in El Paso and Juarez without fetishizing the border space as the primary site of violence. To this end, he depicts El Paso and Juarez not just as contiguous, but as continuous, by moving between them without scene changes. The first scene between Chema and her mother, Amelia, in Juarez cuts to a scene between Chema and her girlfriend, Profesora Alonso, in El Paso, and then moves to another scene between Amelia and Chema in Juarez, where Amelia asks Chema to go see an old friend of hers in El Paso (Alex, Ramses's lover). The link between these scenes is associative, but we do not see Chema move across the border, in fact, the actual border is never depicted on stage. That is not where the trauma lies in this play. Instead we see lovers and friends crossing into Juarez and El Paso in a quotidian manner. Ramses comes to the United States to see Tito/Titus, enacting what Tito/Titus calls the "cross national daddy commute." Tito/Titus crosses into Juarez to see him as well. Chema goes to school in El Paso during the day, and goes back and forth to see her professor girlfriend.

The depiction of the crossing of borders in the play also works against the idea of unidirectional (and seemingly chrononormative) movement over them as an end goal for labor or love. The following conversation between Chema and Profesora Alonso suggests the limits of the borderlands paradigm for understanding quotidian transnational life :

> *Profesora Alonso*: No other city gives you a sky this open.
> Nowhere else can you feel this lost, trapped.
> *Chema*: You can feel it in Juarez, too.
> *Profesora Alonso*: I meant la frontera. Borderlands, the same—
> *Chema*: Except there it's physical, not mental.
> It's not a city, it's a slaughterhouse.
> Everyday they don't kill us, they're just fattening us up.
> For greater pleasure.
> *Profesora Alonso*: Stay here after your show opening tonight.
> *Chema*: No. I have to go back to my mom. One night without me is all she can take.
> *Profesora Alonso*: Why hasn't your family tried to leave Juarez?
> *Chema*: We love Juaritos. It's my city. It's the city that welcomed my mom with her maquiladora arms wide open in the early 80s.
> Going to school here is guilt enough. Are you coming to my show?
> *Profesora Alonso*: Of course. I might be a little late though.
> They kiss. Chema leaves.[16]

Chema rejects a certain iteration of the Juarez-El Paso area by complicating, if not rejecting, the academic idea of the borderlands.[17] Alonso's hailing of the paradigm is tired and well worn, a cliché, as her laconic, almost offhand locution suggests. She gestures to the title of Gloria Anzaldúa's book by default rather than with acuity. Although all Chema does to rebut her here is point out that the feeling of being trapped is "physical" rather than "mental," in Juarez, Cazares's gesture to Anzaldúa has other effects. In the context of the play and its lack of investment in the "border" as a threshold space (in marked contrast to Cazares's other plays), this comment does the work of deemphasizing and defetishizing the border as *the* space of transnational violence.

In *Ramses*, Juarez and El Paso are on the same plane, making them deterritorialized spaces differentially affected by a transnational commerce that rejects the idea that there is a common locatable culture specific to the area that can be allegorized or made metaphorical. By and large the characters' movements argue that circulations of transnational commerce (which includes Chema taking her artworks back over the border into Mexico) articulate the lived experience of the space, rather than a unidirectional migration. Even so, this play harbors no late 1990s-era utopian discourse of the hybrid or the nomad, which often valorizes the constant movement and flexibility inherent to many neoliberal discourses. The recursivity of constant crossing is neither liberating nor oppressive in itself; it simply is. In addition, by resisting the unidirectional narrative of crossing, Cazares eschews the desire to frame these crossings as either tragic or triumphant. Avoiding easy, if painful, resolution means that *Ramses* does not let audiences experience the characters as hapless victims in a futile situation. Nor does it allow audiences to see his characters as heroes whose battle to survive would underscore liberal humanism such that their struggle would be universalized, thus denying the particular vectors of structural inequality in the region. Cazares's rejection of (often straight male) border-crossing narratives is key to exposing the particularity of the neoliberal movement.

Cazares's temporal and spatial vagaries also stand apart from United States narratives of upward mobility and capital accumulation, mainstream Chicano migration narratives, and Mexican national progress narratives based on the centrality of the Mexican Revolution as a solution to inequality. The play acknowledges the coexistence of unidirectional progress narratives—particularly those within Mexican historiography—and the recursive movement of neoliberal commerce. Cazares voices their coexistence through Mama Alma, a character who speaks through the screen to Tito/Titus in the movie theatre he and Ramses use as a safehouse. Alma is deeply invested in the importance of the Mexican Revolution, which she calls "a project against capitalism." She claims that the "migrations from north to south" are "the forgetting" of that revolution.[18] In this, Alma echoes the sentiments of many Mexicans who see migration and the consumption of United States culture as a betrayal of the Mexican Revolution and the recent resurgence of domination by the wealthy the Revolution was supposed to end. She tells Tito/Titus, who is a United States citizen, "This is your blessing, your curse: you must be/breathe two geographies at once. You have no present. Just the past, only the future. That's why you're insane."[19] It's a good line, but the play suggests that although he has to "breathe two geographies at once," and deal with a Mexican past and a United States future, Tito/Titus is not worried about being one or the other. He is not on an identity quest: he moves between borders and hookups; he does not strive in any traditional sense; he is not looking for a better life; he is not trying to find himself.

Tito/Titus keeps his slash-name and does not choose a singular temporal or spatial site. His memory of the Egyptian Theatre,[20] where this confrontation occurs, sketches out the conundrums of postnationalist imaginaries in Mexico, always already dead, yet spectacularly present:

> Where the fuck was The Egyptian movie theater? Since I was a kid it had been closed. I remember only— yes, the two fucking statues of Anubis that flanked the entrance, the permanent poster of the last movie premiered: *Nor From Here Nor From There* from the stupid India Maria.[21]

Once inside, we find a storehouse of movies in the "bowels" of the theatre, where a larger expanse of cinematic history is stored.[22] The Egyptian theatre is a bricolage of different eras and a ruin of the history of transnational media commerce. More plainly, the obsolescence of the poster Tito/Titus remembers marks 1985 as the year the theatre closed, a year when the "ruins" of the Mexico City earthquake exposed the lack of infrastructure in neoliberal Mexico. The theatre's archive tracks with the nationalist period in Mexico, a golden age that began with the centralization of the socialist nation state under President Lázaro Cardenas (1934–40) and ended with the peso crash of 1982. In the Egyptian Theatre in downtown Juarez, the nationalist past lives alongside the postnationalist past (the 1980s), spatially exemplifying their coexistence in neoliberal imaginaries, but this national archive is also the ruined site of Titus's present existence.

The abandoned movie house also references a different ghostly site: a pre-AIDS era cruising site. Popular in gay literature of the 1960s and 1970s, these theatres represent a different golden age. The space's contours were inspired by Gil Cuadros's poem "Conquering Immortality."[23] In that poem, the shuttered but glorious Los Angeles Egyptian Theatre becomes a double for a shuttered but glorious body ravaged by AIDS. In the United States, these buildings are either in ruins, have been rebuilt, or have been repurposed as part of urban (neoliberal) gentrification ventures, marking a striking parallel to their ghostly Juarez twin.[24] The palimpsestic nature of a space that references two golden eras long gone marks the theatre in the Cazares play as both a refuge from and a ruin produced by neoliberal violence. The doubleness of the space (and its temporal dimensions) haunts the scene's revelations about serostatus and involvement in drug cartels. It dissolves by the end of the play, as Tito/Titus and Ramses remain suspended, waiting for an end that we know will happen, but does not yet. This final scene up-ends the idea of national progress, as well as the possibility of escape from the violences of neoliberal narcoentrepreneurship, an end made all the more poignant by Tito/Titus's suggestion that he "could spend a whole lifetime here. Buried underneath 80s debris. Things we thought were important. Things we called progress. Just here with you."[25]

Rather than a domestic (heteronomrative) retreat, however, Cazares offers the threat of the end of the world—a queer eschatology qua Reza Abdoh—as a way to unthink the present. Although Cazares theorizes the end of the world in the play, *the play actually does not end*, suggesting that Cazares thinks about the future as an event located in the present, just as Abdoh did. In *Ramses*, the end of one era and the emergence of the next coexist alongside empires past, collapsing all time and space into one moment, as in Christian eschatology. That Cazares references both the Egyptian era and the Aztec past when he describes the recent history of Juarez, however, suggests a hybrid relationship to cosmology that undoes a purely Christian outlook. As Chema explains of her painting of the Juarez of her childhood (in the 1980s):

> *Chema*: I want people to think about what those first nights were like.
> The panic of the setting sun, of sight disappearing.
> Where sunrise was the ultimate uncertainty.
> Not death. Not our souls
> *Profesora Alonso*: Humans acrifice.
> *Chema*: Yes.
> The death of the entire world.
> Restingon
> avertedby
> the offering of a bloody heart that was still releasing steam in the cold morning air of Tenochtitlan right before dawn.[26]

Specifically referencing the ritual of the new fire, which is a ceremony of renewal to be performed after 52 years in the Aztec calendar, Cazares points out the cycle of destruction and renewal crucial to Mexican cosmology. The new fire ceremony included a sacrifice and had to be done correctly by a priest or the world would end. Ramses's failure to dissolve bodies can bring about the end of the world, or, perhaps, his failure might be the sign of a new world. Following the engagement of Abdoh's *Law of Remains* with the *Egyptian Book of the Dead*, Cazares's *Ramses* also guides its characters over to the other side with spells and revelations. Lydia, the murderous laundress, curses the narcos with the Aramaic "Mene, Mene, Tekel" apocalyptic warning from the Book of Daniel. Tito/Titus calls himself the "Neo-Apocalypsist."[27]

More than canny observation, this statement makes it clear that Tito/Titus is the analogue of the neoliberal world. He is a chronic presence, shaped by the commercial culture of the 1980s, the consumption of licit and illicit drugs, and by participation in the violence of the state. Tito/Titus's reign, unlike Ramses's, might not end, but, then again, it might. It is thinking of the destruction of the world, an act that keeps us in suspension, rather than staging the apocalypse that allows the audience of *Ramses* to think differently.

While there is no doubt that neoliberal institutions profit from an idea of progress that works best within unidirectional time, the actual operations of neoliberal capital do not move on an industrial time-line or follow the strict division of time into the productive time of work and the nonproductive time of leisure. Rather, one is, quite simply, always working, always being entrepreneurial, always burying one's dead. The neoliberal is recursive, a series of financial crises, a constant oscillation between panic and optimism, a cycle that can't be broken. In response, entrepreneurship asks for a constant remaking of the self, an exhausting process that has no end in sight. Cazares offers the possibility of putting these neoliberal projects on pause by imagining a moment to cease moving and making.

Clearly, given its depiction of violence, the end of Cazares's play can be read through a glass darkly. I would offer, however, that imagining an end of the world that manifests as a failure to make violence disappear, where bodies remain to testify to globalized economic violence during the collapse of cosmological and material worlds, does offer the possibility to unthink neoliberal logics and practices. Cazares's end times threaten the success of attempts to erase interconnections between discrete oppressions or to obscure violence by positing it as a natural process or the unavoidable result of capitalist advancement. *Ramses Contra Los Monstruos* allows readers to imagine a transformation in which the necropolitical world can make itself into something else. While the stop-time that Cazares's apocalypse offers halts the recursive chronicity of neoliberal time, his most important contribution in engaging end-times is how he brings space back into the picture. Cazares move to space is important because it allows different vectors of neoliberal history to occupy the same space at the same time.

I argue, then, that *Ramses Contra Los Monstruos* offers the possibility of thinking historiography through the lens of a queer spatial eschatology that engages the idea of end-times without imposing a linear narrative upon the idea of the end (even as it recognizes the misrecognition of neoliberal time as linear). Theologian Vitor Westhalle suggests that the attention to eschatology *in space* questions the very dominance of time over space in post-Enlightenment theological thought, both in its teleological and axiological forms.[28] Quoting from and interpreting the work of Gustavo Gutíerrez, Westhalle claims the importance of a latitudinal perspective:

> The eschatology of the theologies of liberation is not about progress, which suggests a longitudinal paradigm, it is about limits, borders, margins. It is an attempt to make the margins visible, for they are the turning point to another world, a world that can only be devised by those who dare to stand at the threshold and remove the veil that hides the truth beyond it. And herein lies the meaning of the word apocalypse.[29]

Westhalle, then, confounds the difference between eschatology and apocalypse, which, in a temporal theological register imbued with queer theory, are understood as two separate modalities that either represent utopic, future-oriented thought (eschatology) or pessimistic, death-oriented thought (apocalypse).[30] These paradigms emerge with special strength in discourse around and through the "age of AIDS" and are implicit in theories of queer temporality.

Cazares, while neither espousing liberation theology per se nor rejecting queer temporality, also confounds the difference between apocalypse and eschatology as a mode of political critique. Rather than separate the pessimistic (dystopic) theological view from the utopian (remedial) theological view, enacting the kind of binary opposition so key to neoliberal labeling, Cazares decides, instead, to think the two together as a mode of seeing the neoliberal condition. Remember Tito/Titus's words at the beginning of the play: "I dream of the New Apocalypse—I dream. I, Tito/Titus Neo-Apocalypsist—Hear me: Pity our Christian ego. It is not enough to ponder your own death—but of the entire world."[31] Thinking eschatology and apocalypse together, Tito/Titus devises the next world standing at the threshold of his own understanding, and making visible what was hidden until his lover failed to conjure disappearance. By extension, we as audience members and readers are also asked to appear and disappear. If, as in Christian theology, the dead rise at the eschatological moment and place, Cazares evinces this rising up through the refusal of the bodies to disappear into acid. He renders the appearance of neoliberal violence theatrically through the presence of the bodies supposedly destroyed or destroyable. The safe house that Ramses and Tito/Titus inhabit is exactly the opposite of a safe house: it is a kind of chora, a place between places, nations, national narratives, and times that exposes us to violence, rather than saving us from it. It is here that Tito/Titus can see a possible end to the "remaking of death" by refusing its corpses' disappearances. At the same time, Tito/Titus blurs the line between criminal and innocent, HIV+ and HIV-, effectively making us all one—and without identity.[32] Instead of representing a fall from grace in a decaying world, Tito/Titus's relationship with Ramses is a fall *into* grace within the earthly realm, a fall that allows a terrifying vision of possibility, of the very (un)making of that earthly realm through cosmological thought.

Cazares's theology asks historiographers to forego the use of a secular, "rational" humanist, Enlightenment paradigm as a counterforce to neoliberal thought. The lesson here is clear: spatial eschatology is a mode of understanding how the collapse of time, space, and matter can help us see connections between discrete oppressions without reducing them to narrative explanations that would have us believe either in the progress of capitalism over time (which renders spatial difference docile) or in the catastrophic devolution of civilization, which universalizes divergent cultural experiences while placing individualistic notions of blame upon its victims. Theatrical representation of these connections, ironically enough, makes them real. The move to eschatology, deeply embedded in Christian thought, is not an intuitive one. My proposition to think of it as a model of historiography is risky, especially considering the ravages that certain modes of religious expression have wrought on disenfranchised people throughout the Americas. Yet, I would offer that eschatology—in its queer and latitudinal form—allows us to think ourselves out of neoliberal recursivity and to reassert materiality exactly because of its multidimensional collapse of time, space, and matter. In short, eschatology allows us to think neoliberalism in a way that Enlightenment-imbued versions of history do not. My suggestion is made possible not by theorizing a dramatic work, but by allowing dramatic work to theorize. This makes possible doing the historiographical work of resituating dramaturgical structures and their theatricalization—that is, how they produce time, space, and matter on stage—as "infrastructural," rather than merely as "staged signs of previously identified categories." Given the severe reification of things Mexican and American in discourses, historiographies, and representations of advanced capitalism (e.g., United States-Mexican drug wars, free trade, or femicide), this intervention is urgent.

Notes

1. Victor Cazares, *Ramses Contra Los Monstruos*, unpublished play, 2011, 93.
2. Cazares has rewritten the play since I began work on this essay. I have chosen to write about the earlier version of the play, without reference to the revisions made in 2013.
3. Achille Mbembe, "Necropolitics," *Public Culture* 15: 1 (Winter 2003): 11–40.
4. Elizabeth Freeman, *Time Binds: Queer Temporalities, Queer Histories* (Durham, NC: Duke University Press, 2010), xxii.
5. Ibid.
6. Reza Abdoh, "Law of Remains," *Plays for the End of the Century*, ed. Bonnie Marranca (New York: PAJ, 1996), 95–120.
7. I reference and revise Merriam-Webster Dictionary online, s.v. eschatology, http://www.merriam-webster.com/dictionary/eschatology (accessed January 24, 2014).
8. See Lara Nielsen, "Introduction: Heterotopic Transformations, The (il)Liberal Neoliberal," *Neoliberalism and Global Theatres: Performance Permutations* (London: Palgrave MacMillan, 2012), 6; and Claire Fox, *The Fence and the River: Cultural Politics at the Border* (Minneapolis: University of Minnesota, 1999). In brief, this program allows for the duty-free importation of goods into Mexico, if made within Mexican factories into products for export. These factories, however exploitative their labor practices are, benefit both countries by allowing US manufacturers to use cheaper labor to make products and, simultaneously, to ease mass unemployment in Mexico after the bracero program, which had allowed Mexicans to do agricultural work in the United States without legal difficulties, ended.
9. Sergio Gonzáles Rodríguez, *The Femicide Machine* (New York: Semiotexte, 2012),19.
10. Miami sea surveillance, the weakening of the Colombian cartels, and the strengthening of the Mexican once resulted in Mexico taking a larger share of the narcotics business from the 1990s forward.
11. The murders of women from the 1990s to the present in Juarez, Mexico, are referred to as "femicides." See Diana Washington Valdez, *The Killing Fields* (Los Angeles: Peace at the Border Books, 2006).
12. Cazares, *Ramses*, 68–69.
13. I am indebted to Hermann Herlinghaus's formulation, contained in "Placebo Intellectuals in the Wake of Cosmopolitanism: A 'Pharmacological' Approach to Roberto Bolaño's Novel 2666," *The Global South* 5:1 (2011): 101–19.
14. Cazares, *Ramses*, 65–69.
15. Ibid.,65, 93.
16. Ibid.,23–24.
17. Borderlands scholarship includes Gloria Anzaldúa, *Borderlands/La Frontera: The New Mestiza* (San Francisco: Aunt Lute, 1987); Carl Gutiérrez-Jones, *Rethinking the Borderlands: Between Chicano Culture and Legal Discourse* (Berkeley: University of California Press, 1995); Carl Gutiérrez-Jones, "Desiring B/orders," *Diacritics* 25:1 (Spring 1995): 99–112; Hector Calderón

and José David Saldivár, eds., *Criticism in the Borderlands: Studies in Chicano Literture, Culture and Ideology* (Durham, NC: Duke University Press, 1991); and Ramón Rivera-Servera and Harvey Young, eds., *Performance in the Borderlands* (London: Palgrave Macmillan, 2010).
18. Cazares, *Ramses*, 71.
19. Ibid.
20. The Egyptian (Theatre) also alludes to the Egyptian national who was first blamed for the Juarez killings. See Valdez, *The Killing Fields*.
21. Cazares, *Ramses*, 50.
22. Ibid.,54.
23. Gil Cuadros, "Conquering Immortality," *City of God* (San Francisco: City Lights, 1994), 137–50.
24. See Samuel Delany, *Times Square Red, Times Square Blue* (New York: New York University Press, 1999) for more on this phenomenon in New York City.
25. Cazares, *Ramses*, 94.
26. Ibid.,83–84.
27. Ibid.,4.
28. Vitor Westhalle, *Eschatology and Space* (New York: Palgrave MacMillan, 2012). Vitor Westhalle's arguments about the temporal modes of eschatology are too complex to be considered here, yet his reading of eschatology through Foucauldian historiography and postcolonial theory is a model for rethinking time, space, and matter in systemic theology.
29. Ibid.,81.
30. See, for example, "Queer Apocal(o)ptic/ism: The Death Drive and the Human," *Queering the Non/Human*, ed. Noreen Giffney and Myra J. Hird (Burlington, VT and Hampshire, UK: Ashgate, 2008), 61.
31. Cazares, *Ramses*, 4.
32. See, for example, Patrick S. Cheng, *Radical Love* (New York: Seabury Press, 2011).

Bibliography

Abdoh, Reza. "Law of Remains." In *Plays for the End of the Century*. Edited by Bonnie Marranca. New York: PAJ, 1996, 95–120.

Anzaldúa, Gloria. *Borderlands/La Frontera: The New Mestiza*. San Francisco, CA: Aunt Lute, 1987.

Calderón, Hector, and José David Saldivár, eds. *Criticism in the Borderlands: Studies Chicano Literature, Culture and Ideology*. Durham, NC: Duke University Press, 1991.

Cazares, Victor. *Ramses Contra Los Monstruos: Salmos para el fin del mundo*. unpublished manuscript, 2011.

Cheng, Patrick S. *Radical Love*. New York: Seabury Press, 2011.

Cuadros, Gil. "Conquering Immortality." In *City of God*. San Francisco, CA: City Lights, 1994, 137–50.

Delaney, Samuel. *Times Square Red, Times Square Blue*. New York: New York University Press, 1999.

Edelman, Lee. *No Future. Queer Theory and the Death Drive*. Durham, NC: Duke University Press, 2004.
Fox, Claire. *The Fence and the River: Cultural Politics at the Border*. Minneapolis: University of Minnesota, 1999.
Freeman, Elizabeth. *Time Binds: Queer Temporalities, Queer Histories*. Durham, NC: Duke University Press, 2010.
Giffney, Noreen. "Queer Apocal(o)ptic/ism: The Death Drive and the Human." In *Queering the Non/Human*. Edited by Noreen Giffney and Myra J. Hird. Burlington, VT and Hampshire, England: Ashgate, 2008, 55–78.
Gonzáles Rodríguez, Sergio. *The Femicide Machine*. New York: Semiotexte, 2012.
Gutíerrez-Jones, Carl. "Desiring B/orders." *Diacritics* 25, no. 1 (Spring 1995): 99–112.
———. *Rethinking the Borderlands: Between Chicano Culture and Legal Discourse*. Berkeley: University of California Press, 1995.
Herlinghaus, Hermann. "Placebo Intellectuals in the Wake of Cosmopolitanism: A 'Pharmacological' Approach to Roberto Bolaño's Novel 2666." *The Global South* 5, no. 1 (2011), 101–19.
Mbembe, Achille. "Necropolitics," *Public Culture* 15, no. 1 (Winter 2003), 11–40.
Muñoz, José. *Cruising Utopia: The Then and There of Queer Futurity*. New York: New York University Press, 2009.
Nielsen, Lara. "Introduction: Heterotopic Transformations, The (il)Liberal Neoliberal." In *Neoliberalism and Global Theatres: Performance Permutations*. Edited by Lara D. Nielsen and Patricia Ybarra. London: Palgrave MacMillan, 2012.
Rivera-Servera, Ramón, and Harvey Young, eds. *Performance in the Borderlands*. London: Palgrave Macmillan, 2010.
Washington Valdez, Diana. *The Killing Fields*. Los Angeles: Peace at the Border Books, 2006.
Westhalle, Vitor. *Eschatology and Space*. New York: Palgrave MacMillan, 2012.

II

Temporal Matter

5
The Design of Theatrical Wonder in Roy Mitchell's *The Chester Mysteries*

Patricia Badir

The Chester mystery play is a familiar entity to twenty-first-century theatre historians. Much scholarly labor has been invested in the excavation of archival evidence pertaining to the original performances of the cycle play and, as a result, we know a lot about the material, social, economic, and theological components of the play's pageants within the context of late medieval devotional practices and urban oligarchical systems.[1] My goal here, however, is to unmoor our understanding of this play as a medieval thing. I want to do this by placing the Middle English text in proximity to archival material that is distant from anything that could be called either medieval or original.

In 1917 Roy Mitchell, in collaboration with Frank M. Conroy, revived the Chester Nativity pageants at the Greenwich Village Theatre in New York City. Designed as a Christmas entertainment, the adaptation, *The Chester Mysteries*, combined pageant seven, the painters' pageant (*Incipit Pagina Septima de Pastoribus*), and pageant nine, the mercers' pageant (*Pagina Nona: De Oblatione Trium Regum*), both from the late–fifteenth-century text of the Chester cycle. Mitchell would remount this production at Hart House Theatre in Toronto in 1919 as a part of that theatre's inaugural season. These productions were among the first postmedieval revivals of the play and likely the first North American performances.[2] As such, they are manifestations of late nineteenth- and early-twentieth-century medievalism, consistent with the ecumenical spiritualism of theosophy and the anti-industrial aesthetic of the Arts and Crafts movement. These productions were also made possible by the relatively recent availability of antiquarian and scholarly editions of the medieval play.[3] The archive of the Mitchell revival is remarkably rich; it includes annotated play scripts, photographs, programs, reviews, manifestos and articles, journal entries, and personal correspondence that solicit strong affective engagement as they unfold Mitchell's near-fanatical obsession with the medieval play's vitality. I use this material to address two of the initial questions posed to contributors by the editors of this collection: how might we think critically about the contemporary and past historiographical methodologies used to write theatrical and performance histories; and how might we resituate theorizations of the archive, periodization, and the past within our research? I want to suggest that considering historical drama outside of its native performance context makes familiar things strange in productive ways. I am not trying to provide a new reading of the medieval text exactly, but I do want to suggest that the Chester Nativities' remediated form, in all its enchanting complexity, poses the interplay between motion and stillness (and by extension light and darkness) as a possible modality for understanding the dramaturgical design of theatrical wonder that underpins the painters' and the mercers' pageants. Likewise, the medieval text provides experimental material for an emergent modernist theatre seeking to explore alternative spiritualities by releasing the iconic and corporeal materialities of religious plays from the bookish restraints of late-nineteenth-century antiquarianism. It is the conversation taking place between the medieval and the modern that I want to hear. It isn't a conversation that is out of time or of all time. It is neither an original nor a universal conversation, rather, it is multitemporal and variously located—dynamic in a manner that is madly cumulative rather than neatly specific.

In order to enable this project I want to appeal to a theoretical scaffold that supports a different kind of historiography, thus permitting a discussion of the modern production that doesn't lose sight of the medieval text, as studies of modern revivals often do. My work appeals to Jonathan Gil Harris's interrogation of the "time of material culture." Harris would call the remains of medieval cycle drama— the play manuscripts, the accounts, the matter meticulously collected by the REED project—"ethnographic curio[s]" valued because they "materialize [...] moment[s] unfamiliar to us."[4] Harris also claims, however, that historical artifacts can challenge conventional models of temporality and historicity, according to which any object or phenomenon has "citizenship" in a singular historical moment. Drawing on recent philosophy of science, Harris suggests that objects are never of a single moment; they are, instead, "untimely matter," bringing together several or many historical periods at one time. The exemplary instance of the polychronic object is, for Harris, a palimpsest, a multiply marked surface that is not just polychronic (that is, of many times), but also (to use Michel Serres's term) multitemporal, in that it can prompt many different understandings and experiences of temporality, "of the relations between now and then, old and new, before and after."[5] One of the things that the Mitchell archive does to my example of the palimpsest (the Chester Nativity pageants) is force us to acknowledge some of the multiple stopping points on a medieval text's trajectory from then to now and to ask what the exploration of these points might add to our understanding of the text's vitality, that is, to its social and affective engagement with the things and the people that encounter it through time and space.

Harris leans heavily on Bruno Latour's reassembling of "the social" that is dependent on "a tracing of associations" often between heterogeneous, and not necessarily human, things—between people, texts, and performances let's say, or adaptations of texts, or letters and journal entries, or photographs and reviews. My method is to "follow [these] actors themselves," in Latour's terms, that is, to root through the modern archive in order to reconnect the materials of one theatrical past to another, so as to learn how they associate, how they "fit together," and to ask how I might "best define the new association that they have been forced to establish?"[6]

Latour's understanding of "the actor," annotated by Harris, seems particularly suited to the theatre historian's task of trying to make an archive speak or, perhaps more accurately, move. What I want to propose is that in its stillness, in its very two dimensionality, the assortment of media that constitutes the Mitchell archive does more than simply allude longingly to the very thing it cannot reconstitute: the fleeting vivacity of the performed event. Instead, the untimely matter of the archive indexes theatrical motion as the white space between the words of typescript, just as the shafts of light and the composition of set pieces in production photographs expose a dizzying network of associations between the medieval and the modern. Placed in conversation with this archive, the Chester play becomes, in Nicolas Bourriaud's terminology, a *social interstice*, encouraging us to rethink the regionally specific, historically located nature of the original artwork itself. "Artistic activity is a game whose forms, patterns and functions develop and evolve according to periods and social contexts," writes Bourriaud, but this activity is "not an immutable essence," for it is "the critic's task to study this activity in the present," thereby encapsulating the primary dilemma of the historian of art. Bourriaud writes specifically about relational artists working in the 1990s that claimed nothing less than the sphere of human relations as the venue for art. Under this mandate, the artwork is presented as a place of sociality in which untimely experiments take precedence over historical excavation and explanation.[7] I take my cue from the artistic practice Bourriaud is trying to document, that is, I am proposing to think about the Chester Nativity pageants as rematerializing or resurfacing in peculiar and remarkable ways as they establish dynamic relationships with the things and the people that are their unlikely conversationalists in the Roy Mitchell archive.

Roy Mitchell was born in 1884 in Fort Gratiot, Michigan but his connections to Canada were deep: both of his parents were Canadian and he attended the University of Toronto, from which he graduated in 1906. As a young adult, Mitchell developed a twin passion for theatre and for theosophy, two interests that would guide his professional life for the entirety of his career. He joined the Toronto Theosophic Society in 1909 and became one of the founding members of the Arts and Letters Club (ALC) of Toronto, a gentleman's society that would be the first outlet for Mitchell's theatrical activity. Mitchell's aesthetic values were avant-garde, or at least they seemed so to Toronto's conservative audiences, introduced, by his hand, to the likes of Maeterlinck, Yeats, and Tagore. In 1916, Mitchell went to New York to study stage design and soon become the technical director of the Greenwich Village Theatre. It was in this playhouse that he first revived the Chester Nativity plays, in collaboration with Frank M. Conroy.

Mitchell returned to Canada in 1918 to work as the director of motion pictures for the Department of Information in Ottawa. His ALC connections continued to serve him well and, by 1919, he was back in Toronto as the newly appointed first director of Hart House Theatre, Toronto's first "Little Theatre," opened under the auspices of the University of Toronto and financed by ALC member Vincent Massey. Mitchell included *The Chester Mysteries* in both seasons of his tenure at Hart House, and the theatre continued to produce the play for a decade following the director's departure.

Before introducing the archive of *The Chester Mysteries*, I would like to turn to Mitchell's theoretical writing about theatre, always produced in tandem with his theosophical manifestos, for which he is better known today. I do this in order to begin to invent, in Bourriaud's terms, some of the productive proximities between the medieval pageants and their modern iterations. *Creative Theatre*, Mitchell's strange and largely ignored manifesto, was first published in 1929 in New York. In it, Mitchell lays out his theory of theatrical motion in eccentric philosophical and spiritual terms. Theatre needs to be a spiritual experience, a *paradosis* Mitchell calls it, that gives access to "the unlighted chamber above each of us, not finally and forever, but for a re-creating instant." The performance is nothing short of a revelation for performers, technicians, and audiences, "as if filling the senses with form and sound, stirring the emotions to sympathy and shaping ideas to one intense accord." Theatre practitioners make for their witnesses "a causeway into an inner world where they rest in a lightening flash of communion."[8] Access to spiritual insight, revelation, and the stirring of emotion lead to the formation of social bonds, all in an instant.

At the beginning of the Chester painters' play ("The Pageant of the Shepherds"), the first shepherd reflects on his solitude. "But noe fellowshippe here have I," he moans, "save myselfe alonge, in good faye; therefore after one faste will I crye."[9] As it turns out, however, he is not alone; there are three other shepherds in the fields and, eventually, they gather together to complain collectively. They don't, initially, rise above their petty grievances and connect in any genuine fashion (they bully each other and even fight) until they see a star so bright it frightens them ("For to see this light here / a man may bee afright here, for I am afeard").[10] Their senses stirred, they fall to their knees in collective wonder as an angel appears to them singing "Gloria in excelsis Deo."[11] They continue to bicker over the sense and meaning of this strange manifestation, but when the angel speaks to them, compelling them to go to Bethlehem *together*, their emotions are roused to sympathy and their actions shaped to one sole purpose. This is, I think, Mitchell's *paradosis* in its sincerest form.

In Mitchell's and Conroy's adaptation of the Chester play, the action segues from this scene to the mercers' play (also known as "The Magi's Gifts") allowing the shepherds to join the magi at the site of the Nativity. Here the three kings provide an ekphrastic description of what they see before them:

SecundusR ex:
    The starre yt shines fayre and cleare
    Over this stable aye entyre.
    Here is his wonninge withowten were,
    Andhe reinis he ele nt.

TertiusR ex:
    A fayre mayden yonder I see,
    And ould man sittinge at hir knee,
    A child alsoe; as thinkes mee,
    Threepe rsonsthe rinar e.

PrimusR ex:
    I say in certayne this is hee
    That we have sought in farre countree
    Therefore now with all honestye
    Honor will that baron.[12]

Of course the audience sees this scene too, or rather sees the kings seeing it, and, so, the tableaux, breathtaking in its stillness—"three persons therin are"—constitutes the "lightening flash of communion" Mitchell calls for, allowing the play to move the audience as well as the stage witnesses. At this point, the Second Shepherd announces,

    Brethren, lett us all three
    singinge walke homwardlye.
    Unkynd will I never in noe case bee,
    but preach all that I can and knowe,
    as Gabryell taught by his grace mee.[13]

In the medieval text, spiritual motion, born of stillness, is the precondition for physical motion. Mitchell sees this dramaturgical formulation and exploits it: "You have watched an actor alone in the scene and however moved he has been or moving, you have awaited a second because, until there is a second, seen or heard, the courses which are part of the theatre cannot begin. Fire latent in cloud, fire dormant in earth, lightning only the passage between them."[14] My point here is that the medieval Nativity, in such proximity to Mitchell's theory, generates an untimely theory of theatrical wonder. The theatre that works best, Mitchell says, is the theatre "whose soul moves the most, and feet the least."[15] The realization of this statement does not belong exclusively to the medieval or to the modern, but to the social exchange between the Mitchell archive and its medieval muse.

The Archive: Paper

Theatre "lives in its moment of consumption," Mitchell writes, and as a consequence "it has no life before or after. It gestates, it is consumed, it dies and its consumer is integrant to its mystery."[16] This realization prompts Mitchell, in *Creative Theatre*, to wonder "how many people really remember words after they leave the play. Our memories are all of movement."[17] The live event is all there is. It is the spoken word, "the liquid m's, n's, ng's and l's an actor loves," that make a Middle English play meaningful to a modern audience. We must never be misled, Mitchell believes, by the fact that performance is archived in words ("it is words alone we have been able to preserve in an other art medium than our own").[18] And yet, texts are pretty much all that remains of the Chester play: manuscripts, accounts, and editions, in the case of the medieval play; typescripts, reviews, letters, and photographs, in the case of Mitchell's revival—the wonderless paper trails of theatrical vitality held under what Derrida calls "house arrest" in the archive.[19]

Not simply the information provided by the archive is at stake here, however, but how the archive's various medialities interact with a polytemporal, intrinsically social text, creating, in the process, a whole new set of questions and criteria for analysis. Friedrich Kittler states, "What remains of people is what media can store and communicate. What counts are not the messages or the content with which they equip so called souls for the duration of a technological era, but rather (and in strict accordance with McLuhan) their circuits, the very schematism of perceptibility."[20] Mitchell might have been sympathetic to this point of view because theatre's motion, in his articulation, is essentially "a thing of passage and born of passages." Its movements are transmissions or currents between human and nonhuman theatrical agents: stories, directors, stages and settings, actors, technicians, lights, sound and music, audiences and auditoriums. The theatre's textual artifacts can, therefore, be participants in an affective network, moving through time and space, behaving as repositories of acts and articulations that can gesture to the associations, the social interstices, formed among these agents. If, as Mitchell writes, "we face an audience because we believe we can move it not by the single presences of actors but by the fluency with which our presences reach one another," and if a play is "a silent, spectral thing, co-extensive with the book," then might the theatre historian look to books and to words on pages in order to observe how theatrical agents move between them, "as water lives in the spaces of a sponge, or still more as a subtle body might live within, and be co-extensive with, this physical body of ours?"[21] To illustrate what he means, Mitchell imagines a playwright, irritated and disconsolate at rehearsal because a director is misinterpreting his writing.

"[He] thinks it is all wrong. After a while he may learn that the most precious thing he brings to the theater is not words at all but the white paper between them, the silent spaces where he has glimpsed the phantom moving."[22] The trick for the theatre historian, then, is to capture a glimpse of the phantoms—and the associations that they form—in the white paper of the archive.

Kittler has argued that writing "store[s] writing—no more and no less" and that "typewriters do not store individuals."[23] The Mitchell archive, however, suggests otherwise. Three manuscript texts and one published edition of Mitchell's and Conroy's adaptation of the painters' and mercers' pageants survive. The oldest of these texts is the printed edition. It is a booklet entitled, *The Nativity and Adoration Cycle of the Chester Mysteries*, printed and sold in 1917 by Egmont H. Arens, an industrial designer who moved into the publishing business right around the time Mitchell came to New York to work at the Greenwich Village Theatre.[24] Arens's publication (figure 5.1) links *The Chester Mysteries* to a shop, the Washington Square Bookshop in Greenwich Village, that was at the center of American bohemian culture. Arens and his wife and partner Josephine Bell (who was also a designer and radical intellectual) owned the shop and published out of it, establishing a reputation for fine press printing of literature and drama of the American avant-garde, including nine issues of *Playboy: A Portfolio of Art and Satire* (no relation to Hugh Hefner's publication), featuring writers such as Djuna Barnes, E. E. Cummings, Lola Ridge, and D. H. Lawrence. Arens also published artwork by Georgia O'Keefe, Rockwell Kent, and Hunt Diederich. Patrons of the shop included James Baldwin, Dashiell Hammett, Lillian Hellman, and Eleanor Roosevelt. Arens also started a series of plays, under the imprint Flying Stag Plays, which profited from the bookshop's association with the Provincetown Players. The connections go on and on, unveiling an extraordinary network of associations to the curious researcher with Google at her fingertips. One begins to speculate about who attended *The Chester Mysteries* at the Greenwich Village Theatre in 1917 and who bought the Arens publication.[25] With whom did Mitchell discuss *paradosis* and his theories of motion? The charming pamphlet unfolds, dynamically, as a multiplicity of possible meetings, encounters, events, and collaborations that relocate the medieval play at the center of bohemian culture in New York City at the beginning of the twentieth century, thereby challenging all kinds of assumptions—aesthetic, historiographic, and formal—concerning to whom medieval drama belongs or what it can and ought to be.[26]

Figure 5.1 Title page of *The Chester Mysteries* printed and published by Egmont H. Arens for the Washington Square Bookshop, New York (1917). Cover Illustration by Josephine Bell. York University Libraries, Clara Thomas Archives & Special Collections, Roy Matthews Mitchel fonds, 1974–012–002 (017).

The introduction to *The Chester Mysteries* begins by articulating something of the untimeliness of the Nativity pageants. It is only recently, Mitchell observes, that "workers in the theatre have come to realize the dramatic values of the medieval religious plays" that have been, for many decades, imprisoned between the covers of the publications of learned societies and regarded "as mere curiosities and valuable only as university texts for the study of so-called pre-Shakespearean drama."[27] Mitchell's task, as he sees it, is to deliver these texts from "the archaisms of spelling and diction which make them seem unnatural and stilted" and to release the "marvellous [sic] playing qualities as well as a beauty of language and thought which is rare in modern pieces." In his collaboration with Conroy, Mitchell appears to have been striving for a kind of linguistic purity that would strip the play of markers of location and time. This would be an ongoing preoccupation, as later manuscript revisions attest to further efforts to cleanse the text of idiom and dialect in a manner perfectly consistent with the early-twentieth-century fascination with universal manifestations of aesthetic form and theatrical affect: "From the old text into the present one, Mr. Conroy has carried nothing that is not universal, as true today as it was five hundred years ago, and by this process of cutting away what is merely local and excrescent, his figures stand out with a roundness and clarity scarcely evident until the players begin to move and speak."[28] The Nativities' ancientness, oddly, is attributed not to the Middle English original (itself a product of revision over time), but to the antiquarian editions that are faulted for locking the text in its lifeless past. Mitchell's version will be, he thinks, for all times. Of course what Mitchell doesn't recognize, even though his introduction fully acknowledges it, is the line of revision and transmission from medieval manuscript to modern art house printing. Mitchell references George Bellin, the sixteenth-century Cestrian scribe who was responsible for the 1592 manuscript of the Chester play, which is, in turn, the source of Thomas Wright's edition, reviled by Mitchell, but very likely the copy that he had at hand.[29] Mitchell's introduction provides an inadvertent link between the fifteenth-century manuscript and its bohemian revision, revealing for latter-day historians an important conversation between Mitchell's universalizing medievalism and nineteenth-century antiquarianism, a salutatory reminder that, despite Mitchell's efforts, the play remains multiply marked by the hands that have touched it. The Chester pageants are not out of time but rather of many times.

The typescript copies of *The Chester Mysteries*, all more recent artifacts than the Arens publication, take us deeper into Mitchell's protracted engagement with the medieval past. The earliest of these (undated) is the closest to the Middle English text insofar as it preserves many of the older spellings.[30] Yet, the pages unsettle time as the reader witnesses the director modernize as he copies, crossing out final e's and replacing archaic spellings with more familiar ones. We see Mitchell, in pursuit of the universal, excising medieval profanities and striking out by hand, for instance, lines alluding to Joseph's decrepitude. In the margins, we find handwritten annotations as well as the occasional sketch. Manuscript p. 13 (figure 5.2), for example, contains a small rectangle in the margins, inside of which there are three numbered lines, each representing one of the kings. To the right

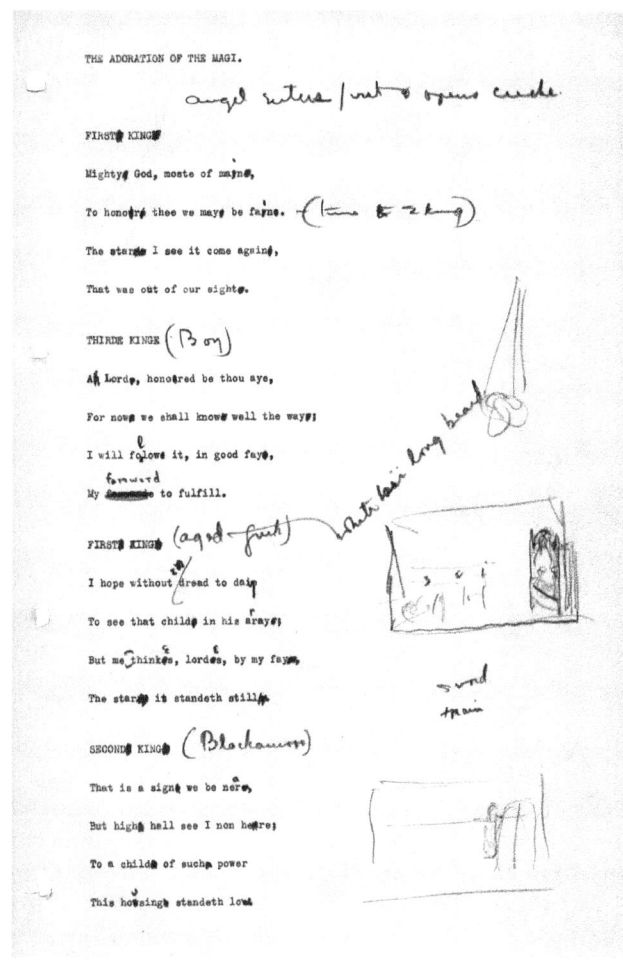

Figure 5.2 *The Adoration of the Magi*. Typescript (f. 13). York University Libraries, Clara Thomas Archives & Special Collections, Roy Matthews Mitchel fonds, 1978–010–001(05).

is a rudimentary drawing of the stable scene. The sketch draws the eye because it displaces the Middle English words and makes a modern stage in the white spaces between them. There are also handwritten instructions (the angel enters and opens the crèche) and descriptions (the first king is aged with white hair and a long beard, the second king is a boy, and the third a blackamoor).

The marks, the notes, and the doodles are, I argue, artifacts gesturing to a vital, moving presence at work in the white spaces of the text. The medieval play is still there, but, in its revised typescript iteration, it comes to life (or to afterlife) as an actor, a mediated entity that is not frozen in time but a living social participant that continues to touch, as it is being touched, not only by the mechanical motion of a typewriter, but also by the traces of Mitchell's moving hand. In the medieval text, the first king states:

> I hope withowt dreade todaye
> To see that childe and his araye.
> But methinkes lordes, by my faye,
> The starre yt standeth still.[31]

The king worries that the star's stillness is an ill omen, a sign of misguidedness or misdirection, until he is reassured by his companion that "that is a signe we be neare." This passage might not be remarkable were it not so heavily marked in Mitchell's script. As it is, surrounded by excisions, annotations, and illustrations, the words become vibrant performers—arresting, like the star, in their stillness on the page.

The leaves of the adaptation seem to activate the wonder built into the medieval play not so much by purging what Mitchell would have called the "dogma and museum-likeness" of medieval philology, but by grappling with it.[32] A twenty-first-century reader handling the typescript might well observe the foreignness of manual type, which now belongs to history. The experience today is not entirely unlike that of the medieval manuscript scholar seeking, as Siân Echard puts it, to "approach the object in its medieval condition—to recover the book—and to trace the evidence of that object's passage from one culture to another."[33] As it moves from manuscript, through much defamed nineteenth- and twentieth-century scholarly editions, into early twentieth-century typescript, only to be modified again by Mitchell's hand—a phenomenon that oddly references the text's manuscript origins—the Nativity play's dynamic encounter with time, space, and media becomes something of a wonder in and of itself. In this sense, the typescript is both a palimpsest that rematerializes the Chester play beneath Mitchell's manual type, and a social interstice in which new associations between the medieval and the modern are made possible. "*The stage is not a picture: It is a place*," writes Mitchell, "you need only examine the marked script of any director to see that it is so."[34]

The second typescript in the archive is cleaner.[35] The stage directions, also in Mitchell's hand, are close to those in the earlier typescript, though more generous in detail. The spelling has been regularized and much of the "medieval" has vanished. This typescript, however, is archived with a much more interesting third text. This text, dating to 1939, is virtually identical to the others and appears to be the last typescript version of the play.[36] In this case, though, there is no evidence of Mitchell's hand in the margins of the text. It is a clean text, obviously prepared for publication, as the paratextual matter, which sits alongside it in the archive, suggests. The manuscript begins with a title page that includes the following line at the bottom of the page: "~~Samuel French, etc~~". The strikethrough is explained by a letter, addressed to Mitchell's wife Jocelyn, from play publisher Samuel French, dated October 25, 1944.[37] The correspondent notes that the editors "are very sorry" but will "not be interested in publishing THE NATIVITY CYCLE at this time." This rejection touches a nerve; if the third typescript puts the play in motion again, the rejection brings it to standstill, as one of the principal makers of theatrical canonicity, Samuel French, returns manuscript to sender.

This immobility is interesting, arresting one could say, because the play the archive revives also understands motion in relation to stillness. At the beginning of the Chester shepherds' pageant, action comes to a stop right at the point when all appears to be lost. The boy, Trowle, refuses to participate in the shepherds' camaraderie, and violence seems imminent:

> Boye, lest I breake thy bones,
> kneele downe and axe me a boone.
> Lest I destroy thee here on these stones,
> Sease, lest I shend thee to soone.[38]

Mitchell writes in his script that first shepherd "lifts his staff" as if to strike at Trowle, but, then, "the star shines suddenly bathing them all in light" and "all remain motionless except to look towards the star." Catastrophe is averted because movement needs to be guided by higher powers to be right. The stillness, initiated by the appearance of the star, forces observation, reflection, and redirection. Mitchell knew that motion could reside in the printed book as "the merest suggestion, existing in the white paper between the speeches, between sentences, phrases, words, and sometimes even between syllables."[39] What the archive reveals, however, is that while papers can be reconceived as agents of frenetic activity, they can also stand still, making their occasional motion seem all the more purposive. When the Chester Nativity pageants are received amid Mitchell's vast network—a network "summoned," as Bourriaud suggests, "by [their] own design"[40]—they are much less the timeless monuments that Mitchell sometimes imagines them to be. They become social things, actors with the ability to stride, to run, to creep, to quiver, *or* to stand perfectly still, "with intense feeling, visible, contractile, extensible—instinct with its own kind of life."[41]

The Archive: Image

There are a number of murky black-and-white photographs that document the sets and costumes of the Toronto productions of *The Chester Mysteries*. Mitchell was appreciative of photography. While he ardently asserted that his theatre was not "a theatre of technology," his affinity for expressionism came from a sense that antirealist painting might embrace the photographer's eye for light in order to stave off the encroaching domination of the movies. "Some experimenter with a talent for essentials," he writes, "could teach us a beautiful use of suggestive elements in a dark field, and give us a speed that could almost rival pictures."[42] Figure 5.3 documents the set of the 1919 production at Hart House designed by J. E. H. MacDonald, but this photograph, like the others in the archive, is disappointing—at least at first.

Photographs of theatrical performance are typically understood as furnishing evidence. As Susan Sontag argues, "A photograph passes for incontrovertible proof that a given thing happened," while photography "has become one of the principle devices for experiencing something, for giving an appearance of participation." The truth of the matter is, however—at least for Sontag—that photographs are *memento mori*: "to take a photograph is to participate in another person's or thing's mortality, vulnerability, mutability. Precisely by slicing out this moment and freezing it, all photographs testify to time's relentless melt."[43] Photography is the antithesis of Mitchell's *paradosis* and the fact that his theatre is largely preserved in photographic form makes for something of paradox. In his response to Sontag's claim that "only that which narrates can make us understand,"[44] however, John Berger points out that readers of photography must aim "to construct a context for a photograph, to construct it with words, to construct

Figure 5.3 Hart House production of *The Chester Mysteries* (1919). Image courtesy of University of Toronto Archives.

it with other photographs, to construct it by its place in an ongoing text of photographs and images." Photographs cannot be considered in a linear way, as illustrations of what happened. Instead, we have to "situate the printed photograph so that it acquires something of the surprising conclusiveness of that which *was* and *is* [...] Such a context replaces the photograph in time–not its own original time for that is impossible—but in narrated time."[45] In other words, photographs must be comprehended as untimely matter, that is, as socially vibrant mediators functioning in a multitemporal network of conversations and alliances.

There is no better interpreter of these polychronic associations than Mitchell himself. On the subject of "old plays," Mitchel observes that "they involve perils," and his primary concern appears to have been to avoid enlisting "experts with a concern for historical accuracy or fidelity to the text, whose feeling for authenticity far outruns their feeling for art." Accordingly, good adaptations of medieval plays are not to be "burdened with too much knowledge of wagons," reproducing "the giggling atmosphere of those college revivals in which the front rows are filled with suitably dressed, orange-sucking spectators." The mysteries of the Nativity, he sensed, belong in churches, "and when they must go to the theatre, it should be to a theatre that reproduces a church [...] there should be no curtain, no footlights, no orchestra in its well."[46] The drive here—a gesture toward an authenticity unfettered by historicism—taps into Mitchell's sense that theatrical practice generally needs to capture something of the mystical quality of late medieval religious experience, an experience that moves the audience to a "Beyond place." Writing in 1930 for *Theatre Arts Monthly*, Mitchell asks his reader to "slip some weekday into a church":

> Let him turn his view past the pier that marks the meeting of nave and transept walls at the left, away into the dusk; then sweep across to the right until his line of sight runs past the other corner, and he will feel the effort of those old Colleges of Builders, creating in stone the seeming of a little world opening into a great one—an embouchement of vision into a Beyond Place.[47]

Mitchell offers several keys here to narrating the archival photographs of his productions: the sweeping gaze of the viewer; the geometry of architecture; and the labor of craftsmen.

The photograph of the set alone is flat. The stained glass window is curious but distant and shows none of the color that light should bring to life. The altar and manger, the spaces of real presence, are also devoid of the essential vitality of the Nativity, yet, we are to

> imagine a play there at the crossing. It could not be a mean play; it would have to be a big one. [...] Imagine the play there making its own magic in its own soul. It need not be a gloomy soul. It might sometimes be a tragic one, but it could just as well be a soul that revealed itself in gaiety, a soul instinct with joy and buoyancy and grace, a soul of laughter and color and light.

Mitchell's theory of motion prompts untimely engagement with medieval theatricality by indexing something of its sacramental quality. "Ours is the only art whose life depends upon its power to conjure up a living something," he writes, "a Presence."[48] For Mitchell, the artist, nothing short of a priest, stands upon the stage altar as a mediator between the material world and things higher than it, moving his audience as he transforms the stuffness of the everyday into the transcendent and the spiritual: "the natural world is incomplete and only beautiful as I read order and beauty into it," he claims.[49]

In the Chester play, presence is no mere metaphor, since the word is literally made flesh:

Garcius:
>
> To Bethlem take wee the waye,
> for with you I thinke to wend,
> that prince of peace for to praye
> heaven to have at our ende.
> And singe we all, I read,
> some myrth to his majestee,
> for certayne now see wee it indeede:
> the kinge Sone of heavon is hee.[50]

Perhaps the photograph seems more colorful now, in proximity to the Chester Nativity scene recast in the mystical shades of Mitchell's ecumenical spirituality. The flat black-and-white image acquires some depth as the words of the medieval play surface, palimpsest like, within the frame of the Hart House proscenium providing what Walter Benjamin calls "a tiny spark of chance, of the here and now, [...] that imperceptible point at which, in the immediacy of that long-past moment, the future so persuasively inserts itself, that looking back we may rediscover it."[51]

Still more can be said about design as captured in this picture. "The architect does not design in tints and shades," Mitchell writes in *Creative Theatre*, "he designs in things—high solids, low solids, forms on which one can walk. He does not have to discern merely the tonal value of a shadow. He has to make something that will produce a shadow." While Mitchell fully rejected the concept of white light on painted scenery, he embraced, along with many modernist painters, the idea of "colored light on neutral scenery, tones of ivory and warm gray that will modify our light without gainsaying it."[52] Mitchell calls his "new theatre" a theatre of "shadow-casters" that deflect, interrupt, and transmit light for light, "our sole mechanical medium of motion."[53] Consistent with this vision, the dramaturgy of the Chester Nativity, one discovers, unfolds as movement from darkness into light: it begins in the shadows (shepherds on gloomy moors), coming later to understand light as a wonderful mystery, and, finally, as a prefiguration of the divine.

Garcius:
>A,Gode sm ightis!
>In Yonder starre light is;
>of the sonne this sight is,
>as yt nowe seemes.[54]

And then later in the play

PrimusPas tor:
>Nowe followe we the starre that shines,
>tyll we come to that holy stable.
>To Bethlem boyne the lymes;
>Follow we yt without any fable.[55]

The photograph becomes even more legible to us, with respect to light and color, when released from the single moment it documents and put into contact with material that reveals the web of associations implicated in Mitchell's artistic practice. The Barnicke Gallery at Hart House in Toronto has in its possession one of J. E. H. MacDonald's design sketches for *The Chester Mysteries* (figure 5.4). This drawing astonishes by adding color to the record, but also through the relationships it establishes among photography, painting, light, and sacramental forms: the horizontal axis of the gray altar breaking up the vertical shafts created by solemn columns (capturing something of both the architect's

Figure 5.4 J. E. H. MacDonald, *Untitled Drawing from Stage Set "The Chester Mysteries of the Nativity and Adoration"* (1919), watercolor and pencil on paper, 14 x 27 cm, Justina M. Barnicke Gallery, Hart House Theatre Collection, University of Toronto.

and the stone mason's craft of which Mitchell makes so much), and the swatches of bright ivory in close proximity to bold color. The image is arresting in its simplicity, but also in the affective affinity it has not just to the Hart House photograph of the stage but also to Mitchell's marginal pen sketch in the earliest of the typescripts.

It is probably a stretch to draw an association between the Shepherds and the Magi portions of the Chester Nativity sequence and the particular crafts of the guilds that produced them. Nevertheless, Chester's shepherds, evocatively, were painters, as were the two artists responsible for the Hart House set designs, both members of the influential Group of Seven, known for landscape paintings that bridged the gap between romanticism and expressionism. J. E. H. MacDonald was also a graphic designer whose work had strong affinities with the back-to-craft medievalism of William Morris, Charles Rennie Mackintosh, and the Arts and Crafts movement. The Group of Seven opened their first major exhibition at the Art Gallery of Ontario the same year Hart House opened, and the members of the Group were frequent exhibitors in the Hart House gallery and in the theatre foyer.[56] The network of association that coalesces around the design of Mitchell's vision for *The Chester Mysteries* can be extended further still. Figure 5.5 is a Christmas card, designed by MacDonald for Vincent Massey. Massey (as noted earlier) was Hart House's greatest patron, and the future head of the Massey Commission, which, in 1951, diagnosed Canada's cultural landscape and recommend the creation of the Canada Council to foster Canadian art. Massey would become the first Canadian-born governor general of Canada in 1952.

There is, however, another point to be made here, one less concerned with the Chester Nativity pageants as social things, acting as inspiring agents in the vibrant ecology of an emergent Canadian modernism. Many of the Group of Seven were invested, as was Mitchell, in the ecumenical spiritualism of theosophy and the mystical writing of Madame Blavatsky. Theosophy, in this context, was a mixture of Western and Eastern theologies that Ann Davis argues appealed to Canadians "attracted to transcendentalism and a liberal Christianity open to mysticism."[57] Theosophy, as taken up by the Arts and Crafts movement, involved a spiritual position-taking that directly challenged the conceptual boundary between the realm of higher spiritual truth and the realm of earthly, material objects. If art objects have an inner life, as the theosopher-artisan J. E. H. MacDonald believed, it is possible to invest the archival vestiges of Mitchell's theatre—the photographs but also the painting and the card—with an iconicity that

Figure 5.5 Christmas card designed and printed for Vincent and Alice Massey, 1922. Robert Stacey Collection, National Gallery of Canada Library and Archives, Ottawa.

is, to the historian of medieval materialities, readily at hand.[58] Might production archives be more easily understood if they were conceived of, and handled, as icons or relics would be? Originally viewed as an expression of piety, the medieval Chester play is reconfigured under Mitchell's direction to stimulate the production of new and fully modern devotional images that draw attention, as icons do, to their craftsmanship, in their experimentation with the spiritual motion made possible by shadow, color, and light.

* * *

The archive of *The Chester Mysteries* is a curious and inviting place because it fully occupies the medieval past, repurposing its matter in its making of its own modern time and space. Medieval and modern artworks live synchronically in the present, in a social encounter with each other that assures no single piece of the past is separable from any other or, indeed, from now. This dizzying activity is the motion of the archive. It is also, for Mitchell, the motion of theatrical revival. "Producing a form is to invent possible encounters," writes Bourriaud, and "receiving a form is to create an exchange, the way you return a service in a game of tennis."[59]

The second typescript in the Mitchell archive—one I have referred to but not yet discussed—includes an epilogue spoken by a figure called the Expositor:

> Within our hearts this prayer, that ye may feel
> How in love's hands time is a little thing
> And so tonight may love your senses bring
> Back to the halls of Bethlehem, the fold
> Where shepherds watched their sheep
> Where angels told
> Of peace on earth, good will to men.
> And ye shall see the coming of the kings
> And by a s tar...
> So lastly shall you see them rise and go
> And the place vacant left.

Theses words are crucial, I think, because one of the things Mitchell's work prescribes is a theatre that moves people—imaginatively and spiritually—through history. His purpose, in his direction of *The Chester Mysteries*, would not have been to return his audiences to Bethlehem in order to experience a biblical moment of origin, nor would it have been to recreate an experience proximate to a medieval Christian's encounter with God made flesh. Instead, I think Mitchell sought to uncover the Middle English play's untimely dimensions—to "see them rise and go" and find "the place vacant left"—in order to locate his study of motion in stillness and his study of time in stasis. The reviews of the first Hart House production of *The Chester Mysteries* confirm that Mitchell's ambitions, though both lofty and fanatical, were not completely mad. One reviewer, for instance, suggested that the play made the audience feel as though "they were taking part in something—like an act of worship, and it was not merely a play that they were watching." It would not be "an exaggeration to state," the reviewer continues, "that no such spell has ever been cast in a local playhouse" and "that the place whereon [the actors] were standing" became something like "holy ground."[60] Another critic found "not a jarring chord" in this "creation of five centuries ago" and reported that it was "a surprise to many to find so perfect and acceptable a setting of the world-old story" presented with "admirable simplicity," giving us "the mind of the fourteenth century in terms that are almost identical with our own." "Every spectator," he concludes, "reads his own soul into the play."[61] "The English drama has traveled a long way since the days of the miracle plays," opines a final critic, "and in the journey it has lost the poetic quality that can be secured by the blending of mysticism and reality. That quality pervades *The Chester Mysteries*."[62]

Each of these reviews oscillates among pasts, gathering up bits and pieces of "old world" sacramentality in order to attach them to a modernist yearning for an unfussy serenity. All of these critics find in Mitchell's production an encounter with the past that is also an encounter with the present, and to look at these clippings now, nearly a century later, only adds dimension to the archival acknowledgments of the Chester Nativity play's untimely depth. For Mitchell, the theatre ought to provide "a gentle kind of exultation." Of *The Chester Mysteries* specifically, he writes:

> The audience weeps, the actors play with streaming faces, and no one seems particularly ashamed of it. It is several minutes after the end of the play before the first spectators stir, and sometimes there will be members of the audience still in their places an hour afterward. Whether this is theatre or religion, I do not know, but I have a feeling that it is theatre in one of the great manifestations that we have lost in our day.[63]

Roy Mitchell sought to recuperate something from the past, a magic, a mystery, a certain kind of wonder, that he felt was lost to modern times. When the medieval history Mitchell was chasing enters into conversation with the modern archive, they become, together, the artwork under investigation. Historical quests are unsettled, since no single image or piece of text can ever belong uniquely to one place or one time. At this moment of recognition—this social interstice, this *paradosis*—the dramaturgical design of the Chester play becomes unmistakably clear: the pageants are palimpsests of theatrical wonder that unsettle fixed notions of periodicity by making it possible for fifteenth-century Lancastrian shepherds to be moved though time and space to an ancient place where they discover the untimely stillness of theNativity.

Notes

1. See, for example, Lawrence Clopper, "The History and Development of the Chester Cycle," *Modern Philology* 75 (1978): 219–46; *The Chester Cycle in Context*, eds. Jessica Dell, David Klausner, and Helen Ostovich (Abingdon, Oxon: Ashgate, 2012); *The Trial and Flagellation of Christ with Other Studies in the Chester Cycle*, ed. W. W. Greg (London: Malone Society, 1935); *The Chester Mystery Cycle: A Casebook*, ed. Kevin J. Harry (New York and London: Garland, 1933); *The Chester Mystery Cycle: Essays and Documents*, eds. R. M. Lumiansky and David Mills (Chapel Hill and London: University of North Carolina Press, 1983); F. M. Salter, *Medieval Drama in Chester* (Toronto: University of Toronto Press, 1955); Peter Travis, *Dramatic Design in the Chester Cycle* (Chicago: University of Chicago Press, 1982). Of particular importance is the work of David Mills, including his edited collection, *Staging the Chester Cycle* (Leeds Texts and Monographs, ns 9, 1985) and the most extensive study of the play to date, *Recycling the Cycle: The City of Chester and Its Whitson Plays* (Toronto: University of Toronto Press, 1998).
2. The first modern performance of the Chester play was William Poel's production of Chester's "Sacrifice of Isaac," paired with *Everyman*, at the Charterhouse in London in 1901. Nugent Monck, a member of Poel's company, staged the first versions of Chester's Nativity, Shepherds, and Magi plays in Bloomsbury Hall, London, in 1906. Monck then proposed, but never produced, a production of the whole cycle that was to be performed over three days at Whitsun 1907. The Shakespearean actor/director Frank Benson, who worked closely with Frank Conroy, also produced a production of the Chester Nativity in the first decade of the twentieth century. The first full-scale revival of the play was in 1951 when the entire play was performance for the Festival of Great Britain. See *Victoria County History: A History of the County of Chester*, eds. A. T. Thacker and C. P. Lewis, vol. 5. 2 (http://www.british-history.ac.uk/source.aspx?pubid=524, 2005): 275–76; D. Mills, "Reviving the Chester Plays," *Medieval English Theatre* 13(1991): 39–51; "'Reviving the Chester Plays': A Postscript," *Medieval English Theatre* 15 (1993): 124–25; http://www.chester-mysteryplays.com/history/abouttheplays.html. For extensive discussion of the play's early revivals, see Mills, *Recycling the Cycle*, 206–11.
3. The first full editions were *Chester Mysteries*, ed. J. H. Markland (London: Roxburghe Club, 1818); *The Chester Plays*, ed. T. Wright (London: Shakespeare Soc. 17. 2 vols. 1843, 1847); *The Chester Plays*, eds. H. Deimling and Dr. Matthews, Early English Text Society. Extra Ser. lxii, cxv (London: Oxford University Press, 1893). For extensive discussion of the play's early print history, see Mills, *Recycling the Cycle*, 199–206.
4. Jonathan Gil Harris, *Untimely Matter in the Time of Shakespeare* (Philadelphia: University of Pennsylvania Press, 2009), 2. See also *Chester: The Records of Early English Drama*, ed. Lawrence Clopper (Toronto: University of Toronto Press,1979).
5. Harris, *Untimely Matter*, 3–4. Harris is working from Michel Serres's conversation with Bruno Latour, *Conversations on Science, Culture and Time*, trans. Roxanne Lapidus (Ann Arbor: University of Michigan Press, 1995), 60.

6. Bruno Latour, *Reassembling the Social: An Introduction to Actor-Network-Theory* (Oxford: Oxford University Press, 2005), 5, 12.
7. Nicolas Bourriaud, *Relational Aesthetics*, trans. Simon Pleasance and Fronza Woods with Mathieu Copeland (Les presses du réel, 2002), 11, 44–45.
8. Roy Mitchell, *Creative Theatre* (Westwood, NJ: Kindle Press, 1968), 6.
9. *The Chester Mystery Cycle*, eds. R. M. Lumiansky and David Mills. Early English Text Society. Supplementary Series 3, 9. (London and New York: Oxford University Press, 1974). vol. I. 126, ll. 41–44. I am referring to the medieval text even when referencing Mitchell's revival. I am doing this deliberately, though perhaps confusingly, in order to fully integrate Middle English play with the materials pertaining to the modern revival.
10. *The Chester Mystery Cycle*, vol. I. 138, ll. 302–305.
11. Ibid., vol. I. 141.
12. Ibid., vol. I. 179–80, ll. 124–35.
13. Ibid., vol. I. 154, ll. 651–56.
14. Mitchell, *Creative Theatre*, 97.
15. Ibid.,256 .
16. Ibid.,5.
17. Ibid.,164 .
18. Ibid.,163 .
19. Jacques Derrida, *Archive Fever: A Freudian Impression*, trans. Erik Prenowitz (Chicago: University of Chicago Press, 1996), 3.
20. Friedrich A. Kittler, *Gramophone, Film, Typewriter*, trans. Geoffrey Winthrop-Young and Michael Wutz (Stanford: Stanford University Press, 1986), xl–xli.
21. Mitchell, *Creative Theatre*, 97, 163.
22. Mitchell, *Creative Theatre*, 164.
23. Kittler, *Gramophone, Film, Typewriter*, 7, 14.
24. *The Chester Mysteries* printed and published by Egmont H. Arens for the Washington Square Bookshop, New York (1917). Cover Illustration by Josephine Bell. Clara Thomas Archives and Special Collections, 1974–012–002 (017).
25. The copy that I consulted belonged to Hugh Poynter Bell. Bell was English but moved to Canada in 1912 and became involved in the management of Hart House theatre. He was the music and art critic for the *Montreal Daily Star* from 1923 to 1949. He was also a composer.
26. Bourriaud, *Relational Aesthetics*, 28–29.
27. Seenote 3.
28. Mitchell, Introduction to *The Chester Mysteries*, 1; Mitchell, Introduction to *The Nativity Cycle of the Play of the Shepherds, The Play of the Kings, The Play of the Shepherd's Offering from the Chester Mysteries. Playing Verison by Frank Conroy & Roy Mitchell* [etc.], typescript, Clara Thomas Archives and Special Collections, York University, Roy Mitchell Fonds, 1974–012–002 (017),2.
29. British Library Additional 10305 (1592). Bellin was also the scribe of another manuscript owned by the Coopers' Company of Chester. There are eight known manuscripts of the Chester Play. See *The Chester Mystery Cycle*, vol. I. ix–xxvii, as well as Mills, *Recycling the* Cycle, 153–98.

30. *The Play of the Shepherds*, typescript, Clara Thomas Archives and Special Collections, York University, Roy Mitchell Fonds, 1978–010–001 (05).
31. *The Chester Mystery Cycle*, vol. I. 175, ll. 13–16.
32. Mitchell, *Creative Theatre*, 9.
33. Siân Echard, "House Arrest: Modern Archives, Medieval Manuscripts," *Journal of Medieval and Early Modern Studies* 30:2 (2000): 186.
34. Mitchell, *Creative Theatre*, 221.
35. Untitled typescript. Clara Thomas Archives and Special Collections, York University, Roy Mitchell Fonds, 1974–012–002 (017).
36. *The Nativity Cycle of the Play of the Shepherds* [etc]. See note 28.
37. Clara Thomas Archives and Special Collections, York University, Roy Mitchell Fonds, 1978–010–001 (05).
38. *The Chester Mystery Cycle*, vol. I. 136, ll. 258–61.
39. Mitchell, *Creative Theatre*, 153.
40. Bourriaud, *Relational Aesthetics*, 28–29.
41. Mitchell, *Creative Theater*, 163.
42. Roy Mitchell, "The Theatre as Laboratory," typescript, Clara Thomas Archives and Special Collections, York University, Roy Mitchell Fonds, 1974–012–001 (05).
43. Susan Sontag, *On Photography* (New York: Picador, 1973), 5, 10, 15.
44. Ibid.,23.
45. John Berger, *About Looking* (New York: Vintage e-books, 1991), 65; emphasis in the original.
46. Mitchell, Introduction to *The Nativity Cycle of the Play of the Shepherds*, 1.
47. Roy Mitchell, "The House of Presence," *Theater Arts Monthly* (1930): 581–82.
48. Ibid.,582.
49. Roy Mitchell, "The Spirit of Modern Art," *Canadian Theosophist* 8:6 (1932): 163.
50. *The Chester Mystery Cycle*, vol. I. 146, ll. 471–79.
51. Walter Benjamin, "Short History of Photography", *Screen* 13, no. 1 (1972), 7.
52. Mitchell, *Creative Theatre*, 228.
53. Ibid.,225.
54. *The Chester Mystery Cycle*, vol. I. 139, ll. 324–27.
55. Ibid., vol. I. 145, ll. 452–55.
56. Their names are Franklin Carmichael, Lawren Harris, A. Y. Jackson, Franz Johnston, Arthur Lismer, J. E. H. MacDonald, and Frederick Varley.
57. Ann Davis, *The Logic of Ecstasy: Canadian Mystical Painting, 1920–1940* (Toronto: University of Toronto Press, 1992), xi–xii, 97.
58. Caroline Walker Bynum, *Christian Materiality: An Essay on Religion in Late Medieval Europe* (New York: Zone Books, 2011), 18.
59. Bourriaud, *Relational Aesthetics*, 23.
60. *Mail and Empire* (1919).
61. *World* (December 25, 1919).
62. *Mail and Empire* (December 24, 1919).
63. Mitchell, Introduction to *The Nativity Cycle of the Play of the Shepherds*, 3.

Bibliography

Benjamin, Walter. "Short History of Photography." *Screen* 13, no. 1 (1972), 7.
Berger, John. *About Looking*. New York: Vintage e-books, 1991.
Bourriaud, Nicolas. *Relational Aesthetics*. Translated by Simon Pleasance and Fronza Woods with Mathieu Copeland. France: Les presses du réel. 2002.
Bynum, Caroline Walker. *Christian Materiality: An Essay on Religion in Late Medieval Europe*. New York: Zone Books, 2011.
Clopper, Lawrence, ed. *Chester: The Records of Early English Drama*. Toronto: University of Toronto Press, 1979.
———. "The History and Development of the Chester Cycle." *Modern Philology* 75 (1978), 219–46.
Davis, Ann. *The Logic of Ecstasy: Canadian Mystical Painting, 1920–1940*. Toronto: University of Toronto Press, 1992.
Dell, Jessica, David Klausner, and Helen Ostovich, eds. *The Chester Cycle in Context*. Abingdon, Oxon: Ashgate, 2012.
Deimling, H., and Dr. Matthews, eds. *The Chester Plays*. Early English Text Society. Extra ser. lxii, cxv. London and New York: Oxford University Press, 1893.
Derrida, Jaques. *Archive Fever: A Freudian Impression*. Translated by Erik Prenowitz. Chicago, IL: University of Chicago Press, 1996.
Echard, Siân. "House Arrest: Modern Archives, Medieval Manuscripts." *Journal of Medieval and Early Modern Studies* 30, no. 2 (2000), 185–210.
Greg, W. W., ed. *The Trial and Flagellation of Christ with Other Studies in the Chester Cycle*. London: Malone Society, 1935.
Harris, Jonathan Gill. *Untimely Matter in the Time of Shakespeare*. Philadelphia: University of Pennsylvania Press, 2009.
Harry, Kevin, J., ed. *The Chester Mystery Cycle: A Casebook*. New York and London: Garland, 1933.
Latour, Bruno. *Reassembling the Social: An Introduction to Actor-Network-Theory*. Oxford: Oxford University Press, 2005.
Lumiansky, R. M., and David Mills, eds. *The Chester Mystery Cycle*. Early English Text Society. Supplementary Series 3, 9. London and New York: Oxford University Press, 1974.
———. *The Chester Mystery Cycle: Essays and Documents*. Chapel Hill and London: University of North Carolina Press, 1983.
Markland, J. H., ed. *Chester Mysteries*. London: Roxburghe Club, 1818.
Mills, David. *Recycling the Cycle: The City of Chester and Its Witson Plays*. Toronto: University of Toronto Press, 1998.
———. "Reviving the Chester Plays." *Medieval English Theatre* 13 (1991), 39–51.
———. "'Reviving the Chester Play': A Postscript." *Medieval English Theatre* 15 (1993), 124–25.
———. *Staging the Chester Cycle*. Leeds Texts and Monographs, ns 9. Leeds: University of Leeds, School of English, 1985.
Mitchell, Roy. *Creative Theatre*. Westwood, NJ: Kindle Press, 1968.
———. "The Spirit of Modern Art," *Canadian Theosophist* 8, no. 6 (1932), 161–68.
Salter, F. M. *Medieval Drama in Chester*. Toronto: University of Toronto Press, 1955.

Serres, Michel, with Bruno Latour. *Conversations on Science, Culture and Time*. Translated by Roxanne Lapidus. Ann Arbor: University of Michigan Press, 1995.
Sontag, Susan. *On Photography*. New York: Picador, 1973
Thacker, A. T., and C. P. Lewis, eds. *Victoria County History*, 2005. http://www.british-history.ac.uk/source.aspx?pubid=524.
Travis, Peter. *Dramatic Design in the Chester Cycle*. Chicago, IL: University of Chicago Press, 1982.
Wright, T., ed. *The Chester Plays*, ed. London: Shakespeare Society. 17. 2 vols. 1843, 1847.

6
Performing *Ruhe*: Police, Prevention, and the Archive

Jan Lazardzig

At the dawn of the nineteenth century, under the influence of that new historical actor the masses, the supervision and surveillance of theatre in the German-speaking world was turned over to the institution that already possessed a certain biopolitical expertise: the police.[1] To understand why theatre censorship fell under the jurisdiction of the police authorities, it is important to clarify the role of *Policey* for the constitution of the modern state. The rediscovery of the antique thematic of *politeia* and *politia* in the late fifteenth century allowed the German terms Policey, *Policei*, or *Pollicei* to appear in urban laws of German territorial states. In the administrative language of the sixteenth century, the notion of Policey suggested *good* public order in the city and country, including, for instance, moral and religious life. In the German use of administrative language, Policey is initially understood as a broadly formulated reference to the interdependency of city, state, and constitution. The Early Modern notion of police primarily suggests an internal-political view of order that can be summed up in three definitions:[2] first, Policey describes a condition of good order for a polity; second, Policey represents law for the respective polity; and third, Policey describes methods for the production and circulation of this good condition or law. All three definitions relate to the responsibility of the individual citizen for the production and maintenance of good order.

In the eighteenth century, the understanding of Policey became so diverse that almost every scholar of Policey theory developed his own notion of what constitutes good Policey.³ The bureaucratic apparatus of absolutism included the Policey of fire, of building, of medication, as well as the Policey of inflation and poverty. This policing of all areas of existence commits the happiness of its subjects to a normalizing, regulating authority. Compared with the present notion of police, it could be said that the Policey of the old order consisted in making police in the modern sense obsolete. The police of the old order were order per se, a role that the modern police only endeavor to maintain.⁴ The transformation of political aims emerging throughout the eighteenth century—from welfare state to control state—parallels a reduction of the broad notion of police, which sees the production and maintenance of good order as both a preventative measure and as welfare work. By the middle of the eighteenth century, Policey no longer described the condition of good order itself, but, rather, *the activities* of controlling authorities.

In the wake of new censorship regulations around 1800 in both Prussia and the Habsburg monarchy, theatre enterprises and managers were obligated to submit all texts intended for performance to (newly established) city police administrations.⁵ The system of police pre- or preventative censorship would remain in force—with a brief interruption in the aftermath of 1848—until after World War I (1918 in the German Empire, 1926 in Austria). As a consequence of this preventative praxis, Vienna and Berlin created what are likely the most extensive literary archives for theatre in the German-speaking world.⁶ The significance of these archives is difficult to overstate, for they present not only a systematic documentation of the dramatic and performance history of the nineteenth century, but further demonstrate what the ruling powers in each case understood as "theatre" (i.e., what they licensed or permitted). Remarkably, the logic behind these powerful archives has, until now, received little attention within the historiography of theatre and censorship. This may be a result of the fact that the imperative of police action and the phantasmatics of police order and organization are closely linked to the history of bourgeois theatre.

In his engagement with the concept of the archive, Jacques Derrida reminds us that the word "archive" combines two principles. On the one hand, it marks a place in which things find their point of departure, be it physically, historically, or ontologically. On the other hand, the archive contains an orderliness or lawfulness that is actualized and executed through authority:

> Arkhē, we recall, names at once the *commencement* and the *commandment*. This name apparently coordinates two principles in one: the principle

according to nature or history, there where things *commence*—physical, historical, or ontological principle—but also the principle according to the law, there where men and gods *command*, there where authority and social order are exercised, *in this place* from which *order* is given—a nomological principle.[7]

Derrida understands the nomological principle, the commandment, not only as the right and responsibility to identify and to classify, but also as the right to unify authority and synchronize it according to *one* principle. Derrida emphasized that, temporally, commandment precedes commencement, thus, before the archive has a place, a home, it has a *nomos*, a law or lawfulness. Should place and law, *nomos* and home, come together in one institution (Derrida speaks of the "toponomology" of the archive[8]), then the nomological principle becomes more or less invisible, and can only be detected with great difficulty.

Following Derrida, the commandment of the police theatre archives is more than the sum of decrees and ordinances, manuals and instructions with which the activity of police officials and censors are regulated.[9] Instead, as I will argue in this essay, it is to be found in the idea of precaution or prevention and acquires its specific legitimacy out of an extensive concordance between the development of theories of the police and theories of theatre reform in the eighteenth century. A common point of reference here involves the social doctrines of the Enlightenment and their artistic objectives.[10] These are referred to both by bourgeois theatre reformers and by the representatives of Cameralism and *Policeywissenschaft*, meaning the study (which emerged as a university discipline in 1727) of policy and administration in and of the enlightened, absolutist territorial state.[11] Of particular influence here are the plans laid out by Christian Wolff (1679–1754), which were later developed most significantly by the state and police theorists Johann Gottlieb von Justi (1717–71) and Joseph von Sonnenfels (1732–1817). Wolff conceives of the stage as a pleasant school for virtue, designed to perfect one's moral education.[12] As a worldly institution for the announcement of bourgeois morality, the stage joins, as complement, its spiritual counterpart, the church. Wolff formulates what would become a recurring topos for a number of bourgeois theatre reformers, from Johann Christoph Gottsched (1700–66) to Johann Elias Schlegel (1719–49) to Gotthold Ephraim Lessing (1729–81), Johann Georg Sulzer (1720–79), and Friedrich Schiller (1759–1805). With von Justi, the pedagogical and disciplinary function of the literary theatre enters into police literature on a broader scale.¹³ The establishment of permanent ("standing") German-speaking stages is understood by the reformers (and, not least of all, as a reaction to the traditional antitheatrical reflexes of local authorities) as being in harmony with the raison d'être of the Enlightened-absolutist state.¹⁴ In terms of practical effects for the theatre, this harmony is seen when, for example, actors and observers are policed through orders and rules, or when the monitoring of effects and the regulation of affects are discussed in terms of police-based concepts.¹⁵

One point of intersection for police precaution and the aesthetic direction of effects and affects is the concept of *Ruhe*.¹⁶ As a result of its polysemic qualities, Ruhe is a term difficult to translate into English. It can be used with reference to both behavior and relationships, and contains kinetic (how to keep calm) as well as sonic (how to keep quiet) significations. At approximately the same time as the Ruhe of the body politic develops into a primary goal and a raison d'être of policing activities, Ruhe becomes a prerogative for a reformed, and hence literary, theatre. For the theatre reformer Lessing, to give but one example, audiences are conceivable only under the condition of absolutely silent attention.¹⁷ The new ideal is the civilized and insightful spectator: he who devotes his attention entirely to the performance, who remains seated or stands quietly and peacefully, who gives himself over rapturously to the theatrical illusion such that text and performance can reach their full effect, who, if need be, produces a gentle tear of emotion or a delicate smile.¹⁸ For both Policey theorists and theatre reformers of the second half of the eighteenth century, Ruhe represents a desirable state, not simply one characterized by a lack of activity.

Ruhe of the Body Politic

The scholarly consensus on the history of the police is that our contemporary conception of the police became codified in Germany and Austria at around 1800.¹⁹ The famous police article (§10 II 17) included in the *Prussian Civil Code* (*Preussisches Allgemeines Landrecht*) of 1794 excludes the Early Modern idea of social welfare from the police's catalogue of duties, confining the task of the police in large part to the prevention of danger. The former period's broad conception of the Policey undergoes a legislative limitation: "The office of the police is to take the necessary measures for the maintenance of public peace [Ruhe], security [*Sicherheit*], and order [*Ordnung*], and for the prevention of imminent danger to the public or individual members of the same."[20] Even if the prevention of danger is here (for the first time) explicitly declared as the primary objective of the police, the preventative orientation of the police goes back much further.[21] This is particularly evident in the imperative of Ruhe, perhaps the most difficult to understand of the "modern" imperatives that make up the police's preventative regime.[22]

In the major eighteenth-century works of Policey studies, the idea of Ruhe becomes a central topic around 1750 (and even more so after the French Revolution of 1789). Ruhe is applied to an understanding of the state, which conceives of the body politic as being fundamentally dependent upon the individual body of the subject, not only in the sense of a *body* politic, that is to say in the sense of the state as a collective singular, as *Leviathan*, but also in the sense of an identity of interests between an individual and a community.[23] Everything that provides for the power and well-being of the state also serves, by means of this almost osmotic logic, the well-being of the individual. "Good Policey" is, thus, not to be understood as an exclusively repressive concept of authority in the Early Modern state. Rather, as Michel Foucault emphasizes in his lectures on governmentality, it is a fundamental concern about sustaining the well-being and the life of the people, and with the improvement of processes and the accumulation of knowledge concerning them.[24] Thus, in the numerous and lengthy treatises on Policey and Cameralism, what is meant is primarily the concrete "know how" for securing health, sustenance, productivity, and infrastructure. What exactly does it mean, however, to be in the state of Ruhe? In what manner is Ruhe produced, and to what end?

Literature on the science of policing deals explicitly with Ruhe in those places where the inner order of the state is injured or endangered through disturbance and disruption, where a breach of public order occurs. In his *Foundations of Policey-Wissenschaft* (*Grundsätze der Policey-Wissenschaft*, 1759), Johann Heinrich Gottlieb von Justi comments on Ruhe in connection with the inner security of the state. In the "policed" state, that is to say the body politic oriented toward harmony, equilibrium, and consistency, the preservation of "inner Ruhe" operates for him as a "primary object of the *Policey*."[25] Ruhe is the result of orderly behavior of subjects in public places.[26] As an instrument of statecraft, Policey must enforce Ruhe with reference to order. In opposition to order, which is capable of being fixed in writing and whose realm of legitimacy is defined in advance, Ruhe aims for a habitual modesty and uniformity (as these relate to order). It is to be understood as the contextual and situational orientation toward order. In securing Ruhe, the preventative regime of the Policey does not aim solely at the (contemporary) policing goal of the prevention of danger, but, rather, orients itself toward the bodily and economic well-being of the subjects. The primary goal is safe-guarding the productivity of the state's citizens:

> The attention of the *Policey* must thus first and foremost be directed towards preserving complete peace [Ruhe] in every city and place. Thus, as soon as a crowd emerges, the police must immediately be present, must investigate the cause of this crowd, must take its initiators into custody or otherwise make this cause cease. They must, through serious measures and arrangements, take special care in particular to prevent disorder and tumult at night, since the hardworking laborers need some rest [Ruhe]. Thus, it is to precisely this end that no parades, festivities or other undertakings which could cause a confluence of people may take place without the foreknowledge and permission of the *Policey*; in this manner, they can be prepared to take the necessary measures against any disorder or debauchery that occurs thereby.[27]

The policing doctrines, distilled from countless regional Policey decrees throughout German-speaking areas, discuss Ruhe predominantly in relation to its absence, namely, in situations of uproar, disorder, and disruption. One reads in Johann Peter Willebrand's *True Notion of the Police* (*Inbegriff der Policey*, 1767): "So that no one in a city is frightened or robbed of his peace [Ruhe] at an unexpected time, the *Policey* will not tolerate anyone drumming or trumpeting without the *Policey*'s permission," for "nothing is more unjust than that the resting [Ruhe] of inhabitants is disturbed during the night by disorderly racket."[28] The Policey's monitoring of the sonic space of the city is carried out by nightwatches.[29]

Public festivities like parades, masquerade balls, and the theatre are continually named as sources for the disruption of Ruhe. In the early Policey and Cameralist doctrines, remarks on the actor are to be found alongside remarks regarding holiday ordinances and measures against debauchery and drunkenness. On the one hand, the concern is with the preservation of Ruhe and morality, on the other, with the safeguarding of the economic interests of a state. Paul Jakob Marperger (1656–1730) writes, for example, in his *Description of Trade Fairs* (*Beschreibung der Messen und Jahrmärckte*, 1710) that the presence of comedians "with regard to the many foreigners who attend fairs should be *ea lege* more or less tolerated, / but that all bawdiness and buffooneries / by which innocent ears might be sullied / should be banned from their theatre."[30] For permanent ("standing") theatres, which in the course of the eighteenth century increasingly took the place of the traveling theatres, Jakob Friedrich von Bielfeld (1717–70) demanded in his *Doctrine of Statecraft* (*Lehrbegriff der Staatskunst*, 1768) that

> the police officials would be required to afford the director of the stage all possible assistance, in order to preserve peace [Ruhe] and order during the performances. The plays were not only to be staffed by sentinels, who in the name of the local authorities would prevent all disorder and commotion; moreover, the police must also illuminate all entrances to the theatre, as well as prevent all the confusion and commotion of the coaches.[31]

The Policey's desire to achieve Ruhe is not, however, external to the theatre, is not some power opposed to it, but, rather, is in accordance with the aesthetic regime of bourgeois theatre reformers.

Within the numerous journals, almanacs, periodicals, and chronicles that determined critical discourse about the theatre in the second half of the eighteenth century, questions of audience behavior were some of the most pressing topics.[32] The *parterre* in particular—often used synonymously for the audience (or *Publikum*, which appears here as a relatively new aesthetic entity)—was the subject matter of countless critiques. At stake was a public addicted to showing disapproval through tapping canes upon the wooden floor (*pochen*) and noise-making, slamming box doors, scraping chairs, greeting seatmates, engaging in chit-chat and criticism in the parterre, hissing, booing, hooting, and jeering in the balcony, indeed, the right to make one's opinion known during the performance through applause or rapping was thoroughly debated.[33] In light of the disruptions that the theatregoer may face, particularly in urban areas, the editor of Gotha's *Theater Kalender* (to give but one example), the most significant German-language theatre journal, argued in 1783 for a Policey law that was to help ensure Ruhe in the theatre: "It would be a very salutary thing if there were to be an express Policey law, particularly in the large cities, where there are always so many unruly people, protecting the civilized spectator who wanted, in accordance with custom, to be silent, from the disruptor of public Ruhe."[34]

The adherence to Ruhe is seen as an indication for the cultivation of taste in the audience as well as its capabilities for criticism. Heinrich

August Ottokar Reichardt (1751–1828) explains this in his *Essay on the Parterre* (*Versuch über das Parterre*, 1775): "How can one judge plays when the spirit of the piece is driven out by noise, [...] when only the eye sees what the ear has not heard and what the inner sense has not perceived?" For Reichardt as well, writing in one of many treatises dedicated to the parterre as the locus of taste, connoisseurship, and critique, constructing a judgment is dependent on the "good order which must prevail in the theatre."[35] It is from this place that the taste of the "crowd," the mass of less- or entirely uneducated spectators, is to be formed.[36] Even as late as 1810, August von Kotzebue demands a "noise Policey" for unruly spectators in Vienna and Berlin.[37]

Regimeso fPr evention

Prevention (from *praevenire* = to preempt) takes as its goal either the inhibition of a certain undesired event or situation, or the limitation of the expected negative effects caused by this event or situation. As a principle of action intended to avoid future evils, prevention is characterized by what the sociologist Ulrich Bröckling calls an "active negativity,"[38] those activities that distinguish themselves through the "absence of positive objectives." From the perspective of prevention, security or health would only be indicated by their absence (as not-illness or insecurity, disorder or unrest). Regimes of prevention would correspondingly be built upon an "affectively highly-cathected lack," which would also serve to produce legitimacy for preventative action.[39] The proliferation of preventative regimes in health, ecology, economy, and security tends toward the limitless, as they must permanently thematize the opposite of what they espouse to achieve. According to Bröckling, these regimes play a significant role in constituting those dangers that they allegedly prevent. Prevention should, according to the paradoxical formulation, "prevent problems which are not yet present." Accordingly, prevention takes its orientation from a "present future," which is to say, from a future that "we today—in the present present—imagine to be more or less likely, as a desired or undesired future."[40]

Bröckling distinguishes between three regimes of prevention. All three regimes draw their rationales, their technologies, and their methods of subjectivization from the realm of health care. The first regime is that of *hygiene*, which installs a disciplinary regime tasked with the elimination of known dangers. Its techniques are based in identification, separation, and purification. The subject of prevention here is conceived as both in need of discipline and essentially disciplinable. The second regime is that of *immunization*. Its model is that of a self-regulating monitoring system whose goal is resilience. Its procedures are based in the mobilization of potentials for self-government. The subject of prevention here is conceived as imbued with both self-responsibility and the capacity to modify itself. The third regime is that of the *precautionary principle*. Its logic consists in constantly reckoning with the worst possible outcome, without knowing precisely what this might look like. This regime requires an extended sovereignty, one that attempts to develop plans and scenarios for that which has been hitherto inconceivable. Its techniques are preemptive and aim to overcome maladies without knowing at all what these might look like.

All three regimes—as I would like to show in the following pages—can be brought under the heading of the preventative imperative of Ruhe. If preventative action distinguishes itself through the absence of positive objectives, then in what manner (which is to say, through which practices and techniques) is the preventative imperative of Ruhe compatible with the objectives of theatre reformers?

Purification: Theatre Censorship

Metaphors of purification and cleaning are, in the wake of Gottsched, ubiquitous among theatre reformers of the eighteenth century.[41] In order to make the stage into an instrument of moral and ethical education, theoretical and practical efforts attempted to overcome all forms of extemporization and the impromptu, which were of particular significance—indeed, constitutive—for the nonliterary *commedia dell'arte*.[42] Extemporization and the impromptu were held to be the source of moral and ethical corruption and were as such disqualified and excluded from the ideal conception of a permanent ("standing") theatre. Taste was to be refined, affects sublimated, and behavior was to be cultivated.

Authors writing in the Policey sciences adopt the idea of the literary theatre as an instrument for the moral education of the public only in the second half of the eighteenth century.[43] Previously, theatre had played a role primarily as a source of income, and, with an eye to the satisfaction and well-being of the citizenry, as a source of entertainment and amusement. In Justi's magnum opus *Basic Pillars of Power and Happiness of the States* (*Die Grundfeste zu der Macht und Glückseligkeit der Staaten*, 1760/61), the educational capacities of the stage enter into Policey literature in a significant way.[44] Justi's text, which explicitly labels "the moral quality or the ethical state of subjects" as a "central object of the Policey," deals exhaustively with the theatre in a section entitled "Of the Delights and Amusements of the People." Comedy is, as he writes with reference to Gottsched's academic address *Plays, and especially Tragedies, are Not to be Banned from a Well-Appointed Republic (Die Schauspiele und besonders die Tragödien sind aus einer wohlbestellten Republik nicht zu verbannen*, 1736), extraordinarily suited "to promote positive moral qualities." Because dramatic productions frequently fail to achieve the aim, however, of uniting entertainment and education, he underlines the idea of a positive custodial role for the stage played by the state:

> The government should appoint a man as overseer of the pieces placed on the program whose taste and insights are as impeccable as his heart is noble, who understands both the rules of the theatre and the tastes and preferences of the majority of the audience, who attempts to unite the one with the other, and who never loses sight, even when faced with the funniest pieces, of the ultimate purpose of comedy, which is to advance virtue and promote good moral values.[45]

Justi imagines an overseer or a directorial figure—in any case, an official—who brings his influence to bear on playwrights and actors in order to advance the desired effects of comedy as an entertaining mode of instruction in virtue.

Other textbooks on the Policey and Cameralism that follow, positively disposed toward the theatre, view its advancement as a public duty and repeat without exception the demand for a governmental supervisor of the stage. This recommendation—realized, for example, in Vienna and Mannheim with the creation of a national theatre—is mostly linked, argumentatively speaking, with the purification of the theatre. Bielfeld calls the purified stage "the best school for morals, language, and general etiquette." He calls for a courtier or "any other respectable civil servant" to act as a steward of the theatre and, in addition, for police officials to attend, with the task of "order[ing] and silenc[ing] during performances."[46] He also lights the front of the theatre and demands precautions against the "confusion and noise of the carriages." According to Willebrand, it is "the duty of the police intendants to ensure specifically that no play is publicly performed that offends the purity of good taste and pure virtue."[47] From the Policey's point of view, the purity of the stage is tied to compliance with poetic regulations: the pieces performed are to be "well-made" and "rule-based."[48] Joseph von Sonnenfels, the ardent reformer and first censor of the Viennese stage, is the first to speak explicitly of theatre censorship (*Theatral Censur*).[49] While there is no mention of state agents in his *Principles of Police, Commercial, and Financial Science* (*Grundsätze der Policey, Handlung und Finanzwissenschaft*, second edition 1767), he puts all possible emphasis on the unavoidability of "theatre censors." They are to review the pieces, allow only censored plays to be performed, and must prohibit all extemporizing, which inevitably leads, according to Sonnenfels, to unseemly gestures and scurrilous behavior.[50]

With Sonnenfels, the thought that the preventative goal of Ruhe and order among the audience could be achieved through censorship of the text becomes fully established.[51] The "active negativity," that is, the abstention from any positive objectives, shows itself here in an (apparently) paradoxical manner, since prevention consists in the unconditional affirmation of the most important goals of theatre reform. The preventative character of these reforms becomes visible precisely in the lack of alternatives to these positive objectives. Thus, Sonnenfels's successor as Vienna censor, Franz von Hägelin (1735–1809), who occupied the office from 1770 to 1804, writes the following in his well-known 1804 censor manual:

> Following the primary rule, theatre is to be a school of morals and taste. Our desire would be that the dramatic authors of these genuine rules, who have so often preached them, would in practice remain faithful to them. However, they seem to forget them when composing their pieces. One must, as with many moralists, lay more worth on their works than theirwor ds.[52]

Despite common objectives, one can observe a significant difference between the authors of theatre reform and police theorists with respect to genre. Policey authors, almost without exception, discuss the pastoral surveillance of the theatre by using comedy as the example (which seems particularly suited to link entertainment and education). In contrast, the central aesthetic positions of the theatre reform movement are developed with reference to the genre that has, poetically, been accorded the highest acclaim since Greek antiquity: tragedy (e.g., Lessing, Sulzer, Mercier, and Schiller).[53] Another form of subjectivization comes into play, particularly against the background of the French Revolution. While the Policey authors, from the perspective of a sovereignty that is, at its core, led by reason, proceed from a subject that is to be disciplined (comedy), theatre reformers take the reasoning, insightful individual (tragedy) as their point of departure. This individual is both capable and worthy of being disciplined because s/he is fundamentally "reasonable."

Immunization: Autonomy

An alternative form of preventative theatre praxis arises in the context of the idealist conception of autonomy shared by Goethe and Schiller at the Weimar court theatre. Ruhe depended upon self-responsibility and self-governance, a conception that can be described by means of the preventative regime of immunization.[54] In a speech entitled *What Can a Theatre in Good Standing Actually Achieve?* (*Was kann eine gute stehende Schaubühne eigentlich wirken?*), delivered before the Palatine German Society a few years prior to the outbreak of the French Revolution, Friedrich Schiller summarized the core principles of a reformed theatre. It was to serve as school for virtues and morals in the state guided by reason. The title of the printed version, *Theatre Considered as a Moral Institution* (*Die Schaubühne als moralische Anstalt betrachtet*, 1785)—which would, in what followed, congeal into an often functionalized (and banalized) formula for the theatre of the Enlightenment[55]—reminds us of Schiller's entry (as ducal counselor) into the institutions of the state.[56] Schiller ennobles the stage through a vision of an aesthetic education led by the dramatic arts, placing it on a level with the highest public institutions of the state. He affords the stage, along with religion and the state, its own form of jurisdiction in passing judgment on despotism and the abuse of power.

Schiller's conception of theatrical reception is structured and grounded anthropologically.[57] As a result, he views the dramatic arts as the highest form of art, precisely because they harmonize the sensible and the reasonable, following the anthropological model of the body/soul connection (*commercium mentis et corporis*). The "aesthetic sense" or "the feeling for the beautiful" consists in an "intermediate state" that connects and balances the extremes of body and soul, the sensible and the ethical, the "animal" and the "more delicate works of the understanding."[58] Educated as a physician, Schiller follows the Enlightenment's dietetic conception of health, which emphasized a balance of extremes, measuredness, equivalence, and harmony.[59] This anthropological conception—which moves in the 1802 edition of Schiller's writings to the beginning of a text on the stage—already contains, in embryonic form, the Weimar courtly theatre's concern with theories of autonomy. In Schiller's preface *On the Use of the Chorus in the Tragedy*,[60] composed in Weimar in 1803 for the book edition of the *Bride of Messina* (*Die Braut von Messina*), the anthropological *commercium* doctrine leads into a reflection on the relationship between the sensible and the ethical, between feeling and understanding, material and form. It results in a conception of Ruhe oriented toward theatre praxis.

Schiller's preface is dedicated to the most experimental and also most hotly contested element of his verse tragedy, the chorus. Although his preface is at least ostensibly concerned with *his* drama, he also offers a more general account of the tasks of art. Schiller sees the audience's desire for delight and pleasure, its striving for enjoyment, as fulfilled "in the freedom of the mind in the living play of all its forces."[61] He takes up, within the framework of theoretical accounts of autonomy, principles which Goethe had formulated two years earlier in his essay *Weimar's Court Theatre* (*Weimarisches Hoftheater*, 1802), one of the manifestos of the classical-idealist theatre. Like Goethe, Schiller proclaims himself to be in favor of a preservation of the artificiality of representation. The spectator should remain constantly aware that he is watching a play, that he is observing "theatre." The illusion of reality—whatever its form—should not take place. Schiller sees the introduction of a chorus as the most distinguished means of achieving this effect. Its capacity to create distance and disrupt illusions will interrupt, inhibit, and ultimately render impossible a psychological identification with the acting characters.[62]

The verse drama *The Bride of Messina or the Hostile Brothers, A Mourning Play with Choruses* (the full title) is an analytic drama along the lines of Sophocles's *Oedipus the King*, and is generally regarded as a paradigmatic example of Weimar Classicism.[63] In a letter to his friend Christian Gottfried Körner, Schiller speaks of a "simple tragedy, following the most rigorous form," with a chorus.[64] Schiller splits the chorus into two parts, which occupy the left and right halves of the stage and stand in, metonymically, for the feuding brothers and the divided city of Messina. According to Schiller's explanation in the preface, the figure of the chorus establishes an opposition to the affective events of the plot. The chorus brings language to life, but *not* as a plot agent. Its task is to reflect on the plot, not to act in it. While language is brought to life, the chorus, at the same time, opposes itself to the action of the plot, as an instance of reflection. In this manner, the chorus produces a Ruhe in the plot, one to which Schiller gives an aesthetic qualification that distinguishes it from a police-like or disciplinary concept of Ruhe:

> Just as the chorus brings life to language, so does it bring calm [Ruhe] into action—but the beautiful and lofty calm [Ruhe] which must be the character of a noble work of art. For the spectator's feelings must retain their freedom even amid the most vehement passion; they must not be the victim of impressions, but rather they must come away serene and clear from the agitations sustained. What common judgment finds objectionable in the chorus, namely that it dispels the illusion and shatters the emotional power of the effects, is just what serves as its highest recommendation. For it is precisely this blind power of passions that the true artist avoids, it is precisely this illusion that he scorns to arouse.[65]

In bringing Ruhe into the dramatic action, the chorus interrupts the affective results of the action on the spectators, who are freed from the coercion of empathy. This same mechanism also holds in reverse form, albeit with slightly modified objectives, for those acting on the stage. It is only in following the chorus's activity as a Ruhe-producing element in the production that the acting figures emerge in their tragic ideality:

> The chorus, by holding the parts separate and by intervening between the passions with its calming [beruhigenden] observations, gives us back our freedom, which would otherwise be lost in the storm of emotional agitation. The tragic persons likewise have need of this respite, this calm [Ruhe], to collect themselves, for they are not real beings that merely obey the force of the moment and represent mere individuals, but ideal personages and representative of their class, who pronounce upon the profound in mankind.[66]

The chorus produces Ruhe and reflection not only *on* the stage, but also *for* the stage. In Schiller's conception, its balancing function brings to fruition both the imaginative freedom of the spectators as well as the ideality of the dramatic figures. With this, the chorus's classical function as a figuration of the audience is actualized in the terms of theories of autonomy. On the one hand, the chorus closes off the stage from the audience, "autonomizing" the dramatic arts. On the other hand, it immunizes the audience, in a sort of affective economy, against the potentially corrupting (which is to say, strictly sensual) effects of thes tage.

Precaution: Imaginations of Disorder

Ruhe, as the writings of Policey authors make clear, is a nonspecific preventative goal, always to be interpreted with respect to time and context. As such, it's hardly surprising that elements of the *precautionary principle* are in no way foreign to the older preventative regimes. Everywhere that a possible danger appears (in literally unmeasurable form), everywhere that preventative foresight consists primarily in the production of fantasies of disorder and *Unruhe*, the border between prevention and *precaution* begins to dissolve. The known danger is replaced by the incalculable, which appears, in turn, to justify all means available. It's just here that the criticism of theatre reform begins, that reform which, with the literization of the stage, also produced the condition for the possibility of its censorship.

I would like to give a final example of the double nature of prevention, which seems to be at stake here, Ludwig Tieck's (1773–1853) meta-theatrical closet play *Puss in Boots* (*Der gestiefelte Kater*, 1797), which takes enlightened literary theatre's self-policing as the object of its play-within-a-play structure.[67] Written at the advent of a modern police administration in Berlin, the play produces and amplifies disorder and Unruhe by using precisely those mechanisms that are meant to regulate and monitor them.

The drama, which appeared in 1797 in a collection of fairy-tales, belongs to a series of meta-theatrical fairy-tale dramas by Ludwig Tieck, which emerged between 1795 and 1804.[68] In fact, Tieck's play offers a *tour d'horizon* of the critical debates surrounding the theatre in the final third of the eighteenth century. References specific to his time appear in recurring snippets of praise for Iffland's naturalistic, detail-oriented style (Iffland is clearly depicted as the actor who plays the cat *Hinze*), parodies of Kotzebue's popular melodramas, and derision for the proto-censorship by theatre criticism and the behavior and self-conception of the parterre. The plot takes as its object a stage version of Perrault's fairy-tale for children, *Le Maistre Chat* (1695). The interior play goes by the same title as the piece that lies before the reader of the drama. The sporadic commentary of the (fictional) public present on the stage, critical of the fictional nature of the play, subjects the veridical illusions of the play—and, beyond that, the conditions of theatrical production and reception themselves—to repeated renegotiations. The drama was published by Tieck under a pseudonym, *Peter Leberecht*, or *Peter Live-right*, a moniker that signals piety, law-abiding behavior, and subordination. The drama reflects the supposed orderliness of the theatre in the mirror of a disorderly, continuously commenting, criticizing, rapping, clapping, whistling, hissing public. The actors—especially the playwright of this piece—react, for their part, to the public's commentary, accusations, and high-volume interventions and subject the latter's expectations to lengthy consideration. This results in the intradramatically motivated transgression of fictional and generic conventions. In a variety of ways, it brings to the fore the confrontation between order and uproar, rule and ruckus, expectation and disappointment, and faithfulness to a text versus extemporizing improvisation.

The place of action is the auditory: "The scene is in the parterre," runs the paratext of the prologue. The parterre public, introduced as a number of distinct characters designated by their trades (Fisher, Miller, Locksmith, etc.), argues volubly over questions of taste, in a satirical representation of the "tone-setters" of the theatre, a narrow stratum of bourgeois theatre connoisseurs, including publicists for the theatre, who are concerned with guiding the taste of the "mob." Tieck ridicules the trendsetters in the parterre who wish to mediate between a group composed mostly of intellectuals and the less or entirely uneducated masses that constitute the rest of the audience. (Fittingly, Tieck bestows the name *Leutner* upon the spokesperson that alludes to *läutern* = to purify, but also to *läuten* = to ring the bell.) Heinrich Schütze reports in his *Hamburg Theatre History* (*Hamburgische Theater-Geschichte*, 1794) that these "tone-setters" (*Tonangeber*) were frequently granted a seat in the first row of the parterre and thus form a parterre within the parterre:

> These self-appointed commentators applauded new, deserving pieces, single, well-acted scenes, and pleasingly spoken passages in the same; they demanded peace, orderliness and silence [*Ruhe, Ordnung und Stille*] whenever undeserved praise or derisive reproach was heard, or any other inappropriate exclamation, whether from the boxes or from the balcony. We do not recall that they abused this self-appointed right in a way that was deleterious to the rest of the public. No one seemed to resent it when, within this circle, [...] a voice was raised, a piece was praised aloud, etc.[69]

Tieck lends their designation as "tone-setters" a literal (and, with that, an inverted) meaning:

> *Miller*: I really want to start pounding.
> *Ringer*: Besides, it's a bit cold. I'll begin.

He pounds his cane on the floor, the others accompany him.
Mower: on the other side. What is the reason for the pounding?
Ringer: To save good taste.
Mower: Well, I certainly don't want to be left out of that. *He begins pounding.*

The inert theatre police of the parterre, as the locus of order and taste, appear here as an instance of groundless opinion and contingency.

Satirical engagement with the preventative regime of Enlightenment theatre reform, however, does not remain solely on the level of the policing of taste. The author functions as a figure of transgression who engages the drama throughout, and who repeatedly breaks through the fictional level of the play within the play. Tieck/Leberecht allows his alter ego, who appears as the "poet" within the interior drama (which shares a name with Tieck's text) to come before the tribunal on taste, represented by the space of the audience, many times. He appears in order to deliver himself over to the effect of the piece's poetics of "nonsense."[70] If at first he succeeds in courting the goodwill of the audience and in calming it down, then, finally, in a paradoxical turn, he becomes the victim of the effect of the drama he has composed. The piece fails and anarchy reigns, and not only in the auditorium. The poet becomes, before everyone's eyes, entirely disoriented by the interplay of the various levels of his own piece. In the end, the semantic field of taste returns once more to the completely undecorated stage and the poet is pelted with rotten fruit and crumpled-up paper (*Epilogue*) and expelled from the theatre. With this, a turn comes to completion that was already foreseen in the *anteludum* by the "opinion-setters," who, as self-proclaimed theatre connoisseurs, had prophesied a descent into disorder and anarchy.

Tieck's meta-theatrical closet drama addresses the regime of Ruhe on different levels. On the diegetic level, it reverses the production process of literary theatre: "from page to stage" turns into "from stage to play." He thus showcases the doctrines of Enlightenment theatre reformers (some 60 years after the symbolical onstage elimination of Harlequin) by letting them go astray. The text's conclusion contains neither the "improvement" of the audience nor the inhibition of uproar on the basis of prescripted behavior. The attempt to preventatively influence sensibility and morality fails. In the course of this failure, however, the author points to the medial presuppositions and generic conditions of his own written text. The scripted withdrawal from the stage (a closet play) performs an abstraction in the most literal sense.

The audience is made visible (audible) under the regime of Ruhe. It is in this regard that the play performs the archive of literary theatre, or, rather, its *commandment*.

Int he Archive(*commencement*)

The preventative imperative (the commandment) of police theatre censorship develops its rationales, its techniques, and its methods of subjectivization from the population and the territorialization policies of seventeenth- and eighteenth-century sovereigns. The date of these policies becoming an archive can be precisely given (1918 and 1926). The transition from a police registry to a document in the custody of the Berlin and Vienna *Landesarchive* creates a strange sort of interstitial space, located between the police's preventative praxis (the avoidance of future evil) and the historical archive (the point of departure for future theatre historiography). When, in 1928, the theatre censorship texts of the Vienna police were transferred to the *Landesarchiv* of Lower Austria, the police reserved the right to have "these documents freely at their disposal." They also required a guarantee that the archived texts would be "available at all times for official use."[71] This border region of distinct rationales has, in a certain sense, never ceased to exist: the police registers and indexes serve today as inventories, and the archive catalogues take their descriptive criteria, as before, from police guidelines. Police praxis for concession, censorship, and monitoring continues to determine, in a fundamental sense, what is both visible and accessible to us as theatre. The continually surprising combination of pedanticism, effort, and painstaking care with which the police's administrative observation of the theatre was carried out in the nineteenth century, under the imperatives of Ruhe, security and order, however, allows something else to become visible in the Ruhe of the archive: the inexhaustible fantasies of Unruhe, of insecurity and disorder that lie at the origin of the archive's order. Documentation of these fantasies is nowhere to be found in the archives; they are hidden behind stereotypical turns of phrase, behind administrative and censorial routines, as well as through the sheer material existence of enormous collections of files. The space of these fantasies distinguishes itself through its particular temporality: the—now past—present futures of preventative thought, which never cease to load the archive with their phantasms. It is probably this space and this time that matter most when entering the literary archive of nineteenth-century theatre.

Notes

Translated by Matthew J. Fraser (Chicago).

1. On the proto-history of the masses in *Policey*-sciences and cameralistics, see Michael Gamper, *Masse lesen, Masse schreiben. Eine Diskurs- und Imaginationsgeschichte der Menschenmenge 1765–1930* (München: Fink, 2007), 52–63. I would like to thank Rosemarie Bank (Chicago), Michal Kobialka (Minneapolis), and Christopher Wild (Chicago) for conversations and invaluable suggestions at different points of the writing process. The research carried out for this essay was made possible by a Feodor Lynen Fellowship of the Alexander von Humboldt Foundation at the University of Chicago.
2. See Peter Nitschke, ed., *Die deutsche Polizei und ihre Geschichte. Beiträge zu einem distanzierten Verhältnis* (Hilden: Verlag Deutsche Polizeiliteratur, 1996). On the premodern concept of Policey, compare Andrea Iseli, *Gute Policey. Öffentliche Ordnung in der Frühen Neuzeit* (Stuttgart: UTB, 2009) with furtherr eferences.
3. The police definition in earlier German social and administrative theory mostly targeted the question of how the sovereign could achieve *good* order and what subject matter is inherent in the term "Policey." See Hans Maier, *Die ältere deutsche Staats- und Verwaltungslehre*, 2nd ed. (Frankfurt am Main: dtv,1980).
4. Ibid.,25.
5. For the introduction and execution of police censorship in Vienna, see Barbara Tumfart, *Wallishausers Wiener Theater-Repertoir und die österreichische Zensur* (PhD diss., University of Vienna, 2003). For Berlin, see Gary D. Stark, *Banned in Berlin. Literary Censorship in Imperial Germany 1871–1918* (New York: Berghahn, 2009). For a comparative perspective on European theatre censorship, see *The Frightful Stage. Political Censorship of the Theater of Nineteenth Century Europe*, ed. Robert Justin Goldstein (New York: Berghahn, 2009).
6. On Berlin, see Dagmar Walach, "Das doppelte Drama oder die Polizei als Lektor. Über die Entstehung der preußischen Theaterzensurbibliothek," *Die besondere Bibliothek oder: Die Faszination von Büchersammlungen*, ed. Antonius Jammers (Munich: Saur, 2002), 259–74. On Vienna, see Erich Forstreiter, "Die Abteilung 'Theater' des Archivs für Niederösterreich," *Das Bundesland Niederösterreich. Seine verfassungsrechtliche, wirtschaftliche und soziale Entwicklung im ersten Jahrzehnt des Bestandes. 1920–1930*, ed. Niederösterreichische Landesregierung (Wien: Landesregierung, 1930), 460–66.
7. Jacques Derrida, "Archive Fever: A Freudian Impression," *Diacritics* 2 (1995): 9; emphasis in the original.
8. Ibid.,10.
9. Compare for the Habsburg Monarchy Tumfart, *Theater-Repertoir*. For Imperial Germany, see Nic Leonhardt, "Im Bann der 'Bühnengefahren'.

Preußische Theaterverordnungen zwischen Prävention und Subversion," *Berlin in Geschichte und Gegenwart* 25 (2006): 31–49.

10. Compare Hilde Haider-Pregler, *Des sittlichen Bürgers Abendschule. Bildungsanspruch und Bildungsauftrag des Berufstheaters im 18. Jahrhundert* (Vienna: Jugend und Volk, 1980).
11. Compare Michael Stolleis, *Geschichte des öffentlichen Rechts in Deutschland. 1. Reichspublizistik und Policeywissenschaft. 1600–1800* (München: Beck, 1988).
12. Christian Wolff, *Vernünfftige Gedancken von dem Gesellschaftlichen Leben der Menschen und insonderheit dem gemeinen Wesen zu Beförderung der Glückseeligkeit des menschlichen Geschlechtes den Liebhabern der Wahrheit mitgetheilet* (Halle: Renger, 1721). Compare Haider-Pregler, *Abendschule*, 40.
13. See Wolfgang Martens, "Obrigkeitliche Sicht. Das Bühnenwesen in den Lehrbüchern der Policey und Cameralistik im 18. Jahrhundert," *Internationales Archiv für Sozialgeschichte der deutschen Literatur* 6 (1981): 19–51. On theatre censorship as a constitutive part of theatre reform, see Peter Höyng, "Die Geburt der Theaterzensur aus dem Geiste bürgerlicher Moral. Unwillkommene Thesen zur Theaterzensur im 18. Jahrhundert?," *Zensur im Jahrhundert der Aufklärung. Geschichte—Theorie—Praxis*, ed. Wilhelm Haefs and York-Gothart Mixa (Göttingen: Wallstein, 2007), 99–119.
14. Compare Haider-Pregler, *Abendschule*, 137–78.
15. Peter Heßelmann, "Der Ruf nach der 'Policey' im Tempel der Kunst. Das Theaterpublikum des 18. Jahrhunderts zwischen Andacht und Vergnügen," *"Das Theater glich einem Irrenhause." Das Publikum im Theater des 18. und 19. Jahrhunderts*, ed. Herrmann Korte and Hans-Joachim Jakob (Heidelberg: Winter, 2012), 77–94.
16. Perhaps the closest equivalent is the Latin concept of *tranquillitas*. Its English translation as tranquility, however, only grasps one dimension of the term—namely, that of inner balance and stability or the *Ruhe* of the soul. In the first century BC tranquillitas developed within the framework of Stoicism and Epicureanism into a philosophical concept for peace of mind or "passivity" of mind. In Cicero, tranquillitas acquires in connection with security and peace additional meaning as an expression of the secured peace of the state (compare Cicero, *de lege agrarian* 1.24; *de officiis* 1.20.69; *de oratore* 1.1.2). As John Hamilton has pointed out, tranquillitas and *securitas* (in the sense of care taking rather than security) are used almost synonymously in Cicero. Compare John T. Hamilton, *Security: Poltics, Humanity, and the Philology of Care* (Princeton: Princeton University Press, 2013). As a concept that refers to relationships, Ruhe can refer to the (domestic) political stability of the body politic, whereby the two elements of Ruhe—the pastoral (to ensure Ruhe) and the repressive (to produce Ruhe)—go hand in hand. As a result of the German term's nuances, I will continue to refer to the preventative imperative of Ruhe (untranslated) in what follows.
17. Peter Heßelmann, *Gereinigtes Theater? Dramaturgie und Schaubühne im Spiegel deutschsprachiger Theaterperiodia des 18. Jahrhunderts, 1750–1800* (Frankfurt am Main: Klostermann, 2002), 1.
18. Compare Georg-Michael Schulz, "Der Krieg gegen das Publikum. Die Rolle des Publikums in den Konzepten der Theatermacher des 18. Jahrhunderts," *Theater*

im Kulturwandel des 18. Jahrhunderts. Inszenierung und Wahrnehmung von Körper—Musik—Sprache, ed. Erika Fischer-Lichte (Göttingen: Wallstein, 1999),483–502.
19. See Alf Lüdtke, *"Gemeinwohl," Polizei und "Festungspraxis."* Staatliche Gewaltsamkeit und innere Verwaltung in Preußen 1815–1850 (Göttingen: Vandenhoek, 1982). For the history of policing, compare also Klaus Mladek, ed., *Police Forces: A Cultural History of an Institution* (New York: Palgrave, 2007).
20. Hans Hattenhauer and Günther Bernert, eds., *Allgemeines Landrecht für die Preußischen Staaten von 1794* (Neuwied: Luchterhand 1996), Part II, Section 17, §10. Translated in Alec Stone Sweet and Jud Mathews, "Proportionality Balancing and Global Constitutionalism" (2008), *Faculty Scholarship Series*, paper 14, http://digitalcommons.law.yale.edu/fss_papers/14. In Austria, a "Circular Explaining the Introduction of the New Police State in Vienna" defined the police in advance of the Prussian Civil Code as follows: "The main object of the police, and that which includes all its branches, is: 'Constant vigilance, so that in the various neighborhoods of Vienna laws and rules are observed precisely, peace and quiet, order, security, and public decency is maintained, and, as far as possible, anything that could be detrimental to the general as well as to the private good is prevented.'" Wolfram Siemann, "*Deutschlands Ruhe, Sicherheit und Ordnung.*" *Die Anfänge der politischen Polizei 1806–1866* (Tübingen: De Gruyter, 1985), 9. From this basic formulation of police justice, *Ruhe und Ordnung* became a political watchword as early as the beginning of the nineteenth century. It served as an antirevolutionary catchphrase for reactionaries unified in the promise of a return to the status quo, a peaceful and secure past. See Wolfgang Frühwald, *"Ruhe und Ordnung"—Literatursprache—Sprache der politischen Werbung. Texte, Materialien, Kommentar* (Munich, Vienna: 1976), 124.
21. Compare Achim Landwehr, "'Gute Policey'. Zur Permanenz der Ausnahme," *Staats-Gewalt. Ausnahmezustand und Sicherheitsregimes. Historische Perspektiven*, ed. Alf Lüdtke and Michael Wildt (Göttingen: Wallstein, 2008), 39–64.
22. To my knowledge, there are to date no studies that engage in greater detail with the conceptions of Ruhe and the body politic. For the juridical vagueness of the concept of Ruhe, compare Andreas Hauser, *Ruhe, Ordnung, Sicherheit: Eine Studie zu den Aufgaben der Polizei in Österreich* (Vienna and New York: Springer, 2000).
23. I refer here and in what follows to the main eighteenth-century works of political and economic science as discussed in Stolleis, *Reichspublizistik und Policeywissenschaft*.
24. Michel Foucault, *Geschichte der Gouvernementalität I. Sicherheit, Territorium, Bevölkerung. Vorlesung am Collège de France 1977–1978*, ed. Michel Sennelart, trans. Claudia Brede-Konersmann and Jürgen Schröder (Frankfurt am Main: Suhrkamp, 2004), lecture 12 (29.3.1978) and lecture 13 (5.4.1978).
25. "It is, so to speak, the tool which wielded by statesmanship in order to render its agenda, measures, and laws efficacious." Johann Heinrich Gottlob von

Justi, *Grundsätze der Policey-Wissenschaft. In einem vernünftigen, auf den Endzweck der Policey gegründeten, Zusammenhange und zum Gebrauch academischer Vorlesungen abgefasset*, 2nd ed. (Göttingen: Vandenhoeck, 1759), 270. In his main work, *Grundfeste zu der Macht und Glückseligkeit der Staaten* (1760/61), these positions remain only in attenuated form.
26. See Ludwig Heinrich Jakob, *Grundsätze der Policeygesetzgebung und der Policeyanstalten*, vol. I (Halle and Leipzig: Ruffsche Verlagshandlung, 1809), 263. Jakob shows that "Ruhe" is to be understood as that "Ruhe" which corresponds to the laws.
27. Justi, *Grundsätze*, 271.
28. Johann Peter Willebrand, *Innbegriff der Policey nebst Betrachtungen über das Wachsthum der Städte. Aus dem Französischen übersetzt und mit einigen Anmerkungen versehen* (Leipzig and Zittau: A.J. Spiekermann, 1767), 241, 240.
29. "With the descent of darkness, a troop of police deploys, occupies the various watch-towers spread throughout the city and fans out into all the streets. In addition to the usual weapons, every man is outfitted with a rattle, with which he rattles every hour and with which he can make a noise which is capable of awakening all residents in the case of fire or other emergency." Jakob Friedrich von Bielfeld, *Lehrbegriff der Staatskunst*, part I, 2nd ed., trans. from the French (Breßlau and Berlin: Korn, 1768), 184.
30. Paul Jakob Marperger, *Beschreibung der Messen und Jahrmärckte* (Leipzig: J.F. Gleditsch, 1710), 203.
31. Bielfeld, *Lehrbegriff*, 202.
32. For the documentation and evaluation of eighteenth-century German-language theatre journals, see Wolfgang S. Bender, Siegfried Bushuven, and Michael Huesmann, eds., *Theaterperiodika des 18. Jahrhunderts. Bibliographie und inhaltliche Erschließung deutschsprachiger Theaterzeitschriften, Theaterkalender und Theatertaschenbücher*, 8 vols. (Munich: Saur, 1994–2005).
33. See Heßelmann, *Theaterperiodika*; Hermann Korte and Hans-Joachim Jakob, eds., *"Das Theater glich einem Irrenhause." Das Publikum im Theater des 18. und 19. Jahrhunderts* (Heidelberg: Winter, 2012).
34. Heinrich August Ottokar Reichardt, "Kann den Schauspielern oder besser dem Direkteur einer Schauspielgesellschaft etwas zur Last gelegt werden, wenn ein Stück, das einem Theil der Zuschauer nicht gefällt, mehr als einmal aufgeführt wird?," *Theater Kalender* (1783): 108. The concept of law is to be understood here in the sense of an ordinance or a decree.
35. Heinrich August Ottokar Reichardt, "Versuch über das Parterre," *Theater Kalender*(1775):54.
36. Heßelmann, *Theaterperiodika*, 77.
37. Anonymous [August von Kotzebue?], "Vom Geräusch im Theater," *Die Biene* (1810):312.
38. Ulrich Bröckling, "Dispositive der Vorbeugung: Gefahrenabwehr, Resilienz, Precaution," *Sicherheitskultur. Soziale und politische Praktiken der Gefahrenabwehr*, ed. Christopher Daase, Philipp Offermann, and Valentin Rauer (Frankfurt am Main and New York: Campus, 2012), 93–96. Bröckling has conducted extensive research on theories and practices of prevention. With

a view to present discourses regarding health, ecology, economy, and terrorism, he conceives of prevention as "the dominant rationale under which contemporary societies organize and negotiate their relationship to the future" (93).
39. Ibid.,94.
40. Ibid.,95.
41. Heßelmann, *Theaterperiodika*.
42. Theatre historians have repeatedly pointed out that the epistemological presupposition from which the history of the reformed literary theatre has been written is that of its successful transformation of stage plays into literature. Nonliterary forms of theatre like the *commedia dell'arte* were vilified and censored by the reformers and subsequently left aside and silenced by historiographers.
43. Compare here and in what follows Martens, "Obrigkeitliche Sicht."
44. On von Justi's biography, see Andre Wakefield, *The Disordered Police State: German Cameralism as Science and Practice* (Chicago: Chicago University Press,2009).
45. Johann Heinrich Gottlob von Justi, *Die Grundfeste zu der Macht und Glückseligkeit der Staaten; oder ausführliche Vorstellung der gesamten Policey-Wissenschaft*, vol. II (Königsberg: Hartung, 1761), 376.
46. Bielfeld, *Lehrbegriff*, 202.
47. Willebrand, *Innbegriff*, 226.
48. See Martens, "Obrigkeitliche Sicht," 46.
49. On Sonnenfels, see Simon Karstens, *Lehrer—Schriftsteller—Staatsreformer. Die Karriere des Joseph von Sonnenfels (1733–1817)* (Wien: Böhlau, 2011).
50. Joseph von Sonnenfels, *Grundsätze der Policey, Handlung und Finanzwissenschaft. Erster Theil*, 3rd ed. (Wien and Kurzbek, 1770), 109. Special attention is accorded to the censorship of puppet shows, as these consisted entirely in a conglomeration of dirty jokes, which were perceived to have a disastrous effect on children, whose dispositions were thought to allow much more direct comprehension than those of adults.
51. It is important however to bear in mind that throughout the second half of the eighteenth century the term "censoring" was used almost synonymously for "critiquing." A famous theatre journal was called *The Dramatic Censor (Der Dramatische Zensor)*. Compare Peter Höyng, "Vier Gründe, warum Theaterzensur im 18. Jahrhundert von der Forschung vernachlässigt wird," *Theater im Kulturwandel des 18. Jahrhunderts. Inszenierung und Wahrnehmung von Körper—Musik—Sprache*, ed. Erika Fischer-Lichte (Göttingen: Wallstein, 1999), 433–47.
52. Carl Franz Hägelin quoted from Carl Glossy, "Zur Geschichte der Wiener Theaterzensur," *Jahrbuch der Grillparzer-Gesellschaft* 7 (1897): 299. For criticism of Glossy's selective use of editions and for supplements of the omitted passages, see Lisa De Alwis, *Censorship and Magical Opera in Early Nineteenth-Century Vienna* (PhD diss., University of Southern California, 2012),7–73.
53. Sulzer, for example, grounds this through reference to Aristotle in his entry on "The Theatre" [Schauspiel] in the *General Theory of the Fine Arts (Allgemeine Theorie der schönen Künste)*. The mourning play is accorded the "highest

utility" because it, on the one hand, "enflames the heart with love for virtue" and, on the other, displays "horrifying examples [...] of vice." Johann Georg Sulzer, *Allgemeine Theorie der Schönen Künste in einzeln, alphabetischer Ordnung der Kunstwörter auf einander folgenden, Artikeln abgehandelt* (Leipzig: Weidmann und Reich, 1771), vol. 2, 255.

54. On immunization in Goethe and Schiller, see Cornelia Zumbusch's comprehensive work *Die Immunität der Klassik* (Berlin: Suhrkamp, 2011). Zumbusch follows the observation that during their time in Weimar, Goethe and Schiller worked on figures of purity, protection, and insensitivity, all of which (in a structural analogy to *immunia ab contagio*) aim at freedom from something.

55. On the vulgarization of this topos, see Kurt Wölfel, "Moralische Anstalt: Zur Dramaturgie von Gottsched bis Lessing," *Deutsche Dramentheorien*, ed. Reinhold Grimm (Frankfurt am Main: Athenäum, 1971), vol. 1, 45–122.

56. Schiller no longer complains about the various failings of theatrical enterprises (as he had two years earlier, in his pamphlet, heavily influenced by Rousseau, *On the Contemporary German Theatre (Über das gegenwärtige teutsche Theater*, 1782). He is, at this time, already the in-house author for the Mannheim National Theatre and signs the text as "Ducal Weimar counselor." Compare Peter André Alt, Schiller: *Leben, Werk, Zeit. Eine Biographie* (München: Beck, 2000), vol. 1, 383.

57. See Carsten Zelle, "Was kann eine gute stehende Schaubühne eigentlich wirken? (1785)," *Schiller-Handbuch. Leben—Werk—Wirkung*, ed. Matthias Luserke-Jaqui (Stuttgart, Weimar: Metzler, 2005), 343–57.

58. Friedrich Schiller, "The Stage Considered as a Moral Institution," *Friedrich Schiller. An Anthology for our Time*, ed. Frederick Ungar (New York, New York: Frederick Ungar Publishing Co., 1962), 263.

59. Ibid.,263.

60. Friedrich Schiller, "Über den Gebrauch des Chors in der Tragödie," *Friedrich Schiller Werke und Briefe in zwölf Bänden.* Vol. 5: *Dramen IV*, ed. Matthias Luserke (Frankfurt am Main: Deutscher Klassiker Verlag, 1996), 281–91. For background, see Georg-Michael Schulz, "Die Braut von Messina oder die feindlichen Brüder. Ein Trauerspiel mit Chören (1803)," *Schiller-Handbuch. Leben—Werk—Wirkung*, ed. Matthias Luserke-Jaqui (Stuttgart, Weimar: Metzler, 2005), 195–214.

61. Friedrich Schiller, *The Bride of Messina. William Tell. Demetrius*, trans. Charles E. Passage (New York: Frederick Ungar, 1962), 4.

62. On the significance of the chorus in the context of antitheatrical debates, see also Christopher J. Wild, *Theater der Keuschheit—Keuschheit des Theaters. Zu einer Geschichte der (Anti-)Theatralität von Gryphius bis Kleist* (Freiburg: Rombach, 2003), 407–19.

63. The premier took place in Weimar on March 19, 1803. The plot, based on no actual event, is situated in the Italian city of Messina at an unspecified time period (likely the eleventh or twelfth century). Following the death of the prince of Messina, combat over succession breaks out between the prince's two feuding sons, Manuel and Cesar. Their mother, the widowed princess Isabella, is able to defuse the conflict through reference to a sister previously unknown to the two brothers. She has been brought up in a cloister, unaware of her

familial line. Following this, both brothers announce to their mother their impending marriages, unaware of the fact that both have, independent of one another, fallen in love with the same woman, their sister. During a coincidental encounter among the three siblings, Cesar stabs his brother to death in a fit of jealousy. Afterward, the familial relationships are progressively revealed. In the end, sister, mother, and chorus are unable to prevent Manuel from killing himself. On the premier, see Bruno Th. Satori-Neumann, *Die weimarische Uraufführung der "Braut von Messina"* (Berlin: Oesterheld 1929).
64. Quoted in Schulz, "Messina," 195.
65. Schiller, *Messina*, 10.
66. Ibid.,11.
67. Ludwig Tieck, "Der gestiefelte Kater. Kindermährchen in drei Akten, mit Zwischenspielen, einem Prologe und Epiloge," *Werke in einem Band*, ed. Peter C. Plett (Hamburg: Hoffmann und Campe, 1967), 243–304.
68. I refer here above all to *Hanswurst als Emigrant. Puppenspiel in drei Acten* (1795), *Ein Prolog* (1797), *Ritter Blaubart* (1797), *Prinz Zerbino oder die Reise nach dem guten Geschmack* (1796, 1797), *Die verkehrte Welt. Ein historisches Schauspiel in fünf Aufzügen* (1798), *Anti-Faust oder die Geschichte eines dummen Teufels* (1800), *Der Autor. Ein Fastnachts-Schwank* (1800). For an overview of Tieck's dramatic work, see Stefan Scherer, "Dramen und dramatische Bearbeitungen," in *Ludwig Tieck. Leben—Werk—Wirkung*, ed. Claudia Stockinger and Stefan Scherer (Berlin: De Gruyter, 2011), 458–75 (with further references).
69. QuotedinHe ßelmann, *Theaterperiodika*, 77.
70. For more on Tieck's poetics of nonsense, compare Winfried Menninghaus, *Lob des Unsinns. Über Kant, Tieck und Blaubart* (Frankfurt am Main: Suhrkamp, 1995),92–190.
71. Letter by the Federal Police Headquarters in Vienna on July 25, 1928. Niederösterreichisches Landesarchiv, Präsidialakten, XIV/197, a1.

Bibliography

Alt, Peter André. *Schiller: Leben, Werk, Zeit. Eine Biographie*. Vol. I. Munich: Beck, 2000.

Anonymous [August von Kotzebue?]. "Vom Geräusch im Theater." *Die Biene* (1810), 307–12.

Bender, Wolfgang S., Siegfried Bushuven, and Michael Huesmann, eds. *Theaterperiodika des 18. Jahrhunderts. Bibliographie und inhaltliche Erschließung deutschsprachiger Theaterzeitschriften, Theaterkalender und Theatertaschenbücher*. 8 Vol. Munich: Saur, 1994–2005.

Bielfeld, Jakob Friedrich von. *Lehrbegriff der Staatskunst*. Part I. 2nd ed. Translated from the French. Breßlau and Berlin: Korn, 1768.

Bröckling, Ulrich. "Dispositive der Vorbeugung: Gefahrenabwehr, Resilienz, Precaution." In *Sicherheitskultur. Soziale und politische Praktiken der Gefahrenabwehr*. Edited by Christopher Daase, Philipp Offermann, and Valentin Rauer. Frankfurt am Main and New York: Campus, 2012, 93–96.

De Alwis, Lisa. "Censorship and Magical Opera in Early Nineteenth-Century Vienna." PhD diss., University of Southern California, 2012.
Derrida, Jacques. "Archive Fever: A Freudian Impression." *Diacritics* 2 (1995), 9–63.
Forstreiter, Erich. "Die Abteilung 'Theater' des Archivs für Niederösterreich." In *Das Bundesland Niederösterreich. Seine verfassungsrechtliche, wirtschaftliche und soziale Entwicklung im ersten Jahrzehnt des Bestandes. 1920–1930*. Edited by Niederösterreichische Landesregierung. Vienna: Landesregierung, 1930, 460–66.
Foucault, Michel. *Geschichte der Gouvernementalität I. Sicherheit, Territorium, Bevölkerung. Vorlesung am Collège de France 1977–1978*. Edited by Michel Sennelart, translated by Claudia Brede-Konersmann and Jürgen Schröder. Frankfurt am Main: Suhrkamp, 2004.
Frühwald, Wolfgang. *"Ruhe und Ordnung"—Literatursprache—Sprache der politischen Werbung. Texte, Materialien, Kommentar*. Munich and Vienna: Hanser, 1976.
Gamper, Michael. *Masse lesen, Masse schreiben. Eine Diskurs- und Imaginationsgeschichte der Menschenmenge 1765–1930*. Munich: Fink, 2007.
Glossy, Carl. "Zur Geschichte der Wiener Theaterzensur." *Jahrbuch der Grillparzer-Gesellschaft* 7 (1897), 238–340.
Goldstein, Robert Justin, ed. *The Frightful Stage. Political Censorship of the Theater of Nineteenth Century Europe*. New York: Berghahn, 2009.
Haider-Pregler, Hilde. *Des sittlichen Bürgers Abendschule. Bildungsanspruch und Bildungsauftrag des Berufstheaters im 18. Jahrhundert*. Vienna: Jugend & Volk, 1980.
Hamilton, John T. *Security: Poltics, Humanity, and the Philology of Care*. Princeton: Princeton University Press, 2013.
Hattenhauer, Hans, and Günther Bernert, eds. *Allgemeines Landrecht für die Preußischen Staaten von 1794*. Neuwied: Luchterhand, 1996.
Hauser, Andreas. *Ruhe, Ordnung, Sicherheit: Eine Studie zu den Aufgaben der Polizeiin Österreich*. Vienna and New York: Springer, 2000.
Heßelmann, Peter. "Der Ruf nach der 'Policey' im Tempel der Kunst. Das Theaterpublikum des 18. Jahrhunderts zwischen Andacht und Vergnügen." In *"Das Theater glich einem Irrenhause." Das Publikum im Theater des 18. und 19. Jahrhunderts*. Edited by Herrmann Korte and Hans-Joachim Jakob. Heidelberg: Winter, 2012, 77–94.
———. *Gereinigtes Theater? Dramaturgie und Schaubühne im Spiegel deutschsprachiger Theaterperiodia des 18. Jahrhunderts, 1750–1800*. Frankfurt am Main: Klostermann, 2002.
Höyng, Peter. "Die Geburt der Theaterzensur aus dem Geiste bürgerlicher Moral. Unwillkommene Thesen zur Theaterzensur im 18. Jahrhundert?" In *Zensur im Jahrhundert der Aufklärung. Geschichte—Theorie—Praxis*. Edited by Wilhelm Haefs and York-Gothart Mixa. Göttingen: Wallstein, 2007, 99–119.
———. "Vier Gründe, warum Theaterzensur im 18. Jahrhundert von der Forschung vernachlässigt wird." In *Theater im Kulturwandel des 18. Jahrhunderts. Inszenierung und Wahrnehmung von Körper—Musik—Sprache*. Edited by Erika Fischer-Lichte. Göttingen: Wallstein, 1999, 433–47.

Iseli, Andrea. *Gute Policey. Öffentliche Ordnung in der Frühen Neuzeit*. Stuttgart: UTB, 2009.
Jakob, Heinrich. *Grundsätze der Policeygesetzgebung und der Policeyanstalten*. Vol. I. Halle and Leipzig: Ruffsche Verlagshandlung, 1809.
Justi, Johann Heinrich Gottlob von. *Die Grundfeste zu der Macht und Glückseligkeit der Staaten; oder ausführliche Vorstellung der gesamten Policey-Wissenschaft*. Vol. II. Königsberg: Hartung, 1761.
———. *Grundsätze der Policey-Wissenschaft. In einem vernünftigen, auf den Endzweck der Policey gegründeten, Zusammenhange und zum Gebrauch academischer Vorlesungen abgefasset*, 2nd ed. Göttingen: Vandenhoeck, 1759.
Karstens, Simon. *Lehrer—Schriftsteller—Staatsreformer. Die Karriere des Joseph von Sonnenfels (1733–1817)*. Wien: Böhlau, 2011.
Korte, Hermann, and Hans-Joachim Jakob, eds. *"Das Theater glich einem Irrenhause." Das Publikum im Theater des 18. und 19. Jahrhunderts*. Heidelberg: Winter, 2012.
Landwehr, Achim. "'Gute Policey.' Zur Permanenz der Ausnahme." In *Staats-Gewalt. Ausnahmezustand und Sicherheitsregimes. Historische Perspektiven*. Edited by Alf Lüdtke and Michael Wildt. Göttingen: Wallstein, 2008, 39–64.
Leonhardt, Nic. "Im Bann der 'Bühnengefahren.' Preußische Theaterverordnungen zwischen Prävention und Subversion." *Berlin in Geschichte und Gegenwart* 25 (2006), 31–49.
Lüdtke, Alf. "Gemeinwohl,' Polizei und 'Festungspraxis.' *Staatliche Gewaltsamkeit und innere Verwaltung in Preußen 1815–1850*. Göttingen: Vandenhoek, 1982.
Maier, Hans. *Die ältere deutsche Staats- und Verwaltungslehre*, 2nd ed. Frankfurt am Main: dtv, 1980.
Marperger, Paul Jakob. *Beschreibung der Messen und Jahrmärckte*. Leipzig: J.F. Gleditsch, 1710.
Martens, Wolfgang. "Obrigkeitliche Sicht. Das Bühnenwesen in den Lehrbüchern der Policey und Cameralistik im 18. Jahrhundert." *Internationales Archiv für Sozialgeschichte der deutschen Literatur* 6 (1981), 19–51.
Menninghaus, Winfried. *Lob des Unsinns. Über Kant, Tieck und Blaubart*. Frankfurt am Main: Suhrkamp, 1995.
Mladek, Klaus, ed. *Police Forces: A Cultural History of an Institution*. New York: Palgrave, 2007.
Nitschke, Peter, ed. *Die deutsche Polizei und ihre Geschichte. Beiträge zu einem distanzierten Verhältnis*. Hilden: Verlag Deutsche Polizeiliteratur, 1996.
Reichardt, Heinrich and August Ottokar. "Kann den Schauspielern oder besser dem Direkteur einer Schauspielgesellschaft etwas zur Last gelegt werden, wenn ein Stück, das einem Theil der Zuschauer nicht gefällt, mehr als einmal aufgeführt wird?" *Theater Kalender* (1783), 102–11.
———. "Versuch über das Parterre." *Theater Kalender* (1775), 47–63.
Satori-Neumann, Bruno Th. *Die weimarische Uraufführung der "Braut von Messina."* Berlin: Oesterheld, 1929.
Scherer, Stefan. "Dramen und dramatische Bearbeitungen." In *Ludwig Tieck. Leben—Werk—Wirkung*. Edited by Claudia Stockinger and Stefan Scherer. Berlin: De Gruyter, 2011, 458–75.

Schiller, Friedrich. *The Bride of Messina. William Tell. Demetrius.* Translated by Charles E. Passage. New York: Frederick Ungar, 1962.

———. "The Stage Considered as a Moral Institution." In *Friedrich Schiller. An Anthology for Our Time.* Edited by Frederick Ungar. New York: Frederick Ungar, 1962, 262–83.

———. "Über den Gebrauch des Chors in der Tragödie." In *Friedrich Schiller Werke und Briefe in zwölf Bänden.* Vol. 5. *Dramen IV.* Edited by Matthias Luserke. Frankfurt am Main: Deutscher Klassiker Verlag, 1996, 281–29.

Schulz, Georg-Michael. "Der Krieg gegen das Publikum. Die Rolle des Publikums in den Konzepten der Theatermacher des 18. Jahrhunderts." In *Theater im Kulturwandel des 18. Jahrhunderts. Inszenierung und Wahrnehmung von Körper—Musik—Sprache.* Edited by Erika Fischer-Lichte. Göttingen: Wallstein, 1999, 483–502.

———. "Die Braut von Messina oder die feindlichen Brüder. Ein Trauerspiel mit Chören (1803)." In *Schiller-Handbuch. Leben—Werk—Wirkung.* Edited by Matthias Luserke-Jaqui. Stuttgart and Weimar: Metzler, 2005, 195–214.

Siemann, Wolfram. *"Deutschlands Ruhe, Sicherheit und Ordnung." Die Anfänge der politischen Polizei 1806–1866.* Tübingen: De Gruyter, 1985.

Sonnenfels, Joseph von. *Grundsätze der Policey, Handlung und Finanzwissenschaft. Erster Theil,* 3rd ed. Wien: Kurzbek, 1770.

Stark, Gary D. *Banned in Berlin. Literary Censorship in Imperial Germany 1871–1918.* New York: Berghahn, 2009.

Stolleis, Michael. *Geschichte des öffentlichen Rechts in Deutschland. 1. Reichspublizistik und Policeywissenschaft. 1600—1800.* München: Beck, 1988.

Stone Sweet, Alec, and Jud Mathews. "Proportionality Balancing and Global Constitutionalism" (2008). *Faculty Scholarship Series.* Paper 14. http://digitalcommons.law.yale.edu/fss_papers/14.

Sulzer, Johann Georg. *Allgemeine Theorie der Schönen Künste in einzelnen, alphabetischer Ordnung der Kunstwörter auf einander folgenden, Artikeln abgehandelt.* Vol. 2. Leipzig: Weidmann und Reich, 1771.

Tieck, Ludwig. "Der gestiefelte Kater. Kindermährchen in drei Akten, mit Zwischenspielen, einem Prologe und Epiloge." In *Werke in einem Band.* Edited by Peter C. Plett. Hamburg: Hoffmann und Campe, 1967, 243–304.

Tumfart, Barbara. *Wallishausers Wiener Theater-Repertoir und die österreichische Zensur.* PhD diss., University of Vienna, 2003.

Wakefield, Andre. *The Disordered Police State: German Cameralism as Science and Practice.* Chicago: Chicago University Press, 2009.

Walach, Dagmar. "Das doppelte Drama oder die Polizei als Lektor. Über die Entstehung der preußischen Theaterzensurbibliothek." In *Die besondere Bibliothek oder: Die Faszination von Büchersammlungen.* Edited by Antonius Jammers. Munich: Saur, 2002, 259–74.

Wild, Christopher J. *Theater der Keuschheit—Keuschheit des Theaters. Zu einer Geschichte der (Anti-)Theatralität von Gryphius bis Kleist.* Freiburg: Rombach, 2003.

Willebrand, Johann Peter. *Innbegriff der Policey nebst Betrachtungen über das Wachsthum der Städte. Aus dem Französischen übersetzt und mit einigen Anmerkungen versehen.* Leipzig and Zittau: A.J. Spiekermann, 1767.

Wölfel, Kurt. "Moralische Anstalt: Zur Dramaturgie von Gottsched bis Lessing." In *Deutsche Dramentheorien*. Vol. 1. Edited by Reinhold Grimm. Frankfurt am Main: Athenäum, 1971, 45–122.

Wolff, Christian. *Vernünfftige Gedancken von dem Gesellschaftlichen Leben der Menschen und insonderheit dem gemeinen Wesen zu Beförderung der Glückseeligkeit des menschlichen Geschlechtes den Liebhabern der Wahrheit mitgetheilet*. Halle: Renger, 1721.

Zelle, Carsten. "Was kann eine gute stehende Schaubühne eigentlich wirken? (1785)." In *Schiller-Handbuch. Leben—Werk—Wirkung*. Edited by Matthias Luserke-Jaqui. Stuttgart, Weimar: Metzler, 2005, 343–57.

Zumbusch, Cornelia. *Die Immunität der Klassik*. Berlin: Suhrkamp, 2011.

7

The Materiality of Memory: Touching, Seeing, and Being the Past in Patricio Guzmán's *Chile, Memoria Obstinada*

Kaitlin M. Murphy

In 1996, exiled Chilean filmmaker Patricio Guzmán returned to his home country for the first time in 23 years. In his suitcase, he carefully packed copies of his internationally renowned three-part documentary, *La Batalla de Chile* (The Battle for Chile), in the hope of showing it in Chile for the very first time. This essay focuses not on *La Batalla de Chile*, although the film plays a central role throughout, but rather on the profound historiographical implications of the film Guzmán created as a chronicle of his return visit: *Chile, Memoria Obstinada* (Chile, Obstinate Memory; hereafter referred to as *Memoria Obstinada*). Made six years after Chile's official transition from dictatorship to democratic governance and halfway between Chile's first and second truth commissions, *Memoria Obstinada* is a complex film that reflects on the role of the past in the present. It is about the interplay between individual and collective memory and the dangers of forgetting, or never knowing in the first place. Writing in the wake of the fortieth anniversary of the 1973 coup about a film made in 1996, I am primarily interested in exploring the following questions: what tactics does Guzmán employ in order to intervene in national consciousness and memory during Chile's post-transition period; how does the film process, negotiate, and map memory; and, finally, how might a close reading of this documentary film allow us to think about the possibilities the materiality of memory offers as a historiographical strategy?

I begin with a brief historical sketch of Guzmán's final days in Chile before the coup, his exile, and Pinochet's dictatorship, then shift to an analysis of Chile's transition to democracy. This lays the groundwork for an exploration not only of the film, its truth claims and performative effects, but also of the historiographical possibilities that emerge when we pay attention to the intimate relationship between matter and memory. As I will argue, although memory and matter (material objects) are often considered antithetical, because memory is subjective and open to change over time whereas the material object never changes (the only thing that may change is how it is perceived), memory and materiality are deeply intertwined. This gives memory matter the potential to produce unique mnemonic effects that refute official historical narratives and resituate memory in the present. Memory and materiality are *not*, therefore, antithetical; rather, closer study of material memory itself (in this case, documentary footage, old photographs, and the walls and physical spaces of reenactments) enables us to explore its employment as a historiographical strategy intended to intervene in the official narrative of Chilean history.

The Near and Distant Past

In 1970, Chilean Salvador Allende became the first democratically elected socialist president in Latin America. The United States was immersed in Cold War ideologies which, coupled with self-serving neoliberal interests, resulted in substantial United States interference in politics in many countries in Latin America. Justifying these interventions as the protection of democracy and the American way of life, the United States worked to impose neoliberal order throughout the south by "helping" the rightwing to undermine and squeeze socialist leaders and engineer coup d'états. Deeply threatened by President Allende, a very popular and powerful socialist president, the United States offered assistance to Chile's conservative and land-owning elites to overthrow him. Previously accustomed to power and opposed to President Allende's socialist project, they accepted and began a series of financial, congressional, and public attacks against his regime.[1]

Without any knowledge of what the future would bring, Guzmán, then a young and newly minted filmmaker, set out to document this era of change in Chile. With three friends, several 16-mm cameras, and limited film stock, Guzmán's film team developed a plan they hoped would enable them to be in the right place at the right time. Their strategy was to document events taking place at the main factories, the universities, and the government palace because these locations were all major meeting points for the strikes and rallies taking place across Santiago. With this approach, Guzmán and his crew documented the vibrant euphoria of President Allende's supporters, and the growing fear and resentment of his opponents. In what amounted to roughly 20–25 hours of raw footage, Guzmán and his team recorded the onslaught of crippling strikes, protests, political undermining, and right-wing congressional blockades against President Allende. Of this period, Guzmán later stated: "Through the lived experience of the film, we all came to understand what it means to live through a revolutionary process—what ideological struggle really means, what fascism looks and feels like, what it means for the enraged middle class to rise up against the workers, and how invisible imperialism can be."[2] As Guzmán's team filmed General Pinochet's military takeover of the Chilean government, cameraman Leonard Hendrickson was shot and killed. In *La Batalla de Chile*, we see a military official turn, point his gun straight at the camera, and fire. The camera jolts and Hendrickson tries to lift it, then slumps slowly to the ground.[3] As we later find out in *Memoria Obstinada*, on the day of the coup, Guzmán and the rest of the crew were captured by the military. Guzmán was taken to the National Stadium, which was to become the first of Chile's concentration camps. His uncle Ignacio hid the raw footage in a trunk in his home, later giving it to people from the Swedish embassy to smuggle out of the country.[4] As the Swedish officials drove toward the port city of Valparaiso several hours away, with the intention of putting the reels on a ship to Sweden, they were terrified they would be caught. After being stopped several times by the police, they managed to make it through, only to reach the ship and not be allowed aboard, due to the quantity of trunks they were carrying with them. Fortunately, the captain directed that all the trunks be allowed on board as private diplomatic material, and the ship steamed away from Chile with Guzmán's film reels safely onboard.

Exile

After several weeks, Guzmán was released from detainment and fled to exile in Paris. He met the boat carrying his film reels when it docked in Stockholm three months later. He wasn't allowed to board the ship, but later received a call from the head of the Swedish Film Institute to come retrieve his footage, which had been thrown into a pile on the floor of the Institute basement. Miraculously, not one reel had gone missing (he had carefully numbered all of his reels in Chile, making it possible to be sure). Guzmán returned to Paris and went to work. It took him about eight months to reach the conclusion that it wasn't one long film, but, rather, a documentary in three parts[5] that would come together to form the deeply analytical and political *La Batalla de Chile* trilogy. Making the documentary gave him a sense of purpose in exile, and he believed in its importance for himself, the larger diaspora of Chilean exiles, and people still suffering in Chile. Guzmán reflected that it was only when he finished the film that he fully grasped that he was in exile; he "had no country, no topic, nowhere to go. I had no future, nothing...When I finished the film, I felt what they felt when they left Chile. I fell into a deep depression that lasted six years."[6]

Meanwhile, back in Chile, General Augusto Pinochet's dictatorship was in full force. During Pinochet's first three months in office, over 1,200 people were killed or had disappeared, and over 250,000 were detained for political reasons.[7] In the seventeen years of dictatorship that followed, over 200,000 Chileans went into exile, over 30,000 were detained and tortured, and approximately 3,200 were killed by the military and the secret police.[8] During this time, Chileans experienced extreme censorship and what Nelly Richard describes as the decimation of the earlier frameworks of Chilean identity, culture, and community. Through its surveillance of language and other forms of expression, Pinochet's dictatorship worked to suppress the very production of meaning.[9] Artistic practice was either halted or hidden, cultural spaces were shut down and institutions dismantled, and many artists fled the country. Jorge Muller Silva, a close friend of Guzmán's and the director of photography on *La Batalla de Chile*, was detained, tortured, and never seen again. Guzmán's films, which had received numerous awards and critical acclaim, were formally banned in Chile, and his life in exile continued.

The Transition

Toward the end of 1988, Pinochet allowed a plebiscite for democratic elections to take place and unexpectedly lost by 55 percent to 43 percent. He agreed to step aside, providing certain conditions were met: the new leaders had to work within the bounds of the 1980 Constitution Pinochet had implemented vastly limiting possibilities for governmental reform. He would remain the commander in chief of the army for the next eight years, after which he would become a senator for life. He rearranged the judicial system, ensured the military had the majority of power, and gave the military impunity. This was agreed to by the incumbent Concertación party and in 1990 President-elect Patricio Aylwin took office, ending Pinochet's seventeen years of authoritarian rule (as president). The new democracy was fragile, haunted by the dictatorship and the very real threat Pinochet continued to pose. As a result, the transition was marked by a certain historical continuity between the dictatorship and the new democracy. Fearful of conflict, the government chose to focus on reconciliation and moving forward, leaving the past behind. Within a few months of taking office, President Aylwin convened the first of Chile's truth commissions, *La Comisión de la Verdad y Reconciliación* (the National Commission for Truth and Reconciliation).[10]

Chile's 1990 commission understood reconciliation as one of its primary goals (as reflected in its name). When the commissioners began their work, Pinochet explicitly warned them not to "touch a single hair of a single soldier," nor to attempt to override the laws, giving him and the military immunity, that he had implemented prior to leaving office.[11] The commission worked for nine months gathering and compiling information. As Greg Grandin notes, however, it ultimately took national cohesion as its primary mandate and framed the 1973 coup as a "tragic but necessary intervention that prevented complete national collapse."[12] Not only was there no perpetrator accountability or individual responsibility assigned, the nature of the "truths" the commission chose to address sharply limited its ability to comprehensively and legitimately report on the human rights violations that occurred during the dictatorship. The principal acts documented by the commission included torture resulting in death, execution by government forces, use of undue force resulting in death, death of combatants and noncombatants immediately after the coup, and killings for political reasons. Crimes not covered included forced exile, torture not resulting in death, and illegal detention so long as the person survived.[13] In other words, in order to be counted as a victim, you needed to have died. While such documentation would signal glaring omissions by any commission, it was an especially egregious accounting in Chile, where the overwhelming majority of victims were tortured but survived (had the commission used the universally accepted United Nations definition of torture, it is estimated they would have found roughly 400,000 victims). The result was that the majority of experiences of survivors were not validated or acknowledged by the commission.

Vast omissions were characteristic of the state of memory at the time. While Pinochet's regime had expressed more interest in erasing the past than in remembering it, postdictatorship human rights discourse focused on memory as the cornerstone of reconciliation. Because Pinochet continued to pose a very real and present threat, public discourse around memory and human rights was stunted, leaving the question of responsibility for and to memory (or the lack of it) largely unanswered. This led many to criticize what they perceived as cowardice, avoidance, and what Nelly Richard calls the official "techniques of forgetting."[14] Tomás Moulian, described the early 1990s postdictatorship period in Chile as a time of forgetting, during which "obligatory amnesia was decreed so that nothing could perturb the 'virtuous' official memory of the period of military rule."[15] Chile's commission held no public hearings, named no perpetrators, and sealed the archives. The exercise of justice that marked Chile's fractured transition was paralyzed by tensions between remembering and forgetting, acknowledgment and forced silence. These constrictions continued to plague Chile far beyond the crippled memory project of the truth commission.

It was to this Chile that Guzmán returned in 1996, when he flew to his homeland for the first time since fleeing into exile 23 years earlier. Although his films were internationally known and among the most highly lauded and awarded of Chilean films, they remained undistributed in Chile. Guzmán had never been able to find a distributor willing to promote them, even though the ban on Guzmán's films had officially ended with the dictatorship. When Guzmán wrote to 40 high schools, asking permission to show *La Batalla de Chile* and then interview the students, he received almost all rejections, along with the explanation that to show the film "would be negative, and that it was necessary not to reopen old wounds."[16] Undeterred, Guzmán arranged to informally screen *La Batalla de Chile* in several places. *Memoria Obstinada* documents the results of these screenings, and of remembering.

The Film

Memoria Obstinada opens to a black screen and silence. City traffic honks and blares in the background, and the title briefly appears on the screen. The words disappear into darkness, a car honks twice, and there is complete silence. Then:

To my daughters Andrea and Camila

The screen is abruptly ruptured by pure chaotic noise and the sights and sounds of screaming fighter jets circling and attacking a large stately building, causing huge clouds of smoke and debris to swirl wildly in the air. The raised Chilean flag hanging in the front, at the highest point of the building, waves softly in the gusts of the assault, and words appear on the screen once more:

> 11th September 1973
> Santiago, Chile

Behind these words, we see the fighter jet circle and fire at the building again, and the flag and building disappear into the billowing smoke. The jet circles yet again, and through the shrieks of its attack we hear the sounds of the grand building crumbling. For anyone familiar with Patricio Guzmán's work, this footage is instantly recognizable. It documents the morning attack on La Moneda Presidential Palace that was the beginning of General Augusto Pinochet's coup d'état and violent and oppressive rule, and the last day of President Salvador Allende's government and life.[17]

This sequence sets the stage and tone for the remainder of *Memoria Obstinada*, which interweaves black-and-white archival footage from *La Batalla de Chile* with new documentary footage of Chile in 1996. This new footage takes three forms. First, throughout the film, Guzmán includes multiple first-person testimonial interviews, often with individuals who also appeared in the 1973 footage. Second, Guzmán integrates contemporary conversations and interviews conducted with high school students after the screenings of *La Batalla de Chile*. Third, much of *Memoria Obstinada* is devoted to staged reenactments and returns to "the scene of the crime," upon which I will focus in detail later in this essay. These diverse elements are contextualized with Guzmán's voiceover narration and bound into a single narrative. Whereas *La Batalla de Chile* is event-driven, strongly descriptive, and fundamentally political, *Memoria Obstinada* is reflective and focused on individual subjectivity. *Memoria Obstinada* is intended to bring both the viewers *of* the film and the people *in* the film into experiential contact with the past, in a manner similar to what Alison Landsberg calls "prosthetic memory." Prosthetic memory emerges "at an experiential site such as a movie theater or museum [...] the person does not simply apprehend a historical narrative but takes on a more personal, deeply felt memory of a past event through which he or she did not live."[18]

Suturing in memories for younger generations, making them witnesses to the past, while simultaneously interviewing the survivors of that past, would appear to be exactly Guzmán's goal in staging viewings of *La Batalla de Chile*. The students we see in *Memoria Obstinada* are in what Marianne Hirsch calls the "postmemory" generation—the generation after the one that directly experienced the trauma.[19] These students have no first-hand memory of the coup. Because of the pervasive veil of silence thrown over history after the coup and the fractured political sphere during and after the dictatorship, most appear to have learned a heavily revised historiographical narrative of the period. By showing *La Batalla de Chile* and interviewing both survivors and the younger generation (both side of the memory coin), Guzmán is working to educate and create dialog, but also to create engaged and invested witnesses.

Memoria Obstinada asks the questions what does it mean for a culture to remember, and what are the risks in a culture of forgetting?

Throughout the film, we hear the first movement of Beethoven's Moonlight Sonata, specifically in those moments where Guzmán seems to be insisting on the importance of the struggle to remember. The sonata does not play through; rather, it is a broken melody of which the spectator hears the slow sonorous beginning, over and over again, much as memory is broken and fragmented in Chile. At the very end of the film, we discover where the music is coming from: Guzmán's now elderly uncle Ignacio, the sole surviving family member, is playing the piano and struggling to remember the full sonata. When asked why he hid the film that later became *La Batalla de Chile*, Ignacio replies, "I knew I had to do it, not only for you, but for what it meant, for being able to remember after."

The sonata scene in *Memoria Obstinada* is immediately followed by footage of one of the more poignant vewings of *La Batalla de Chile*. Guzmán was able to arrange a scene that addresses Ignacio's statement about the importance of memory. Students of Ernesto, a fevered union organizer in *La Batalla de Chile* turned much quieter professor in *Memoria Obstinada*, watch the film in stunned silence, tears rolling down their faces. While Guzmán has held a number of other screenings prior to this, these students are hit by the film in a way none of the other audiences were. They express anger at not knowing this history, loss for what could have been, guilt for not understanding what was at stake, and pain for what was lost. Some sob uncontrollably, inconsolable in their grief, while others sit silently, tears pouring from their eyes.

By juxtaposing the scene featuring his uncle, the memory keeper, with the younger generation, and specifically the group of students most affected by the film and their ruptured recognition of themselves as part of the damaged aftermath of history, Guzmán seems to be emphasizing both the importance of memory as a part of our everyday lives and the need to remember. Uncle Ignacio made the choice to fight for memory through the preservation of *material* memory, which is the heroic choice in this film. Without him, *La Batalla de Chile* would never have been made, and Guzmán's life would have been profoundly different. *La Batalla de Chile* is more than that, however, because the history it documents is so at odds with the official history taught under the dictatorship that, prior to this film, the anti-Pinochet version of history was well on its way to being erased. In this sense, *Memoria Obstinada* is an extremely cogent argument for the need to employ materiality in the effort to preserve memory. Certainly, it is important to remember, but Chile's recent history shows that it is possible for a state and society to suppress (for those who lived it) and erase (for the postmemory generation) certain memories. The matter of memory, the effort to document and record, the lengths to which people go to preserve their memories in material form is what makes the correction of state suppression of memory possible in the first place. As memory matter, then, the documentary film and the old photographs of the missing (which Guzmán looks at with survivors) are more than mere objects *of* memory. While individual memories may be more fluid and fragile, gradually morphing as time passes, and matter—such as film footage and photographs—may on the surface stay unchanging, memory and matter are in fact deeply intertwined. Material memory is the provocation and the *producer* of a set of mnemonic effects that in turn create an interactive historiographical space that blends individual memories and knowledge into what might be considered *communities* of memory, framed around the learning, reflecting, and debating inspired by the collective action of viewing the film and photographs. In *Memoria Obstinada*, the students who watch *La Batalla de Chile* are *changed* by it. This is where memory matter becomes historiographical strategy.

Student interviews are juxtaposed with those of the survivors in the film, survivors from both sides of the political debate. Guzmán includes an interview with a teacher, who in the early 1970s was not an Allende supporter. In the film she sits quietly below her boisterously debating young students, and softly reflects:

> At the time, I was in the university. I also participated. I was not from the right wing itself, but in a certain way I agreed that something had

to happen in Chile, that things should not continue the way they were. I was wrong, I was wrong. Now, I think differently. To recognize that one has been wrong is very hard, especially once one understands the cost. I can tell you that at the time of the coup, in the morning in which it happened, I was happy, but because I did not have the consciousness at that moment of what it was going to mean later. Two days after the coup, my point of view was different, and when time passed, obviously, it became even more different.

Throughout the film, Guzmán constructs juxtapositions such as these, between past and present, memory and ignorance, youth and middle age, exile and home, between what Chile was and what it has become.

Certainly, much of the film seems to be an effort to understand a homeland irrevocably altered by years of dictatorship, frozen by fear and silences, haunted by the past. Avery Gordon describes haunting as a constituent element of modern social life, and a phenomenon that is much more complicated than it is typically understood to be.[20] She writes, "Haunting describes how that which appears to be not there is often a seething presence, acting on and often meddling with taken-for-granted realities," with the ghost as "just the sign, or the empirical evidence if you like, that tells you a haunting is taking place." She continues,

> The ghost is not simply a dead or a missing person, but a social figure, and investigating it can lead to that dense site where history and subjectivity make social life. The ghost or the apparition is one form by which something lost or barely visible, or seemingly not there to our supposedly well-trained eye, makes itself known or apparent to us, in its own way, of course. The way of the ghost is haunting, and haunting is a very particular way of knowing what has happened or is happening. Being haunted draws us affectively, sometimes against our will and always a bit magically, into the structure of feeling of a reality we come to experience, not as cold knowledge, but as a transformative recognition.[21]

Haunting, understood to occur in the space between, for example, our ability to describe the logic of state terror and the way people actually *experience* it and its aftereffects, gives us a way to think about the merging of the visible and the invisible, the dead and the living, the past and the present, and how they interact to inform the individual and collective experience.[22] Gordon's goal is to consider how we might reckon with what modern history has rendered ghostly, and how we might begin to "develop a critical language to describe and analyze the affective, historical, and mnemonic structures of such hauntings."[23]

Guzmán's filmic project seems to be driven by similar desires. The result is an intensely political project that directly addresses silences, absences, and unknowing, and works to give ghosts and their memories audibility and visibility, going directly against the official narratives of national history. The film gathers diverse and fragmented memories, experiences, forgettings, and fears and creates a collective narrative intended both to document and make an intervention into the absences and silences that mark the public sphere. Certainly, Guzmán's film is not interested in simply elucidating the politics of the times; it is a deliberate practice of uncovering, articulating, and, indeed, *producing*m emory.

What Guzmán chooses *not* to include in the film, by way of processing, negotiating, and mapping memory and truth claims during the postdictatorship period, is also striking: the politics of the transition period. There is no mention of the *Concertación* government's neoliberal policies, the ongoing political disputes surrounding human rights violations and the trials of military officers, or the struggles of the memory rights organizations to find those who were disappeared and to build public memory sites.[24] The truth commission, the foremost official memory project of the transition, literally gets *no* mention. This absence is incredibly striking. Why would Guzmán make a film that works to explore and document the state of memory in the postdictatorship period, a film based in large part on embodied and verbal testimonial reflection, and not make *any* mention of the biggest official memory project? I interpret this decision as a deliberate repudiation of the flawed political transition process and as an argument for the importance of focusing on individual memories and hauntings that exist, often unrecognized and unseen, in the larger social memory sphere.

By focusing on individual memory, not just on the part of those who remember, but also (importantly) those who don't, and then situating them all within a shared context, Guzmán is able to portray the ways in which the legacies of past events—and their attempted erasure— deeply influence and manifest in the present, affecting daily life with a force that is powerfully tangible. The film deals with the matter of memory (and *is* the matter of memory) across time and generations, but it doesn't stop there because *Memoria Obstinada* is not merely *about* memory, it is an intervention *into* memory—into what people remember, how they remember, and what those memories mean. The film emphasizes that personal memory is always connected to social narrative (just as social memory is connected to the personal), and that the self and the community are the imagined products of a continued and ongoing process. A project within a project, this film is intended to change the status of both memory and truth claims about the past in the present. *Memoria Obstinada* is highly sophisticated and works on multiple levels. On one level, by showing *La Batalla de Chile* and conducting group discussion afterward, Guzmán is suturing memories into a younger generation and creating witnesses to the past. Certainly, not all the students agree with the politics in *La Batalla de Chile*, but by asking them to watch it, and then think and talk about the past and its role in the present, Guzmán is working directly against the culture of forgetting and silence. On another level, he uses multiple techniques to extract and engage with memory in his interviews with survivors. He shows them photographs and old film footage, alternatingly asking them to remember, reembody, reperform, and reenact the past. He also returns to specific locations and "scenes of the crime." Like a memory prism, Guzmán's film takes in diverse, fractured memories and refracts them sharply outward in narrative form. As a strategic intervention, his film is designed to work in and on the public sphere, not just passively reflecting or elucidating the politics of the times, but, instead, by participating in an ecosystem of storytelling and storysharing. By structuring *Memoria Obstinada* in this manner, Guzmán interpolates the viewer into the film, not merely as a viewer, but as a witness to the past and the present in Chile. It is a marvelous sleight of hand: by looking through the visual lens at staged spectatorship and various performance strategies *in* the film, the film itself is, in turn, possessed of an embodied, performative visuality. By honing in on the very matter of memory—the 1973 footage and photographs, and the affective resonances they call forth in the subjects of the *Memoria Obstinada* – Guzmán both returns to the past and brings the past firmly into the present. Opposed to an analysis of memory matter as static and permanently historical (belonging to the past), this temporal maneuver demonstrates the unique ability of material memory to function historiographically. Memory matter, employed in the service of critical inquiry and political projects, can create a dialogical space that illuminates hidden pasts and lost futures, a process that helps to shape memory and, importantly, identity in the present.

Remembering, Returns, and Reenactments

In addition to the film screenings and interviews, Guzmán creates reenactments of past events and actions. These reenactments are meant to evoke an absence, as a means to "see" what is no longer there and/or is hidden, and as a way to give the ghosts of dreams, people, and politics audibility and visibility. Rebecca Schneider defines "reenactments" as battles concerning the future of the past, and the efforts to redo a piece "exactly the same as a precedent piece...to stand again in its footprint, in its precise place."[25] The past is a "future direction in which one can travel," stretching out "before us like an unfamiliar landscape waiting to be (re)discovered."[26] Merleau-Ponty writes that "by thus remaking contact with the body and with the world, we shall rediscover our self, since, perceiving as we do with our body, the body is a natural self, and, as it were, the subject of perception."[27] By playing with these staged intersections of time and space in order to tell his tale, Guzmán loosens the ties that separate the past and present and works to give body and voice to a past that no longer physically exists, except through representations of that world and in memory. These reenactments enable the viewer to experience the past firsthand, for the first time (as a second time).

The first moment of reenactment in *Memoria Obstinada* occurs directly after the opening (reperformed) footage of the bombing of La Moneda Presidential Palace. The visual and audio of the attack dissolves to the image of Juan, one of President Allende's bodyguards, who was at La Moneda the morning of the coup and is one of the few who defended President Allende to survive. Juan begins by reflecting. He remembers that he was unarmed, used as a shield, shot in the stomach, and pushed down the stairs on his back, before eventually being transported to and held at the National Stadium, alongside Guzmán and hundreds of others. As Juan speaks, he and Guzmán look at old photographs and footage that shows Juan lying in the street after being pushed down the stairs, a callous act that may have inadvertently saved his life.

Juan agrees to return with Guzmán to La Moneda for the first time since the coup. Disguised as a member of Guzmán's film crew, Juan carries a tripod camera, which he clutches nervously to himself as though it might provide protection from bullets ripping through an unexpected wrinkle in time. We watch as Juan verbally and physically remembers the day of the coup. In a hushed, secretive whisper, he recounts to Guzmán where he was standing and goes to stand in that spot. He gestures to indicate the direction from which the soldiers first attacked. Juan recounts how there were only 36 people defending President Allende, and how most of his best friends died that day. Step by step, Juan remembers, relives, and reenacts his experience of that morning. With Guzmán prompting him, Juan recalls how he ran across the courtyard while being shot at from above. As he crosses the courtyard, he looks up nervously, as though expecting to see shooters pointing rifles at him. There is a sense that the past and the present are being lived simultaneously, as the emotions brought on by the act of physically remembering and reliving the past threaten to overwhelm Juan.

The film shifts to a group of other former bodyguards, who are thumbing through old photographs of themselves. They work to remember, attempting to identify ghostly soldiers and civilians in the faded black-and-white images. Ghosts seem to surround them as they point to person after person, and softly remember their fate: shot "*that*" day, dragged away and never seen again, disappeared. Disappeared. Disappeared. Disappeared. The lines between dead and alive, past and present, then and now, are blurry, and the individual and collective remembering seems to be, above all, a form of living.

This multilayered recollection is not about exact replication of past actions. Rather, it emphasizes that the attempt to retrieve and relive memories of the past through reenactment as a form of embodied narration is wholly and simultaneously both the *retrieval* and the *construction* of memory. Memory is embodied and generated, for the subjects *in* and the viewers *of* the film alike. Furthermore, the shared remembering, both in the case of the conversation between Juan and Guzmán that takes place in the palace, and that of the group of guards, aids in the retrieval and spreads the burden of the past's return.

The next major reenactment scene opens with the sounds of the anthem of the *Unidad Popular* (President Allende's political party) and the image of bodyguards walking alongside an empty car as it drives slowly down the street, their inside hands resting protectively on the car as they move forward. The film cuts to black–and-white footage of President Allende in the car, anthem playing, bodyguards walking alongside while crowds cheer. The film returns to the present-day reenactment and the empty car and empty street. The loss of President Allende and his dreams for Chile deeply haunt this reenactment. The reperformance of the embodied gestures of the bodyguards is devastating, as they slip back into practiced movements that seem second nature, yet so uncanny and at odds with the absence of the meaning that the president and the pulsating crowd gave their bodies in the black-and-white footage. Unreconciled loss and pervasive surrounding silence seem to inhabit these men and pour out of their bodies as they walk through empty streets and protect an empty car. The replacement of bodies, music, and dreams with emptiness and ghosts points to the presence of absence in the wake of the historical trauma of the coup. This scene is simultaneously the reenactment of the gesture and *also* the enactment of embodied memory, caught in temporal slippage. Their bodies do it again, and they do it for the first time. The corporeal nature of this wrinkle in time/space is profound and haunted. By emphasizing the practiced nature of the gestures as powerful corporeal remembering and mourning, Guzmán stages an uncanny encounter with President Allende's ghostly presence/(of)/absence and bears witness to the embodied memories of his bodyguards. In doing this, Guzmán seems to suggest that these embodied memories rest, dormant, just below the skin, ready to rise up at the slightest provocation.

In one of the most personal scenes of the film, Guzmán returns to the National Stadium, the site of his own detention. He goes with a friend, a man named Alvaro, who in the days after the coup had volunteered to be a doctor to the prisoners and secretly carried messages to the outside world. As they walk through the cold underbelly of the stadium, Alvaro muses in a hushed tone that it was a sinister, fearful place, full of death and pain. The eye of the camera flickers around the empty hallways and walls of the stadium. The camera view changes to handheld, eyelevel, as the viewer watches Guzmán walk slowly down a ramped hallway toward a large grated door. The doctor recalls that one day he went to the stadium and Guzmán was his next patient. Guzmán asks in a distant voice, "And was I afraid?" The doctor replies gently, "No."

The scene then shifts to footage of people in the stadium bleachers while armed and helmeted soldiers walk toward them. Guzmán begins to narrate: "In 1973, thousands of people passed through this stadium. It was the first wave of terror to wash over Chile." The image cuts to soldiers walking in the stadium, through a door and into a security backroom. They don helmets with face protection and riot gear. This image is intercut with a black-and-white photographic still of police in the same uniform. Except for the color of the image, it could be the same policemen. The photographic still shifts to another, this time of the police standing in the stadium hallway pointing a gun at young woman, her hands raised above her head. We return to color, and the police are lined up to begin marching. Guzmán cuts back to black-and-white riot footage from *La Batalla de Chile*, and we see the police attack the crowds. Back again to the contemporary footage, the police—almost indistinguishable from the police of the past—circle out into the stadium and stand facing the crowd. It eventually becomes evident they are at a soccer match, seemingly there to ensure the unruly crowd stays contained. There is a strange layering of multiple stadiums in time; the stadium where thousands were detained, including Guzmán, the stadium that is known as a site of intense horror and violence, and the seemingly unaware youth of the present. As the soccer fans' energy builds, they scream team anthems, climb fences, and throw smoke bombs; their joy feels riotous. There is a staggering uncanniness in how closely the militaristic surveillance, with its undercurrent of potential violence, replicates that of the past. Guzmán, in his own painful memories, brought with him a witness, someone who could narrate Guzmán's own story to and *for* him. The palpable unease Guzmán seems to feel in the stadium, the site of such personal psychological and physical terror, is amplified by the seeming ignorance of the soccer fans under such heavy police surveillance. Peculiarly, the success of the reenactment comes from the performance of power of the anonymous, choreographed police corps. The gestures that carry the memory, the power, performed by their anonymous bodies, give this scene meaning. The viewer does not need to know who the individual police are in order for the reenactment to be effective. This discordant overlapping of the stadium in distinct layers of time again serves to point out the divide between the past and present in Chile.

The embodied remembering activated by the reenactments illuminates a powerful form of memory matter felt and expressed within and through bodies, one that is concurrently ephemeral and enduring. As Merleau-Ponty observed, it is indeed by perceiving with the body, and restoring contact with the body and with the world, that the Selves are rediscovered.[28] By using bodies to call forth ghosts and different time-space intersections, Guzmán is working both in and outside of time, using loss and memory to anchor himself in space and give his workm eaning.

Memory, History, Truth

In certain respects, *Memoria Obstinada* is strangely contradictory. It is strongly grounded in the politics of a time and place, but its author had to leave his home country in order to make it, and it was abroad that all of his films first gained recognition. Guzmán is an insider/outsider, working on the present/past. *Memoria Obstinada* is profoundly based on the experiences of live bodies, but intensely focused on ghosts and haunting. It is wholly about the aftermath of the dictatorship and memory, yet does not explicitly address any of the official transition processes. Intent on deconstructing mainstream narrative constructions of history that exclude the full spectrum of Chileans' lived experience, Guzmán blurs the lines between personal, collective, and political. He positions memory as both borne out of individual circumstances and shaped by collective consciousness and shared social processes. In so doing, his film performs the very repositioning and reframing of memory he argues Chile so desperately needs.

By combining photographs, old footage, reenactments, and interviews, Guzmán uses material memory like a prism, giving diverse memories and practices of remembering audibility, visibility, and a role in the present. He blurs the lines between individual and shared memory and knowing, and exacerbates the sense of dislocation, of being simultaneously in the past and the present. As an exile returning to his country years later, looking for traces of knowing and being that are *in* the present, but are also *of* the past, the film engages material memory to create a sense of being simultaneously inside and outside memory, time, and space. Guzmán portrays these three not as ontological and epistemological superstructures, but as sites of contention open to competing claims of authorship. This materializing of the past is destabilizing (i.e., it sets its audiences on edge), and into this opening, Guzmán inserts his truth claim: we are made who we are by our personal and collective histories, yet we are also the makers of our history—something for which, in Chile, one must actively fight.

By bringing people into experiential and meaningful contact with the past via diverse engagement with material memory, and by making them feel a part of it—or, perhaps more precisely, it a part of them— Guzmán's film is, in effect, a historiography whose function is to *be* a mode of thinking, of seeing, and of touching the past. His film studies time, space, and matter, but by focusing on the very materiality of the historical event, his film in turn *produces* and creates new intersections among time, space, and matter. As Rancière writes, "The dream of a suitable political work of art is in fact the dream of disrupting the relationship between the visible, the sayable, and the thinkable...It is the dream of an art that would transmit meanings in the form of a rupture with the very logic of meaningful situations."[29] This methodical mapping and negotiating of time and place through memory, in bodies and in matter, goes directly against the silences and absences in the official narratives of national history.

As Guzmán's film and work illustrate, there is immense historiographical value in bringing individual memory, matter (including physical space), and official histories into contact and conversation with one another. If official histories, by definition, sublimate and attempt to make transgressive or previously suppressed memories disappear, then the critical role of the historiographer is to investigate the ways in which transgressive memory persists, whether through lived experience, stories passed down through generations, or the mnemonic potency of physical objects and spaces. Projects such as this one challenge scholars and artists alike not merely to investigate, but to question what happens when material memory and embodied memory are made visible and audible enough to trouble official histories. What new communities of memory might be created? What new political possibilities might emerge? The historiographical project, in the hands of people concerned with matters of social and political justice, can be as much about laying the foundation for alternate futures as it is about documenting the multiplicity of our pasts. Memory matter is an argument for why memory *matters*. It is exactly through studying the relation between memory and materiality that we may begin to illuminate how the intersections among time, space, and matter work on, and create, history and truth.

Notes

1. See Greg Grandin, "The Instruction of Great Catastrophe: Truth Commissions, National History, and State Formation in Argentina, Chile, and Guatemala," *American Historical Review* 110:1 (2005): 46–67; and Tomás Moulian, "A Time of Forgetting: The Myths of the Chilean Transition," *NACLA Report on the Americas* 32:2 (1998): 16.
2. Guzmán, quoted in Julianne Burton, *Cinema and Social Change in Latin America: Conversations with Filmmakers* (Austin: University of Texas Press, 1986),66.
3. The camera was later grabbed by protesters and hidden in the gutters so the military wouldn't find it. Guzmán received a phone call that night to go pick it up.
4. While he was filming, Guzmán didn't keep the footage at his house because he felt it was too dangerous. Instead, every week he went to his Uncle Ignacio's house with eight–ten reels and hid them in a large trunk. The military searched Guzmán's home five times but never found the footage. Guzmán's friends knew that if Guzmán was arrested, they were to take the reels to the Swedish Embassy (Guzmán had a contact in the Swedish Embassy through a Chilean filmmaker, Sergio Castilla, who was married to a Swedish woman, Lilian Indseth, then secretary to the ambassador).
5. The three parts are *The Insurrection of the Bourgeoisie* (1975), *The Coup d'État* (1976), and *The Power of the People* (1979).
6. José Carlos Avellar, *Interview with Patricio Guzmán* (Brooklyn, NY: Icarus Films, 1997), np.

7. Neil Kritz, *Transitional Justice: How Emerging Democracies Reckon with Former Regimes* (Washington DC: United States Institute of Peace Press, 1995), 454.
8. Chilean National Commission on Truth and Reconciliation, "*Report of the Chilean National Commission on Truth and Reconciliation*" (1991): http://www.usip.org/files/resources/collections/truth_commissions/Chile90-Report/Chile90-Report.pdf (accessed August 2012).
9. Nelly Richard, *The Insubordination of Signs: Political Change, Cultural Transformation, and Poetics of Crisis* (Durham: Duke University Press, 2004), 17.
10. Though historically truth commissions can trace their roots to the judicial realm, truth commissions are not trials. Transitional justice has evolved into a hybrid practice that involves sanctioning research to outline patterns of abuse and to establish a record of a finite period of a country's past. In many respects, a truth commission is a research project with wide-ranging and far-reaching goals for what that research will accomplish. They are defined by four primary elements. First, they are temporary bodies established to investigate widespread, systematic human rights violations that occurred during a finite period of time. This can include violence committed both directly and indirectly by the state and by armed opposition and guerilla groups. Second, through the investigation of individual cases, a truth commission's goal is to develop an archive that establishes a larger picture of systematic patterns of violence. Third, truth commissions receive a mandate from an authoritative body, usually either or both the executive and legislative branch of government, however, fourth, they are autonomous bodies set apart from the existing institutions of the state and the major parties to past conflicts. This differentiation is an essential component of their legitimacy and ability to contribute to a transition process. Beyond these key elements, truth commissions vary widely and approach the politics of transition in distinct ways, including negotiating the question of publicly naming perpetrators, amnesty programs, symbolic and economic rehabilitation of victims, and the building of monuments and memorials. Priscilla B. Hayner, *Unspeakable Truths: Transitional Justice and the Challenge of Truth Commissions* (New York: Routledge, 2010), 11.
11. Kritz, "*Transitional Justice*," 454.
12. Grandin, "The Instruction of Great Catastrophe," 49.
13. Priscilla B. Hayner, *Unspeakable Truths: Transitional Justice and the Challenge of Truth Commissions* (New York: Routledge, 2010), 317.
14. Nelly Richard, *Cultural Residues: Chile in Transition*, trans. Alan West-Durán and Theodore Quester (Minneapolis: University of Minnesota Press, 2004), 25.
15. Moulian, "A Time of Forgetting," 16.
16. Thomas Miller Klubock, "History and Memory in Neoliberal Chile: Patricio Guzman's Obstinate Memory and the Battle of Chile," *Radical History Review Radical History Review* 85 (2003): 274.
17. This visual footage has now become the official visual memory of the coup and is shown on repeat in the *Museo de la Memoria* (Museum of Memory) in Santiago.
18. Alison Landsberg, *Prosthetic Memory: The Transformation of American Remembrance in the Age of Mass Culture* (New York: Columbia University Press, 2004), 2.

19. Marianne Hirsch, *The Generation of Postmemory: Writing and Visual Culture After the Holocaust* (New York: Colombia University Press, 2012), 4.
20. Avery Gordon, *Ghostly Matters: Haunting and the Sociological Imagination* (Minneapolis: University of Minnesota Press, 1997), 7.
21. Ibid.,8.
22. Ibid.,23.
23. Ibid.,18.
24. Developing memorials and public memory sites has been one of the central goals for many of the human rights groups in Chile.
25. Rebecca Schneider, *Performing Remains: Art and War in Times of Theatrical Reenactment* (New York: Routledge, 2011), 16.
26. Ibid.,22.
27. Maurice Merleau-Ponty, *Phenomenology of Perception*, trans. Colin Smith (London: Routledge, 2002), 239.
28. Ibid.
29. Jacques Rancière, *The Politics of Aesthetics: The Distribution of the Sensible*, trans. Gabriel Rockhill (London: Continuum, 2004), 63.

Bibliography

Avellar, José Carlos. *Interview with Patricio Guzmán*. Brooklyn, NY: Icarus Films, 1997.
The Battle of Chile. Directed by Patricio Guzmán. Brooklyn, NY: First Run Icarus Films, 1975, 1976, 1979.
Bengoa, José. *La Comunidad Reclamada: Identidades, Utopías y Memorias en La Sociedad Chilena*, 2nd ed. Santiago: Catalonia, 2009.
Benjamin, Walter. *Illuminations*. New York: Harcourt, Brace & World, 1968.
Burton, Julianne. *Cinema and Social Change in Latin America: Conversations with Filmmakers*. Austin: University of Texas Press, 1986.
Chile, Obstinate Memory. Directed by Patricio Guzmán. Brooklyn, NY: Icarus Films, 1997.
Chilean National Commission on Truth and Reconciliation. "*Report of the Chilean National Commission on Truth and Reconciliation.*" 1991. http://www.usip .org/files/resources/collections/truth_commissions/Chile90-Report/Chile90 -Report.pdf. Accessed August 2012.
Gordon, Avery. *Ghostly Matters: Haunting and the Sociological Imagination*. Minneapolis: University of Minnesota Press, 1997.
Grandin, Greg. "The Instruction of Great Catastrophe: Truth Commissions, National History, and State Formation in Argentina, Chile, and Guatemala." *American Historical Review* 110, no. 1 (2005), 46–67.
Hayner, Priscilla B. *Unspeakable Truths: Transitional Justice and the Challenge of Truth Commissions*. New York: Routledge, 2010.
Hirsch, Marianne. *The Generation of Postmemory: Writing and Visual Culture After the Holocaust*. New York: Colombia University Press, 2012.
Klubock, Thomas Miller. "History and Memory in Neoliberal Chile: Patricio Guzman's Obstinate Memory and the Battle of Chile." *Radical History Review Radical History Review* 85 (2003): 272–81.

Kritz, Neil J. *Transitional Justice: How Emerging Democracies Reckon with Former Regimes*. Washington DC: United States Institute of Peace Press, 1995.

Landsberg, Alison. *Prosthetic Memory: The Transformation of American Remembrance in the Age of Mass Culture*. New York: Columbia University Press, 2004.

Merleau-Ponty, Maurice. *Phenomenology of Perception*. Translated by Colin Smith. London: Routledge, 2002.

Moulian, Tomás. "A Time of Forgetting: The Myths of the Chilean Transition." NACLA Report on the Americas 32, no. 2 (1998), 16–22.

Rancière, Jacques. *The Politics of Aesthetics: The Distribution of the Sensible*. Translated by Gabriel Rockhill. London: Continuum, 2004.

Richard, Nelly. *Cultural Residues: Chile in Transition*. Translated by Alan West-Durán and Theodore Quester. Minneapolis: University of Minnesota Press, 2004.

———. *The Insubordination of Signs: Political Change, Cultural Transformation, and Poetics of Crisis*. Durham: Duke University Press, 2004.

Schneider, Rebecca. *Performing Remains: Art and War in Times of Theatrical Reenactment*. New York: Routledge, 2011.

III

MaterialSpa ces

III

Materialspaces

8

Adorno, Baroque, Gardens, Ruzzante: Rearranging Theatre Historiography

Will Daddario

Historico-philosophical Introduction

To think critically about contemporary and past historiographical methodologies used to write theatrical and performance histories, one must think again about the purpose and the possibilities of historiographical praxis. If we are to believe the followers of Leopold von Ranke and E. G. Collingwood, historiographers aim to duplicate the charge of historical detectives: to discover what really happened. Thomas Postlewait, for example, states in *The Cambridge Introduction to Theatre Historiography*, "We seek the past event rather than the present engagement."[1] To seek the event and to know what happened requires objectivity on the part of the researcher akin to that found, ostensibly, in the laboratory sciences where the observer, present at the event, has the benefit of direct observation. By distinction, the historian, because of her absence at the event, must interrogate eyewitness accounts and secondary source material, careful always to verify the authenticity of the claims to truth made by the originator of the theatrical event or its subsequent commentators. While careful not to adopt the objectivity of laboratory sciences wholesale, Postlewait desires to fuse self-reflexive historical research with calculating scientific endeavor.[2]

Without wishing to contest the benefit of self-reflexivity, I would like to call into question the purpose of deductive, empirical, pseudoscientific historical research methodologies by claiming that contemporary historiographers will never be able to posit answers or, indeed, consider what constitutes a historical "answer," by doggedly policing the authenticity of an event. Instead of asking, "What really happened?"—a question that leads to constative declarations of identity and fixity—I argue that a reinvigorated and theoretically nimble critical historiography concerns itself with, simultaneously, the materiality of the event under question and the encounter with the event in the archive and/or the repertoire. Therefore, I would phrase the questions emerging from such a concern as follows: what is the nature of the historical riddle presented by the object(s) of inquiry and what are the stakes of deciphering certain historical riddles in the present moment? Beyond the content of a specific play or performance, or the supposed intention of an artist, playwright, or author, what do we make of the unintentional reality of historical material that reveals itself through figures of speech, seemingly nonsensical asides, and vulgar or base humor, on the one hand, and, on the other hand, *pace* Michel de Certeau, those "shards created by the selection of materials, remainders left aside by an explication that come back, despite everything, on the edges of discourse or in its rifts and crannies"?[3] A critical historiographical practice seeking to move beyond the limits of logical positivism does not concern itself primarily with what happened, but with how we produce an understanding of the historical event and how we think through the materiality of the encounter with that event.

The details of this encounter and reinvigorated historiographic practice, along with answers to those questions, appear through an engagement with Theodor W. Adorno's historico-philosophical thought. In *Aesthetic Theory*, for example, the philosopher acknowledges that "according to an almost universally accepted terminology, material is what is formed. It is not the same as content [*Inhalt*]."[4] Developing this idea through the discourse and performance of music, Adorno claimsthat

> its [i.e., music's] content [*Inhalt*] is in any case what occurs…content is everything that transpires. Material, by contrast, is what artists work with: It is the sum of all that is available to them, including words, colors, sounds, associations of every sort and every technique ever developed. To this extent, forms too can become material; it is everything that artists encounter about which they must make a decision.[5]

Building on Adorno's assertions, might we begin to imagine the materiality of the encounter between historiographers and historical fragments as something akin to the encounter between artists and all those materials about which they must make decisions? In this way, historiographers would never presume to work upon or exercise power over the past. Rather, they would work with historical material to compose an image of past events developed through subjective reason, but that reason would have to comport itself to the colors, sounds, and associations presented by the historical objects themselves. Though perhaps enthused by the possibility of arranging historical elements in exciting and unexpected ways, the historiographer-as-artist would also always be slowed by the particularity of the material, coerced into acting as collaborator or conduit, and compelled to consider the conditions that make her historical endeavor possible.

In what follows, I would like to turn to Adorno's insight, offered in his posthumously published inaugural lecture to the philosophy faculty of the University of Frankfurt in 1931, in order, first, to further flesh out the key elements of the artistic, historiographic practice glimpsed in the paragraph above, and, second, to stage a brief encounter with the theatrical practice of Angelo Beolco (aka Ruzzante). Due to its enigmatic nature, which stems mostly from the Paduan dialect in which Ruzzante performed and the esoteric references grounded in the sixteenth-century, lower-middle-class worldview contained within his texts, Ruzzante's theatre practice has remained on the periphery, if not fully in the shadows, of theatre-historiographical studies in the United States. I will argue, however, that artistic, historiographic interpretation, motivated by an Adornian mode of thinking, produces a vivid image of Ruzzante as a comedian whose enigmatical and political humor comes into view alongside a reconsideration of the Baroque. Working through Adorno will not only facilitate our encounter with Baroque Ruzzante, it will also help us to understand the materiality of Ruzzante's spatial and linguistic encounters with his adversaries.

The path to Ruzzante and the Baroque starts with Adorno's 1931 lecture, titled "The Actuality of Philosophy." Actuality, in this sense, does not concern a fixed identity for philosophy; rather, it poses the question "whether, after the failure of the last great efforts, there exists an adequacy between the philosophic questions and the possibility of their being answered at all."[6] The answer is that, yes, one can answer those questions, but the method of actualizing philosophy's potential lies in the encounter between objective material and subjective thought—the true locus of philosophy—which unfolds by eschewing all recourse to science (e.g., Kant, Bergson), on the one hand, and all totalizing philosophies of Being (e.g., Heidegger), on the other. In this lecture in particular, Adorno establishes science as that to which philosophy cannot acquiesce. The difference between the two modes of thinking emerges in the way "that the separate sciences accept their findings, at least their final and deepest findings, as indestructible and static, whereas philosophy perceives the first finding which it lights upon as a sign that needs unriddling. Plainly put: the idea of science (*Wissenschaft*) is research; that of philosophy is interpretation."[7] The first of three derivations from a rigidly empirical historiographical procedure concerned primarily with what really happened occurs in this distinction. A critical, creative historiography requires philosophical interpretation, as opposed to the idea of research, understood in an extremely specific sense, one "which assumes the reduction of the question to given and known elements where nothing would seem necessary except the answer."[8]

Philosophical interpretation assumes as its object neither manifest intentions nor reality concealed within objects, but, rather, that which Adorno names "unintentional reality." Existing in counterpoint to the facts tracked down by the deductive historian, unintentional reality appears within artifacts that, as if by accident, have been smuggled into the present moment in forms as diverse as obscure monologues, puns, architectural drawings, and gardens. Unintentional reality presents itself as historical images that, when arranged into critical constellations and approached through a dialectical materialist mode of thought, illuminate the unintentional truths of objective reality thereby making visible the riddle of the past. Unintentional reality is not the answer to the riddle of the past, that is, it does not reveal the Real, but, rather, it is a shock of light that illuminates the riddle momentarily. The fleeting and ephemeral existence of the lighting negates the permanent, enduring riddle of the past by revealing how that-which-is can only become visible through that-which-is-but-only-for-a-moment. As such, philosophy "persistently and with the claim of truth, must proceed interpretively without ever possessing a sure key to interpretation; nothing more is given to it than fleeting, disappearing traces within the riddle figures of that which exists and their astonishing entwinings."[9] In other words, embracing philosophical interpretation means renouncing axiomatic methods that would try to guide the historiographer through diverse terrains, always with the same map, and choosing, instead, to work out from within the unique labyrinth of each historical fragment.

Walter Benjamin, Adorno's friend and the source of many thoughts in "The Actuality of Philosophy," provides a clear example of this philosophical enterprise in the *Arcades Project*.[10] Benjamin did not seek to deduce the purpose or intention of the Arcades from statements made by the architects or from official releases made by Parisian city-planning officials. Rather, by assembling a seemingly haphazard collection of images, references, quotations, and historical objects, he located the spirit of the Parisian Arcades within the minute details of historical material. Though Adorno did not agree with Benjamin on the final form of the *Arcades Project*, Benjamin's mode of thinking clearly embodied the main claim presented by Adorno in "The Actuality of Philosophy": "Interpretation of the unintentional through a juxtaposition of the analytically isolated elements and illumination of the real by the power of such interpretation is the program of every authentically materialist knowledge."[11]

The second derivation from deductive historical research occurs here, in the consideration of the archive. For Adorno, as well as for Benjamin, the archive is the arrangement of historical images. It makes little sense to talk about content when speaking of arrangement, since an arrangement has no content as such. Rather, arrangements require an attention to form and technique, to *how* one assembles and reassembles various materials. Whereas positivist historians and historiographers would like to find within archives facts and objects that give way to the unimpeachable truths of a historical situation, Adorno collects various materials to assemble a unique archive for each inquiry and to produce an understanding of the past attuned to the dialectical process active within each object. Historical images are never givens, "Rather, they must be produced by human beings and are legitimated in the last analysis alone by the fact that reality crystalizes about them in striking conclusiveness."[12]

But wait. If historiographers adopt the process of philosophical interpretation posited by Adorno, are they not embarking on a project of producing history? Does this word "production" not sound uncomfortably similar to "invention"? Is Adorno's materialist production of historical, unintentional reality through the juxtaposition of analytically isolated elements no more than fantastical invention? Yes and no. The term "invention" played its part in the history of the dialectical arts, particularly in Rudolph Agricola's *De inventione dialectica* (*Of dialectical invention*, 1479, published 1515), where the word encompassed the all-important act of, first, finding and ordering the right arguments needed for proving a statement and then discovering truth itself. A wealth of invention, however, was, for Agricola, a troubling sign, "something given to ungoverned and almost mad intelligences."[13]

Refunctioning this specific understanding of the term, then, one might say that while Adorno's philosophical interpretation does not amount to making stuff up, it does require the ability to skirt the madness alluded to in Agricola's term "wealth of invention," so as to prepare a truly dialectical inquiry. In this sense, "invention" requires a disciplined art to guide it such that the invention gathers itself at some point and commences judgment (i.e., the act of argumentation), a glimpse of and, perhaps, a move beyond the limits of knowledge.

Adorno himself acknowledged the history of the *ars inveniendi* (the art of invention) into which he was stepping:

> If the idea of philosophic interpretation which I tried to develop for you is valid, then it can be expressed as the demand to answer the questions of a pre-given reality each time, through a fantasy which rearranges the elements of the question without going beyond the circumference of the elements, the exactitude of which has its control in the disappearance of the question.[14]

Here, Adorno shifts from "invention" to "fantasy" and transitions from the formal Aristotelian dialectic tradition leading back through the likes of Agricola into his own negative dialectical procedure. This shift marks the third and final Adornian historiographical derivation for which I would like to advocate. In the place of a scientific, research-driven quest for the answer to the question of 'what really happened,' I would propose, following Adorno, an understanding of historiographical practice as disciplined fantasy. The fantastical dimension lives within the act of invention inherent in the process of arranging historical images into critical constellations. In this act of fantasy, one needs discipline to discern the "circumference of the elements" one has collected. The historiographer cannot choose to say just anything about the material under consideration. To the contrary, he or she must listen to the proposal made by the historical material itself and, in that way, give over the power of subjective reasoning to the irrationality of the object. Adorno's term for this act of listening, which according to Birgit Hofstaetter equates directly (in *Negative Dialectics*) with the act of philosophy, is *Verhaltensweise* (comportment). That word contains within it another word, *Weise*, meaning "melody" or "tune." To listen to the proposal made by historical material in a disciplined way would be to tune oneself into the object under consideration and, simultaneously, to attend to one's own comportment toward that object so as to maintain critical self-reflexivity.[15] To write history through disciplined fantasy would be to play the past *quasi una fantasia*. The dialectical movement between rational subjectivity and irrational objectivity so integral to philosophically interpreting the materiality of the encounter, then, also constitutes the motivating force of this disciplinedfantas y.

Fantasizing Baroque

The rest of this essay will transpire as a philosophical interpretation of Ruzzante's theatre practice, aided by a selective collection of Baroque historical images, the point of which is to pursue a dialectical materialist historiography concerned not with what really happened, but, rather, with stretching the limits of what and how one may think about Baroque theatre and Ruzzante's theatre. Remaining with Adorno requires abandoning the Baroque as content, that is, as a time period that contains specific qualities—and, instead, imagining the Baroque as a mutable series of arrangements—for example, a puzzle, the pieces of which may be assembled in multiple ways to reveal different pictures. Accordingly, questions such as what is the Baroque or when did the Baroque occur do not concern me. These questions stem from the type of research Adorno shuns, research that "assumes the reduction of the question to given and known elements where nothing would seem necessary except the answer." Questions like these suppose that there is *a* Baroque that one might fix in *a* time (between 1600 and 1750 CE, for example) in order to isolate specific historical objects as epitomes of *the* Baroque time and place identified.[16] What other arrangements are possible?

Numerous scholars and philosophers have served as guides to this question by moving away from analytical frameworks that would fix the Baroque and flatten it into an intelligible historical form.[17] In one such example, "Barocco: storia di un concetto" ("Baroque: history of a concept"), Otto Kurz arranges the Baroque through an etymological excavation of the word itself and discovers not a permanent historical phenomenon but a shifting, unstable, and quasi-mythical concept housing numerous stories and possibilities. Baroque appears to him as the irregular pearls that sixteenth-century jewelers preferred for their grotesque appearance that so delighted the wealthy citizens of Italy and Portugal.[18] In seventeenth-century texts, such as letters penned by the Italian librarian Antonio Magliabecchi, Kurz discovers the term *barocco* as a synonym for "fraudulent usury" or "cheat."[19] He also finds reference to a *barocco* that signifies the practice of absurd reasoning such as that found in Medieval (Aristotelian) logical exercises.[20] Kurz contends that despite all those references, "baroque," as we understand it today, comes from the name of the painter Federigo Barocci (aka Federico Fiori, 1528–1612) and that its first usage in Italian comes from the *Dizionario delle Belle Arti* (1797) of Francesco Milizia, who defines the term and gives a list of Baroque artists: "it is the superlative of the bizarre, the excess of the ridiculous. Borromini gave [such] delusions, but [also] Guarini, Pozzi, [and] Marchione in the Sacristy of [Saint] Peter are baroque."[21] "Baroque" also denotes a particular style devised by Jesuits, whose use of theatricality in their conversion tactics was well known to the sixteenth- and seventeenth-century world.[22] By the end of Kurz's essay, any certainty about a stable Baroque identity has faded away beneath a mess of historical records, traces, and images.

The mess constitutes a fantastical arrangement that shifts the Baroque from a concrete historical period or a neatly defined architectural/artistic style into a historical riddle. It is important for theatre historiographers to phrase this riddle correctly, thus, the question is not "what does a Baroque theatre practice look like," but "what theatre practices reveal dented, grotesque forms, like that of the Baroque pearl?" What theatre historical texts contain characters or historical figures speaking through a convoluted or abstruse, irregular logic, and where might we find a theatrical version of the *trompe l'oeil* common in painting? To fantasize Baroque means to follow the direction in which these questions point and to imagine or visualize a theatre practice whose specificity comes into view by asking all and each of these questions.

Ruzzante's theatre practice, I argue here, comes into focus by fantasizing Baroque in this way. To ground his practice in its time and place, however, it is helpful to add one more Baroque trope to the arrangement gathered by Kurz. This trope, while familiar, presents another level of complexity because it appears within a labyrinthine philosophical treatise of considerable imagination: Gottfried Wilhelm Leibniz's 1714 text *La Monadologie*. "Each portion of matter" he writes there, "may be conceived as like a garden full of plants and like a pond full of fishes. But each branch of every plant, each member of every animal, each drop of its liquid parts is also some such garden or pond."[23] It is not the case that Leibniz named his philosophy Baroque, but, rather, that within his philosophy it is possible to find a complexity similar to the concept of Baroque mapped thoroughly by Kurz. In Leibniz, as thinkers like John Law and Gilles Deleuze have pointed out, one finds the multifaceted nature of Baroque peculiarity transferred from the particularity of pearls, logical arguments, paintings, and theatrical styles into the materiality of the entire world. Law has suggested that Leibniz's map reveals "an imagination that discovers complexity in detail or (better) in specificity, rather than in the emergence of a higher level order.... It is an imagination that looks down rather than up."[24] It is as if, when scrutinizing the refraction of light off the iridescent surface either of an irregular pearl, or the mental involutions of an abstract logical argument intended to deceive, or a painting whose *trompe l'oeil* effects shuffle the boundary between pictorial space and the viewer's space, one comes into contact with the "gardens within gardens" that make up the world.

Wrested from the typical constellation of Renaissance theatre studies—the poetic style of Bembo, the dialogue forms mastered by Pietro Aretino, the treatises on court behavior by the likes of Baldasarre Castiglione—and arranged within this new constellation of grotesque asymmetry, abstruse logical formulations, *tromp l'oeil* effects, and gardens within gardens, Ruzzante's theatrical activity begins to appear as a Baroque social practice. Neither a historical truth vouchsafed through archival records nor a political program driven by the intentions of the artist, this practice comes to light as the unintentional reality glimpsed within a profoundly unfunny comedic performance.

Ruzzante

What did Ruzzante have to work with? What was his material? Born in the late fifteenth century to a middle-class, educated Paduan family, Ruzzante had the sonority of his Paduan dialect which, as a performer, would have marked him as a *villano* (villager) in Venice or as a native in his own home territory. He had words, profanity, and neologisms, for example, that he utilized to shock and assail his auditors and spectators. He had acquired forms of short plays, *scenarii*, that he transformed into his own short works for the stage. Associations abound among these sounds, words, and *scenarii*—sexual, political, and philosophical associations with which Ruzzante played and through which he baited his audiences. That material, about which Ruzzante made the decisions that would shape his theatrical works, becomes the inheritance of the historiographer, who can begin to assemble an image of Ruzzante by supplementing Ruzzante's own texts and language with the reviews of his work (recorded by audience members), the specificity of the spaces in which Ruzzante performed, even the symbols and insignias embroidered on his costume that marked Ruzzante as belonging to a specific theatrical troupe. By assembling all of these fragments into a critical constellation of Ruzzante's theatrical practice, his words and gestures begin to transform themselves from lascivious and nasty quips into cunning, though oblique, arguments. The images on his sleeves turn into double entendres, laced with aggressive insinuation. The spaces in which he performed become gardens in which Ruzzante planted himself, like a weed, and his theatre practice, over all, reveals itself as a proliferation of gardens within gardens.

The labor of the gardener, the state of the perfect garden, and the measures taken to protect that state all appear in Ruzzante's theatre practice as efforts linked to navigating through and surviving in a world in which he did not make the laws. These gardens are not metaphorical. While certainly a trope within his work, gardens—actual, physical gardens—abound in Ruzzante's time and space. The University of Padua, for example, an institution with which Ruzzante had an unofficial affiliation as a bastard child within an educated family, was renowned at the time for its study of botany. As Matteo and Virgilio Vercelloni reveal in their book, *The Invention of the Western Garden: The History of an Idea*:

> On June 29, 1545, the Senate of the Venetian Republic decreed that a *giardino dei semplici*—that is, a garden of medicinal plants, or physic garden, constituting the first botanical garden in Europe—should be established in Padua, on the Venetian mainland. For centuries, Padua had been the seat of a famous university where the study of botany had been grounded in ancient learning: thus the new botanical garden, a site of experimentation and observation, was a manifestation of an epistemologicalr evolution.[25]

More than an aesthetic study, then, scholars in Padua and Venice understood the garden as a point of access to the wonders of the natural world. In his own mode of speech, Ruzzante claimed as much, in such aphoristic gems as the following from his play *La Moschetta*: "Because I'm telling you, this world is like a vine, and what is natural is the stake: while the stake stands, the vine gives fruit; when the stake doesn't hold, the vine falls on its ass on the ground."[26]

Ruzzante was frequently invited to gardens to perform his plays and to entertain nobles and visiting dignitaries. Citing the diaries of Marin Sanudo, Antonella Pietrogrande relates to us that Ruzzante performed in the gardens of Giudecca around February 7, 1526, and, prior to that, on February 7 and 13, 1515. These gardens were frequently used as settings for theatrical performances and were sizable enough to appear on the remarkable map of Venice created by Jacopo de Barbari in 1500.[27] The Vercellonis supplement this picture of Ruzzante's playing space, observing, "These gardens were arranged according to principle—the interrelation of their constituent elements—on the model of the *hortus conclusus*."[28] Stemming from the medieval monastic horticultural tradition, a *hortus conclusus* was marked by enclosure, symbolic, sacral, and actual: the garden itself was walled off from the exterior of the monastery, then the garden was subdivided into multiple sections and beds. The *hortus conclusus* existed as microcosm, a world within the world, a garden within a garden.[29]

Ruzzante belonged to a number of troupes within the *Compagnie delle Calza* (literally, Companies of the Sock) during the years he performed in Venice, the most notable of which were the *Ortolani* (gardeners) and the *Zardinieri* (aka *Giardinieri*, gardeners/farmers). Between 1520 and 1526, the Paduan performer pops into Sanudo's diaries, marked always by the insignias of the *hortus conclusus* on his outfit, which aligned him with his Gardening troupe.[30] Like snapshots from a camera, Sanudo's diary entries assemble a montage of Ruzzante's activities over the years. On February 16, 1520, he performed with the *compagni Zardinieri* before a crowd gathered in the home of Domenico Trevisan. Sanuto wrote that before dinner he saw "a comedy by Paduans in the style of the peasants, one [actor] had the last name Ruzante and one Menato and it was done well."[31] In January 1521, Ruzzante and Menato appeared again at a "sumptuous feast sponsored by the [company of] Gardeners in Ca' Pesaro."[32] The same pair of Paduans appeared once more in Ca' Contarini da Londra where they performed a "comedy in the rustic style with the compagni Zardinieri."[33] On May 5, 1523, at "a solemn feast offered by the *compagni Ortolani* in the Ducal Palace for the wedding of doge Antonio Grimani's nephew," Sanuto recorded that Ruzzante performed a comedy "molto discoreta," that is to say, an unacceptable comedy for such a high-profile crowd.[34] The vulgar Ruzzante of Sanudo's account, insinuating himself into a private interior space, resembles the Baroque, grotesque pearl: sometimes he was valued for his "dis-correct" humor and sometimes his comedic malformation was more trouble than it was worth.

The comedy for the doge's nephew was unacceptable to Sanudo, but probably not unanticipated; the gardens and images of shovels or other phallic instruments sewn onto Ruzzante's clothing, after all, contained multiple levels of meaning. The *hortus conclusus*, for example, referenced a pious site of monastic scholasticism and prayer, but it also represented a secret "garden" (read: vagina) into which Ruzzante and his male colleagues would like to drive a "shovel" (read: penis). Ludovico Zorzi is, thus, within the orbit of Ruzzante's theatrico-gardening practice when he asserts that "the agricultural symbols of the *Compagnie della Calza* referred generally to the *hortus conclusus* of refined delights and 'virtue,' into which they intended to withdraw and with which they would distinguish themselves from the profane crowd."[35] At the same time, these delights were frequently proposed as unambiguously sexual, and Ruzzante's troupes, as one can see in many of Sanudo's quick critiques, sought to distinguish themselves by telling the dirtiest jokes possible.

Jokes aside, the heft of Ruzzante's theatre practice materializes through an examination of his gardening practice, which flashes into focus by shuffling through his repertoire and adding the *Prima* and *Seconda Orazione* to the this growing historical constellation (*First Oration, ca. 1521, Second Oration, ca. 1527*). The topography of those performances offers another set of gardens within gardens. Working from largest to most intimate, we see that the biggest garden, Padua itself, housed an area called Asolo containing the Villa Barco of Caterina Cornaro, a private, walled-off space where Ruzzante sought to plant himself.

The villa dominated the natural setting within which it was built. Saskia de Wit's description of features common to late Renaissance villas offers a good starting point for an analysis of this villa in particular:

> The spatial composition of the Late Renaissance villas consists usually of a principal axis slung off which are a number of autonomous interior and exterior spaces. Placing parts separately so that they cannot be taken in from one vantage point encourages movement on the part of the observer. As a result the route takes its place in the plan's organization as a structuring element. The polarities of the *hortus conclusus* return in an ambiguity active on various levels. Thus, wilderness and order are made to relate by bringing the wilderness (the *barco*, or *bosco*) within the garden boundaries.[36]

Moving from general to specific, Pietrogrande provides a glimpse of this Ruzzantian performance site: "A true and proper courtly garden, loaded with humanistic themes, is the Barco of Caterina Cornaro, in the countryside of Altivole, at the feet of the Asolani hills; fallen into complete ruin, today all that remains is half of a porch of a barn."[37] In the time of Ruzzante, the villa would have shown scars from fires caused by the Emperor Maximillian whose troops had tried to steal Padua away from the slowly weakening Venetian Republic.[38]

It was within that villa that Ruzzante held court through his *Prima Orazione*. Whereas the villa's autonomous interior and exterior spaces suggested a route through which guests could travel and acquire multiple viewpoints of the estate, Ruzzante attempted to root himself in front of the Oration's addressee, Cardinal Marco Cornaro, the Bishop of Padua, thus stabilizing the audience and offering only one viewpoint from which to look at the world. That view of the world would reveal exactly what the wall around the villa blocked from sight: famine, hunger, and poor living conditions for Ruzzante's Paduan compatriots.

Part one of the address allowed Ruzzante to praise his native Padua, to show off his own Paduan dialect, and to offer a false sense of comfort to the honored guest. Part two of the address made Ruzzante's agenda clearer by focusing all eyes on the cardinal (in whom rested the power to make changes to the disciplinary systems governing the conduct of the working classes) and then delivering an irregular, logical argument, slightly asymmetrical but still aimed at making a point. To further rack focus, Ruzzante landed a direct and unequivocal blow: "And then I almost shit from laughing, when they said that you are a great man. But they don't see you...You're just a small man, right? You are a great small man, and not a great man."[39] As if that was not enough, Ruzzante prefaced his argument by continuing to belittle the man in purple as well as his ecclesiastical office:

> So they say you are Cardinal, and that as Cardinal you are one of those who guards the gates to Heaven, but I don't think that's right. I think those people have never seen it, Heaven, or the gates...Now, I'll tell you: Cardinal means a great rich man, that in this world can do as he likes, and when he dies (because we all die), even if you haven't been all that good, you can go straight to Heaven, and if the gate is barred, you "unhinge" it [*la scardinate*], and you enter straight by any means and everyhole.[40]

Ruzzante's addition of the prosthetic "s" before the word "cardinal" enacted a clever pun. By emphasizing the etymological similarities between cardinal and "*scardinate*" (literally, "to unhinge"), Ruzzante identified the Paduan bishop as a duplicitous gatekeeper who would use his status in the church hierarchy for his own salvation. This oration, then, was not an eclogue or a poem that would entertain the cardinal and celebrate his rise through the ranks of the church. It was, rather, a profane prayer offered up in the style of direct argumentation to a man whose purple uniform could not hide the fact that he was flesh and blood and capable, in principle, of overlooking the class distinction between himself and the man insulting him in public. This must have been Ruzzante's hope, since part three of the oration consisted of a direct request for changes in the laws of the church governing the bodies and souls of the good people of Padua. In total, there were seven requests that ranged from changing the regulations for working on holy feast days and permitting one to eat before Sunday Mass, to a demand for higher powers to castrate all philandering priests and to establish the right to take multiple spouses. Ruzzante accompanied each request with a brief rationale. For example, when lobbying for a dispensation from fasting for all peasants, Ruzzante explained that it is tiring to digest stone, inferring that peasants have resorted to eating rocks as a means for staving off hunger.[41] In the case of philandering priests, he explained that it was not entirely the priests' fault. The flesh is fragile, he suggested, so who can blame them, but the children that come of the sexual encounter become an economic burden to the cuckolded father and that weight was too much to bear.

Through his *Prima Orazione*, Ruzzante revealed the plight of the people outside the garden to the only person who could feasibly make changes capable of benefitting their lives. By rooting himself in front of the cardinal and taking up several minutes of his time, first to berate him and then to demand changes to religious law, Ruzzante developed a picture of the enforced sobriety inflicted upon the rural Paduans that he had come to represent. The image of the peasant that came into focus for the cardinal was of a malnourished laboring body whose economic means of subsistence was preempted or directly caused by the demands of the church. The effect of the image, however, was not potent enough. No changes came from the tenure of Cardinal Marco Cornaro.

Ruzzante appeared in the same room a few years later in front of Marco's brother, Francesco, who had taken his place. That time around, in the *Seconda Orazione*, Ruzzante's tone was harsher and the jokes almost completely absent. In their place appeared a concern not with the bodies of the people suffering outside in the fields, but with the affective forces of the universe. The world, for Ruzzante, was falling apart and the cause was the neglect of even the most basic of personal needs on the part of the religious authorities.

Ruzzante opened with an ambiguous statement: "For what is given by nature, well, just try to do otherwise; after all, when something must be, it seems that men and women and all the reversed world [*el roverso mondo*] get down and help make it be...[and] when something must freeze, it'll freeze in August."⁴² While Ruzzante's introductory words seemed to vouch for the power of nature to keep the world spinning, the rest of the oration offered a counterargument to that opening claim. The proof: all of life's fun has disappeared. There were no more bounties in Padua. The paucity of food had even degraded love and copulation, thus proving that nature's powers had a limit: "In conclusion, this world has become like an untended garden. Look around and see if you see any lovers. I can tell you that hunger has fucked love up the ass. Nobody dares to love anymore, since no one can handle the cost."⁴³

If the *Prima Orazione* depicted a scene of violent contradictions, the *Seconda Orazione* portended complete existential despair. The frankness of Ruzzante's speech and the lack of any story, characters, or organizing fictitious scenario set these two theatre pieces outside of the typical genres of theatrical performances of the time. If they were not plays or even theatrical monologues, what were they? By recalling the spatial palimpsest of gardens, I am tempted to call them scenographic interventions. They were political acts of taking place that began once Ruzzante infiltrated the innermost rooms of the villa and rooted himself in front of his audience and culminated in the composition of a portal through which residents of that interior could see beyond the villa's walls.

By painting such abrasive imagery with his words, Ruzzante chipped away at the wall around the compound that neatly distinguished the cultivated interior from the wild of the countryside. The resulting holes were windows that served two purposes. They created a view of the hardships experienced by peasants and they allowed for famine, pestilence, and unhappiness to enter. Much like *tromp l'oeil* paintings, Ruzzante's windows were made possible by a trick of the eye and a forced perspective. Against the wishes of his audience, who perhaps would have preferred a light comedy, Ruzzante revealed the social situation of rural Paduans and demanded that his esteemed spectators looked out beyond the walls of their charming estate. Here, Ruzzante is playing with Enzo Cocco's notion that "in order to explore the form of the garden, it is necessary to undertake a double journey—inside and outside—and to examine the dialectic tension developing at its boundaries. The 'ideal' configuration of the enclosure must take into account what is contrary to it."⁴⁴ If the two Cardinal Cornaros and the events organizers wanted to invite Ruzzante into their garden, then they would have to invite the outside—the lives of the people Ruzzante represented as a native *villano*—insideas we ll.

Fantasizing Baroque Ruzzante

By assembling the image of a Baroque Ruzzante in this essay, I do not seek to replace one historical periodization within another.[45] Rather, by fantasizing with Kurz and Leibniz, and by disciplining that fantasy with Adorno's request to interpret the unintentional through the analytic isolation of diverse historical elements, I want to propose a method for rearranging theatre historiographical practice that can answer the questions I posed in the introduction to this essay. What is the nature of the historical riddle presented by this object of inquiry? Ruzzante's riddle is: What's so funny? Adorno challenges us not to solve that riddle but to reveal "the change-causing gesture of the riddle process," which, in this case, has as much to do with us in the present as it does with what occurred in Ruzzante's garden.[46] Yes, the humor Ruzzante directed at the cardinals seems tacitly to pose the question "What's so funny?" in order to expose underlying conditions, while also revealing the answer: "Very little anymore, thanks to you." Equally as important, however, is the realization that, by asking that question of Ruzzante's theatre practice, we change the process through which we glimpse Ruzzante. We begin to think Ruzzante anew, not only as a figure in the historical trajectory of comedic form or humanoid evolution, but as an artist engaged in the act of reclaiming space through a type of sceno-gardening.[47]

Destroyed by the wars aimed at crippling Venice's power and the strict rules authorized by that same power, the Paduan countryside, Ruzzante's home, had become an unweeded garden. Beyond the hope of restoring Padua to its original state of splendor, Ruzzante's performances in the Villa Barco suggested that the "upside down" world would never again sit right-side up. In such a new worldly configuration, a comedic theatre practice became a chance to reveal, through laughter, the unfunniness of the new world, which had gradually been blocked from the sight of those people who had the power to intervene. Unintentional reality reveals itself there, in and as that which has been blocked from view.

Theatre historiographers do not inherit one Ruzzante, faithfully transmitted through fragments now stored within various archives. Rather, we produce encounters with Ruzzante through the arrangement of archival scraps that we assemble each time we attempt to interpret his historical image. Choosing to arrange his practice as an operation of taking place and as an act of sceno-gardening presents the possibility that Ruzzante's spatial maneuvers, within the private homes of his audiences, contain more truth than the words he spoke. The phrase "Baroque Ruzzante," in other words, does not denote a specific historical actor; it names the action of developing Ruzzante's spatial activity through an Adorno-inspired philosophical interpretation: "to Baroque Ruzzante."

By stepping outside the temporal boundaries of historical periodization and attempting to Baroque Ruzzante in this way, I hope to engage the historiographical complexity of this historical figure. Gardens, in the form of historically specific locations, insignias, proper names, and plays-on-words, surround and support the historical figure of Ruzzante. The polyvalent meanings of his jokes, coupled with his method of insinuating himself into the walled-off and private garden spaces of his spectators and hosts, require an equally complex interpretive approach. One finds such an approach in the historico-philosophical mode of thought named by Adorno, whose predilection for interpretation over research provides a critical model for engaging with all of Ruzzante's gardens. Once we jump over the wall and into those gardens, a world of Baroque fragments opens up and reveals new elements of Ruzzante's theatre practice, elements such as his deployment of a theatrical *tromp l-oeil* capable of (disjunctively) fusing interior private worlds of privilege with exterior scenes of desperation. Furthermore, garden-space, a name one might use to denote the historical sites of Ruzzante's performances, offers itself as a political stage buttressed by a dialectical tension between interior and exterior.

To engage a figure like Ruzzante, who dealt in double entendre and played with audiences, historiographers must also play. There may, indeed, be an ethical imperative here, one that leads back to Adorno's 1931 address, namely, that each historical object requires its own approach. The historiographer must first learn how to understand the object and then craft a method of interpretation tailored to that object. Beyond that, the possibility exists that all historical objects require historiographers to engage in the *ars inveniendi* of philosophicalthinking.

Notes

1. Thomas Postlewait, *The Cambridge Introduction to Theatre Historiography* (Cambridge; New York: Cambridge University Press, 2009), 120.
2. Ibid., 115: "At least the experimental scientist can make a direct observation of an event, thereby having an interpretive advantage over the historian, whose event is always absent."

3. Michel de Certeau, *The Writing of History*, trans. Tom Conley (New York: Columbia University Press, 1988), 4.
4. Theodor W. Adorno, *Aesthetic Theory*, trans. Robert Hullot-Kentor (Minneapolis: University of Minnesota Press, 2006), 147.
5. Ibid.,147–48.
6. , Theodor W. Adorno, "The Actuality of Philosophy," *Telos* 31 (Spring 1977): 124.
7. Ibid.,126.
8. Ibid.
9. Ibid.
10. See Benjamin, *The Arcades Project.* trans. Howard Eiland and Kevin McLaughlin, ed. Rolf Tiedemann (Cambridge, MA: Harvard University Press, 2002) 204. For more on this notion, see Michal Kobialka, "Tadeusz Kantor: Collector and Historian," *Performance Research* 12, no. 4 (Spring 2007), 78–96.
11. Adorno, "Actuality," 127.
12. Ibid.,131.
13. Cited in Marta Spranzi, *The Art of Dialectic between Dialogue and Rhetoric: The Aristotelian Tradition* (Philadelphia, PA: John Benjamins, 2011), 87.
14. Adorno, "Actuality," 131.
15. Birigt Hofstaetter, "Adorno and Performance: Thinking with the Movement of Language," *Adorno and Performance*, eds, Will Daddario and Karoline Gritzner (London: Palgrave Macmillan, 2014), 155–170.
16. I'm thinking of Baur-Heinhold and Freund.
17. In addition to Kurz and Law, whom I reference in the next couple of pages, check out Benjamin's *The Origin of German Tragic Drama*, trans. John Osborne (New York: Verso, 2003); Cozzi's *Venezia barocca: conflitti di uomini e idée nella crisi del Seicento veneziano* (Baroque Venice: conflicts of men and ideas in the crisis of seventeenth century Venice) (Venice: Cardo, 1995); Deleuze's *The Fold: Leibniz and the Baroque*, trans. Tom Conley (Minneapolis: University of Minnesota Press, 1993); and Martin's *Baroque* (Oxford: Westview Press, 1977).
18. Otto Kurz, "Barocco: storia di un concetto," *Barocco europeo e barocco veneziano*, ed. Vittore Branca (Venezia: Sansoni, 1962), 16. All translation of Kurz are my own.
19. Ibid.
20. Ibid.,17.
21. Ibid.,22.
22. Ibid.,29.
23. Gottfried Wilhelm Leibniz, *The Monadology*, trans. Robert Latta (London: Forgotten Books, 2008), 16.
24. John Law, "And If the Global Were Small and Noncoherent? Method, Complexity, and the Baroque," *Environment and Planning D: Society and Space* 22 (2004): 19.
25. Matteo Vercelloni and Virgilio Vercelloni, *The Invention of the Western Garden: The History of an Idea*, trans. David Stanton (Glasgow, Scotland: Waverly Books, 2009), 56.

26. Ruzzante, *La Moschetta*, trans. Antonio Franceschetti and Kenneth R. Bartlett (Ottawa, Canada: Dovehouse Editions Inc., 1993), 117.
27. Antonella Pietrogrande, "Giardino e luogo scenico nell'epoca di Ruzante," in *Atti del Convegno Internazionale di Studi per il 5th centenario della nascita di Angelo Beolco il Ruzante*, ed. Piermario Vescovo, *Quaderni veneti* 27–28 (Ravenna, Italy: Longo, 1998), 71–72.
28. Ibid.,42–43.
29. Vercelloni and Vercelloni, *Garden*, 23.
30. Pietrogrande, "Giardino e luogo scenico," 71–72. For details of the insignias, see Molmenti and Ludwig, *The Life and Works of Vittorio Carpaccio*, trans. Robert H. Hobart Cust (London: John Murray, Albemarle Street, W., 1907), 93–95.
31. Marin. Sanuto, *I diarii*, ed. J. J. Henry Scarisbrick, vol. 28 (London: Robert W. Scribner, 1879–1903), 264.
32. Sanuto, *Diarii*, vol. 29, 536–37.
33. Sanuto, *Diarii*, vol. 33, 9.
34. Sanuto, *Diarii*, vol. 34, 124.
35. Ruzante, *Teatro*, ed. Ludivco Zorzi (Torino [Turin]: Giulio Einaudi, 1967), 1591. All translation from this volume are my own.
36. Rob Aben and Saskia de Wit, *The Enclosed Garden: History and Development of the Hortus Conclusus and Its Reintroduction into the Present-Day Urban Landscape* (Rotterdam: 010 Publishers, ca. 2001), 87.
37. Pietrogrande, "Giardino e luogo scenico," 68–69.
38. Ibid.,69.
39. Ruzante, *Teatro*,1194.
40. Ibid.,1196.
41. This was also a clever reversal of the parable in the Bible that tells of the Devil's attempt to break Jesus's fast in the desert by trying to convince Jesus to turn stones into bread. From Ruzzante's perspective, the cardinal had turned bread into stone. For more on this, see Will Daddario and Joanne Zerdy, "When You Are What You Eat: Ruzzante and Historical Metabolism" *Food and Theatre on the World Stage*, eds. Dorothy Chansky and Ann Folino White (New York: Routledge, 2015).
42. Ruzante, *Teatro*,1208.
43. Ibid., 1210. This is my own artful translation. On the difficulty of translating Ruzzante's obscenities, see Nancy Dersofi, "Translating Ruzante's Obscenities," *Metamorphoses: A Journal of Literary Translation*, http://www.smith.edu/metamorphoses/issues/links/dersofitranslating.html.
44. Enzo Cocco, "Natura e giardino in Rousseau," *Pensare il giardino*, eds. Paola Capone, Paola Lanzara, and Massimo Venturi Ferriolo, *Kepos Quaderni* 2 (Milan: Guerini, 1992), 53.
45. An example would be an attempt to replace the "late renaissance" periodization found in the works of Linda Carroll and Ronnie Ferguson with a new Baroquepe riodization.
46. Adorno, "Actuality," 129.
47. On artistic evolution and liminoid performance qualities, see Linda Carroll, *Angelo Beolco (Il Ruzante)* (Boston: Twayne Publishers, 1990), 17 and 37.

Bibliography

Aben, Rob, and Saskia de Wit. *The Enclosed Garden: History and Development of the Hortus Conclusus and Its Reintroduction into the Present-Day Urban Landscape.* Rotterdam: 010 Publishers, c.2001.
Adorno, Theodor W. "The Actuality of Philosophy." *Telos* 31 (Spring 1977), 120–33.
———. *Aesthetic Theory.* Translated by Robert Hullot-Kentor. Minneapolis: University of Minnesota Press, 2006.
Baur-Heinhold, Margarete. *The Baroque Theatre: A Cultural History of the 17th and 18th Centuries.* New York: McGraw-Hill, 1967.
Benjamin, Walter. *The Arcades Project.* Translated by Howard Eiland and Kevin McLaughlin. Edited by Rolf Tiedemann. Cambrdige, MA: Harvard University Press, 2002.
———. *The Origin of German Tragic Drama.* Translated by John Osborne. New York: Verso, 2003.
Carroll, Linda L. *Angelo Beolco (Il Ruzante).* Boston: Twayne Publishers, 1990.
de Certeau, Michel. *The Writing of History.* Translated by Tom Conley. New York: Columbia University Press, 1988.
Cocco, Enzo. "Natura e giardino in Rousseau." In *Pensare il giardino.* Edited by Paola Capone, Paola Lanzara, and Massimo Venturi Ferriolo. *Kepos Quaderni* 2. Milan: Guerini, 1992. 53–56.
Cozzi, Gaetano. *Venezia barocca: conflitti di uomini e idée nella crisi del Seicento veneziano* (Baroque Venice: conflicts of men and ideas in the crisis of seventeenth century Venice). Venice: Cardo, 1995.
Daddario, Will, and Joanne Zerdy. "When You Are What You Eat: Ruzzante and Historical Metabolism." In *Food and Theatre on the World Stage.* Edited by Dorothy Chansky and Ann Folino White. New York: Routledge (forthcoming).
Deleuze, Gilles. *The Fold: Leibniz and the Baroque.* Translated by Tom Conley. Minneapolis: University of Minnesota Press, 1993.
Dersofi, Nancy. "Tranlating Ruzante's Obscenities." *Metamorphoses: A Journal of Literary Translation* (1996). http://www.smith.edu/metamorphoses/issues/links/dersofitranslating.html.
Ferguson, Ronnie. *The Theatre of Angelo Beolco (Ruzante): Text, Context and Performance.* Ravenna, Italy: Longo Editore Ravenna, 2000.
Freund, Philip. *Laughter and Grandeur: Theatre in the Age of Baroque.* London; Chester Springs, PA: Peter Owen, 2008.
Hofstaetter, Birigt. "Adorno and Performance: Thinking with the Movement of Language." In *Adorno and Performance.* Edited by Will Daddario and Karoline Gritzner. London: Palgrave Macmillan, 2014. 155–170.
Kobialka, Michal. "Tadeusz Kantor: Collector and Historian." *Performance Research* 12, no. 4 (Spring 2007), 78–96.
Kurz, Otto. "Barocco: storia di un concetto." In *Barocco europeo e barocco veneziano.* Edited by Vittore Branca. Venezia: Sansoni, 1962, 15–34.
Law, John. "And If the Global Were Small and Noncoherent? Method, Complexity, and the Baroque." *Environment and Plannin D: Society and Space* 22 (2004), 13–26.

Leibniz, Gottfried Wilhelm. *The Monadology*. Translated by Robert Latta. London: Forgotten Books, 2008. July 24, 2009. www.forgottenbooks.org.

Martin, John Rupert. *Baroque*. Oxford: Westview Press, 1977.

Molmenti, Pompeo, and Gustav Ludwig. *The Life and Works of Vittorio Carpaccio*. Translated by Robert H. Hobart Cust. London: John Murray, Albemarle Street, W., 1907.

Pietrogrande, Antonella. "Giardino e luogo scenico nell'epoca di Ruzante." In *Atti del Convegno Internazionale di Studi per il 5th centenario della nascita di Angelo Beolco il Ruzante*, Edited by Piermario Vescovo, *Quaderni veneti* vols. 27–28. Ravenna, Italy: Longo, 1998, 63–75.

Postlewait, Thomas. *The Cambridge Introduction to Theatre Historiography*. Cambridge; New York: Cambridge University Press, 2009.

Ruzzante, *La Moschetta*. Translated by Antonio Franceschetti and Kenneth R. Bartlett. Ottawa, Canada: Dovehouse Editions Inc., 1993.

———. *Teatro*. A cura di. Edited by Ludivco Zorzi. Turin: Giulio Einaudi, 1967

Sanuto, Marin. *I diarii*. Edited by J. J. Henry Scarisbrick. London: Robert W. Scribner, 1879–1903.

Spranzi, Marta. *The Art of Dialectic between Dialogue and Rhetoric: The Aristotelian Tradition*. Philadelphia, PA: John Benjamins, 2011.

Vercelloni, Matteo, and Virgilio Vercelloni. *The Invention of the Western Garden: The History of an Idea*. Translated by David Stanton. Glasgow, Scotland: Waverly Books, 2009.

9

A Critique of Historio-scenography: Space and Time in Joseph-François-Louis Grobert's *Del 'Exécution dramatique*

Pannill Camp

As Michel Foucault said in 1980, "A whole history remains to be written of *spaces*,"[1] and while other academic fields may be able to abide without confronting this challenge, theatre and performance are too profoundly saturated with spatial relationships to allow us to avoid engaging with space directly. Historians of theatre and performance may find this incitement particularly daunting because theatre space is an unusually complicated historical object, in part because it must be comprehended in relation to other categories of space, including the peculiar spaces theatre *represents*, and in part because time is always implicated on multiple levels in the statements historians make about theatre space. Ideas about time infiltrate historical writing as forms that inflect interpretations of the past—circular, positivistic, and chiliastic notions of time, for instance, give a particular bent to the thoughts that historians produce about a given development in the history of theatre space. Further, because theatre unfolds in practice— which is to say, it is an activity with a conspicuous duration—its own models of space are irreducibly tied to models of time. Perhaps most vexing, these aspects of theatre and performance history covertly infiltrate each other.

Histories of theatre space today encompass diverse methods and conclusions. One prevalent view sees theatre design and scenery evolving along with industrial technology, engineering, and the physical understanding of sensory perception. Standard textbooks contend that theatre design became rationalized after the science of acoustics advanced in the nineteenth century.[2] This view bends the "main line of development" of Western theatre architecture away from baroque style toward buildings and scenic practices that mastered visual and auditory perceptual dynamics.[3] Today, however, many reject this positivist narrative. A tradition of criticism originating in performance studies holds that the frontal, divided, and physically rationalized ideal of theatre space exemplified by the Bayreuth Festspielhaus is as much a result of ideology and the architectural tactics of political and economic power as it is the natural result of technological progress.[4]

Diversity of thinking about the forces that shaped modern theatre space partly results from no single model of historical space prevailing in theatre and performance studies. Recent generations of scholars have applied a variety of analytical models to theatre space, often importing thinking from theories of architecture. Semiotics, phenomenology, and Marxist/materialist thought have all shown value as critical frameworks with which to analyze the actual and potential functions of performance spaces.[5] These lines of thought comprise a versatile set of approaches to theatre space, but there has been comparatively little debate about their merits and blind spots. This can be explained, in part, by the fact that the tools theatre and performance scholars have brought to the task of examining theatre space are borrowed from other fields. Theatre and performance studies must ultimately write the history of its own spaces, and this entails both accounting for the unique properties and functions of theatre space and identifying the peculiar historiographical parallaxes to which this enterprise is susceptible.

Overview

This essay aims to identify a parallax that arises from theatre's unique status—especially during the modern era—as a generator of particular spatial comprehensions and experiences. Before explaining this function of theatre space in greater detail, critiquing a tendency in historical writing about theatre that stems from it, and proposing a way to allow future histories of theatre space to overcome its distorting effects, it is necessary to elaborate some key premises that guide my thinking. I have been influenced by Henri Lefebvre's idea of space as a social product. Lefebvre contends that although space is produced through social interaction, subject to the operations of state and capitalist power, it is capable of supporting resistance to these operations.[6]

He and other neo-Marxist thinkers reject the claim that space is an immutable, objective fact or a transcendent ideality and comprehend it, instead, as an ongoing process of transformation.[7] His account of space has also begun to make inroads in theatre historiography.[8]

I am inspired by Michal Kobialka's recent call to pursue a "spatial historiography," which exposes the contradictions in what conventional theatre histories have portrayed as coherent theatre spaces, but the *critique* that I will elaborate here is foremost meant to explain how such contradictions have come to be masked in the first place. Currents in materialist thought inform this critique. As Lefebvre explains, in Marxist thought, critique functions as "critical knowledge" with practical consequences, rather than merely as criticism.[9] The first step to escaping naive views of theatre space—such as the notions that it is reducible to theatre architecture, that it has gradually come to converge with the way that space really is, or that it is an inert and transparent medium in which theatrical events are situated— is to investigate latent tendencies in historical writing about theatre. While my project is informed by neo-Marxist thinking, historians of diverse political commitments are equally susceptible to the tendency I describe in what follows.

My argument has two components. First, I contend that theatre is a social activity that is uniquely and centrally involved in the production of particular, historically bounded, comprehensions of space. This is the case because theatre space is *synthetic* in a way that other categories of space are not. Theatre synthesizes space both by fusing different layers or components of space with each other and by integrating the practice of representing space with the practices of representing time and arranging matter, including bodies. My account of the first of these two synthesizing operations relies, to a large degree, upon Lefebvre's idea of "theatrical interplay," wherein "bodies are able to pass from a 'real', immediately experienced space (the pit, the stage) to a perceived space—a third space which is no longer either scenic or public. At once fictitious and real, this third space is classical theatrical space."[10] In other words, theatre not only brings spatial concepts, symbols, and images together, it sends objects and bodies through multiple layers of space in the presence of spectators. The components of Lefebvre's triad, to be sure, coexist in many spaces. A hospital waiting room comprises a particular representation of space, evident in the rectilinear and physical thinking of its designer. It is also a spatial practice that can be grasped in the paths that connect it to adjacent spaces and the data concerning who enters it and the physical traces they leave in it. The hospital serves as a representational space determined by the artistic, poetic, illicit, dreamt, or otherwise imaginative engagements that it happens to situate. Such spaces commonly allow the three layers of space to glide along without troubling each other, allowing the consciousness of space to recede. Theatre, by contrast, draws the diverse elements of social space into a visible and audible mangle. It forces its witnesses and practitioners to contend with space deliberately.

Theatre synthesizes space not only by forcing its layers to interact conspicuously, but also by drawing the representation of space and the representation of time into similarly overt negotiations. The unities of time and place, which rationalized each other in neoclassical debates, amounted to an attempt to understand the mutually implicating experiences of extension and duration.[11] Theatre, however, synthesizes spatial experience by means of embodied practice as well as intellectual exercise. Theatre artists fabricate spatial perceptions by manipulating machines, bodies, and other materials. They forge space itself by producing sensations of concrete things programmed by abstract conceptions of the relationships between space and time and between space and matter. Theatre's role in synthesizing space arises from the collisions it requires both between different layers of socially produced space and between space and the extraspatial elements of theatre practice that render the experience of space concrete.

I use the term "synthesis" to denote the operation through which theatre propounds specific comprehensions of time in part because theatre generates space through combinations (of distinct components of space, of space with time, of space with matter, and of concepts with perceptions). Synthesis carries additional connotations that are also appropriate to my argument: artificial or imitative. The comprehensions of space that theatre generates are indeed artificial, not in the sense of being false, but, in keeping with Alfred Sohn-Rethel's notion of the synthetic, in the sense of being man-made, abstract, and separated from nature.[12] Though theatre practice is a social machine that produces concrete sensations and spatial and temporal perceptions, these experiences are, in the modern era, determined by abstractions of time and space and, thus, are synthetic in multiple senses of the word. The next section of this essay, by examining a practical manual of theatre from 1809 that drew dogmatic conclusions from Enlightenment reforms of theatre space, illustrates how theatre produces synthetic space.

The second component of my argument concerns the implications that theatre's synthetic operations hold for theatre historiography.

Edward S. Casey's influential account of the attenuated category of "place" attributes to modern philosophy the transformation of modern space into abstract relations.[13] I reject the premise that theatre theory and practice are epiphenomena of the history of philosophy, and attend to theatre's considerable role in forging diffuse and durable spaces. Theatre practice determines and promotes specific historically contingent understandings of space and time. These ways of comprehending space generate norms of spatiotemporal experience that hold sway in extratheatrical domains, including philosophy and historiography. The norms of spatial and temporal experience that theatre helps generate are in turn adopted by historians in the form of premises about the nature of space and time.

For these reasons, theatre history is susceptible to a peculiar form of parallax: recognizing in historical artifacts familiar characterizations of the nature of space itself, theatre historians tend to write affirmative histories of certain theatre spaces. Failing to examine their own ideas about space, they regard such objects of study as progressive, correct, or as coming into line with the way space "really" is, while their histories remain unconscious of the way those artifacts of theatre space helped promulgate the spatial ideology that makes such affirmations possible. Historians who hold unexamined assumptions grounded in the abstract space that has prevailed in the modern era tend to praise theatre practices that embrace instrumental uses of mathematics and geometry, and empiricist accounts of the senses.[14] This sort of historiographical delusion is not restricted to any particular ideological posture; positivist theatre histories are no more inclined to affirm the historical developments that covertly supplied their presumptions about the nature of space than are those who see modern theatre architecture and scenography as tools of domination. I conclude this essay by arguing that it is only through a refusal to see past theatrical articulations of space as correct—that is, through the cultivation of a historiographical analogue to what Theodor Adorno called "nonidentity"—that theatre historians can guard themselves against the parallax that results from what I call historio-scenography.

Synthetic Space and Time in Grobert's *Del 'Exécution dramatique*

Modern philosophy has questioned whether space exists in itself, whether it subsists a priori in the mind (as what Kant called a form of intuition), and whether and to what extent our experience of space depends upon cultural conventions.[15] Theatre historians are not obliged to take positions on such metaphysical and ontological questions, but those who view theatre as something beyond a literary tradition must contend with the nature of space as a historical category and as an integral element of theatre practice. Some theatre historians treat space either as an immutable physical fact (a transparent medium in which scenic arts are practiced) or as a synonym for the word "stage."[16] Recently, scholars inspired by Lefebvre's contention that space is a manifold social product have begun to treat theatre space as something both abstract and concrete, and as subject to historical modification.

Lefebvre sees space as profoundly mutable over long spans of history: "'Our' space...remains qualified (and qualifying) beneath the sediments left behind by history, by accumulation, by quantification."[17] The history of social space, in other words, has witnessed macro-shifts in prevailing qualitative categories of space. Lefebvre, in conformity with some materialist thinkers and historians of philosophy, believes the prevailing spatial quality of the modern era to be abstraction. Abstract space, in this account, is a state-instituted "product of violence and war" propelled by a capitalist logic of transactional equivalences.[18] The conceptual equipment of abstract space allows dilapidated residential neighborhoods to be seen as exchangeable for new retail spaces and parking. Abstract space is putatively homogenous and void—an inert container—but it helps give rise to certain kinds of objects and relations. To dispel the apparent homogeneity of abstract space, Lefebvre identifies certain "aspects of elements" of abstract space that give it its latent morphology: Euclidean "geometric" contours; a preponderantly visual or "optical" logic; and a "phallic" quality that "symbolizes force" and emphasizes perpendicular forms.[19] Abstract space embraces the modern state's and capitalism's spatial operations, and forms the foundation for Lefebvre's analysis of contemporary spatial experience.

Marxist thinkers attribute the modern rise of abstract space to the ascendance of capitalist economic relations, which promulgated abstract thinking to serve commodity form.[20] While, in the broadest sense, capitalism may indeed lead to the production of particularly abstract spaces, it does not do so solely through what we think of as economic activity (labor, management, transportation of commodities, exchange, etc.). Cultural and aesthetic practices (admittedly, not without an economic dimension) also render space comprehensible. Because of its unique capacity to synthesize the components of socially produced space with each other and with time and matter, theatre spreads particular understandings of space, and did so to an unrivaled degree until screened representations became the most popular spatial mass medium in the twentieth century. During different epochs, moreover, the space theatre distributed underwent qualitative modifications. In the eighteenth century, for instance, theatre participated extensively in the ascendency of abstract space by fabricating perceptible spatial experiences for mass gatherings in urban centers.

Lefebvre could not have invented a figure to illustrate the theatrical synthesis of abstract space more perfectly than Jacques-François-Louis Grobert, the French artillery colonel and *homme des lettres* who wrote *De l'Exécution dramatique*. This 1809 treatise calls for the systematic reform of theatre buildings, in particular their interior stage equipment (*matériel*).[21] Born to French parents in Algiers in 1757, Grobert served in the French artillery service in the 1790s and in Napoleon's expedition to Egypt, about which he wrote a popular description of the pyramids at Giza and an opera, *La Bataille des Pyramids* (1803).[22] His analyses of theatre space are meticulously geometric and overwhelmingly visual in their focus. The "phallic" element Lebfebvre associates with abstract space appears not only in Grobert's discussion of perpendicular lighting angles on stage, but also in his 1803 military treatises, one on a machine for measuring the barrel velocity of projectiles and the other on the feasibility of invading Great Britain.[23]

Grobert's foray into theatre space was a self-conscious continuation of late-eighteenth-century reforms. As part of a sweeping movement to modernize French theatre architecture, unified perspective scenery was effectively dislodged from architectural treatises on theatre design in favor of a conception of space derived from physical optics. Grobert cites his Enlightenment predecessors, Pierre Patte, who pioneered a concept of theatre architectonics rooted in biomorphic forms, and Boullet, machinist of the Paris Opéra.[24] Despite previous architectural and theoretical mutations, however, painted perspective scenery remained widely practiced, in part because of technical inertia, but also because even the most strident eighteenth-century advocates of new design practices could not conceive of its elimination. It thus fell to Grobert to call for the systematic replacement of painted flats and the stage machinery that supported them with three-dimensional and practical stage settings. Such reform was warranted by what he called "the idea of the inseparable error of theatrical perspective."[25]

Grobert's was not the first criticism of sets painted in perspective. By the 1780s, theatre space was not only conceived of as a rectilinear space of light and sound propagation, it was increasingly perceived as a field of experimentation as well. Grobert cites Sigaud-de-Lafond's air purity experiments, which found that the atmosphere in Paris playhouses was no cleaner than the air in the "least healthy rooms in the Hôtel Dieu" hospital.[26] Grobert's conception of theatre space is the very model of abstract space in the Lefebvrian mold. Rationally and empirically transparent, theatre spaces lend themselves to geometric and visual analysis. The abstraction Grobert ascribes to theatre space, moreover, carries backward and forward in time. The playing spaces of Greece and Rome, in his view, have "no need of a geometric demonstration" to reveal their faults, which are related "to the direction of visual rays." Grobert's critique of modern perspective scenery, the first sweeping theoretical broadside against the practice, finds error creeping into spectators' vision as they find themselves separated from the ideal "*point de distance*" in three dimensions: distance, horizontal obliqueness, and elevation.[27]

Grobert's project for the reform of scenography thus requires merging the imaginative and perceptual aspects of theatre practice (scenery) with spatial abstractions. He thoroughly and precisely explicates the visual effects of chassis placement, the incidence of real and painted light, and the forms of fictional shadows. The perceptual norms Grobert defends are rooted in the conception of theatre space he inherits from his eighteenth-century predecessors: the transparent, uniform field of optical rays. In Lefebvrean terms, then, the colonel aims to synthesize the lived space of theatre with a particular conceived space. Another synthetic tendency accompanies Grobert's attempt to merge these spatial components, since, in order to render abstract space sensible, to distribute it to spectators in the form of lived experience without deforming it, theatre must represent space in concert with a corresponding conception of time.

Grobert believes that the "exact imitation of nature" fosters theatrical illusion, and this especially holds in the case of light, since "veritable illusion can only be born from the distribution of light exactly imitating that which strikes surfaces lit by the sun."[28] This belief commits him to attend rigorously to natural light, since theatre's material factors, to his mind, must be directed incessantly to fostering illusion. While light in the abstract is a momentary traversal of space, natural light is always in flux, thus, he concedes, even ideal stage lighting and stage sets in relief will fall short of the natural effect, so long as scenic lighting fails to move. Shadows, even those cast on three-dimensional scenery, will remain static, and the absurd convention "that the sun is immobile during a representation that is supposed to last twenty-four hours" will remain unchanged.[29]

Spectatorial experience, then, relies upon conformity to minute spatio-temporal correspondences. Grobert describes a production of Jean-François Le Sueur's *Ossian, ou Les Bardes*, the third act of which depicts a dream in which spirits walk through the air and in the upstage distance. To avoid the absurd effect of full-sized actors towering over miniature painted landscapes, Grobert relates, children in costume played the upstage specters, and were directed to move slowly, since, "they believed that the diminution of size and of speed would produce the illusion of distance."[30] To manipulate spatial appearances in this way, he adds, one must engage time with a cognizance of scale: "The slowness of movement should be proportionate to the distance of the eye of the spectator."[31] Theatrical space and time implicate each other, but the relationship between them is also rationally calculable, thus, actors attempting to convey distance are governed by an exact proportionality between size and speed of movement.

Grobert's project to reform scenic equipment is, like the Enlightenment theories that preceded it, self-consciously inscribed in theatre history. Grobert comprehends his theory in the context of the progressive sweep of historical theatre space; thus, the disposition of theatre buildings imposes a "primitive conception" onto modern theatre, whose "shocking" deviations from verisimilitudes amount to a scandal for human advancement.[32] Grobert credits the "progress of enlightenment" with eliminating gaudy decorations in theatre halls, but is stunned by the *insouciance* of spectators who accept deviations from the appearance of nature on the stage "in an enlightened century."[33] His consciousness of the way the art of scenery is situated in history cranes into the future as well: "will not posterity, which sooner or later corrects our mistakes, have cause to blame these errors on a century with so much right to override those that came before it?"[34]

Grobert's technical project—to reform the material conditions of stagecraft in conformity with a new prevailing representation of space—and his historical project—to inscribe such reforms in a progressive conception of time—are not driven by separate imperatives. The time that unfolds in Grobert's spatial analysis of historical change is progressive and accumulative. The future exposes and abandons the errors of the past. In its broad strokes, this temporality conforms to what Agamben has called nineteenth-century "pure chronology." It is structured by before and after, and its meaning is supplied by "the idea […] of a continuous, infinite progress."[35]

While we might initially presume that Grobert's articulation of a particular understanding of space and time reflects his passive uptake of concepts produced by philosophic or economic discourses, Grobert's theatrical activity, in fact, produces a particular historical consciousness. His "*opéra-melodrame*," *The Battle of the Pyramids*, promoted the French imperialist view of recent history. The play proceeds through a series of detailed scenic images, beginning in a Turkish salon on whose walls are written Koranic verses and ending with French invaders and Egyptians "delivered from barbarous tyranny," surrounded by genies and personifications of Hope and Abundance, in a "tableau that expresses admiration and joy."[36] The libretto describes stage sets and aspects of the pyramids in great detail, prescribes the placement and movement of lighting instruments, and calls for such details of mise-en-scène as horses and donkeys. When Grobert laments that the Porte Saint-Martin theatre could not accommodate the livestock that would have helped his spectacle attain "*l'exacte vérité*,"[37] he has identified historical accuracy as the stakes for scenographic reform.

Grobert's program for the reform of theatre space, then, synthesized a way of comprehending space by engaging with both fine grain temporal experience and broad trajectories in historical consciousness. His agenda is primarily spatial, but it is saturated with temporal thinking. In this, Grobert is an early indicator of major themes in nineteenth-century mise-en-scène, such as the use of scenery "*en relief*" and practical rather than painted scenery. The innovations often attributed to later artists—Madame Vestris, the duke of Saxe-Meinengen, David Belasco—put into practice the scenery-in-relief that Grobert called for in the first decade of the nineteenth century.

Grobert's late-Enlightenment approach to theatre architecture has propagated widely. George C. Izenour considers the nineteenth century to have produced the first "rational solution" to theatre auditorium sightlines, in the form of John Scott Russell's "Treatise on Sightlines and Seating," which carries out an algebraic analysis of visual rays.[38] Echoing Grobert's rhetoric of enlightened progress, Izenour explains the development of Western theatre design as the accumulation of increasingly refined technical knowledge, an unabashedly positivist view of the development of theatre space in the West. Deviations from this path, such as the postwar trend toward asymmetrical seating plans, are compared to "contagious diseases," destined to be eliminated.[39]

Critique of Historio-scenography

The space that emerges from the pages of *De l'Exécution dramatique*—a faintly militarized version of the visual field that architectural reformers attached to theatre near the end of the eighteenth century—corroborates Lefebvre's historical account of abstract space. It also demonstrates that such a space existed within theatre theory and practice at the onset of the nineteenth century. Even as it shores up Lefebvre in a general way, however, Grobert's treatise exposes limitations in the way that Lefebvre understands theatre, in showing that theatre space is not insulated in an aesthetic category of spatial experience, but is, instead, produced in contact with other kinds of space.

While Lefebvre claims that theatre brings multiple components of socially produced space into intimate proximity, forcing bodies and objects to simultaneously situate themselves on conceived, perceived, and lived planes, his cursory treatment of the topic misses crucial aspects of theatre's place in the broader history of modern spaces. Lefebvre not only takes insufficient account of the way theatre space interacted with its nontheatrical counterparts, his account of theatre fails to see the way that theatre functioned to *produce* space, to fabricate particular spatial experiences, and to sustain them over time. He associates the concept of mise-en-scène with socially produced space in general. "Nature's space is not staged,"[40] he says, but if theatre space in the modern era was not an insulated and exceptional case, it was also not merely one space among many. Theatre space is neither reducible to a place for display and the actualization of social order, nor to an arena of embodied political communication, nor to a rarified heterotopia, though it serves all of these functions. Theatre fabricates experiences in which space takes on specific qualities for masses of spectators.

The case can be made that theatre is a major site of spatial synthesis, combining space, time and material into overtly artificial but coherent experiences in which assumptions about the nature of space are embedded. Theatre is unique among historical spaces in that it ceaselessly engages conceptions of space as they are articulated, renders these conceptions into material, sensate representations, and submits them to perception in the context of social interactions. Theatre actualizes representations of space in a "mangle of practice," which determines, explicates, and negotiates spatial formations that elsewhere are permitted to glide by each other as if on separate strata.[41]

Theatre actively participates in the production of persuasive ways of comprehending space, rather than passively absorbing spatial concepts generated by other discourses and technologies. One indication of this process is that new debates and practices for representing time and space on stage tend to appear at the leading edge of phase shifts in the history of space. Just as the "town" became a dominant political site in the sixteenth century,[42] for example, Sebastiano Serlio applied a perspective scenic device to extend the visual contiguity of urban centers and to reinforce their status as paradigmatic *loci* of dramatic action.[43] In France, the intensive debate over classical unities—especially of time and space—which led to formal guidelines for theatrical representation, coincided both with intensive efforts to consolidate central state power and with the initial publication of Descartes's *Discourse on Method*, in which a geometric conception of space supported a mechanistic model of nature. Rather than passively absorbing and reproducing conceptions of space brought to coherence by philosophy or political theory, theatre forges enduring spatial formations out of its own resources and makes them coherent within the flux of spectators' lived experience.

While theatre's role in generating particular ways of understanding both space and its relationship to time amplifies theatre history's importance within the broad history of spaces, it also presents a particular pitfall for theatre historians, one that is evident in George Izenour's praise of the nineteenth century's "triumph of rational auditorium design."[44] Such adulation is one symptom that the historioscenographic parallax may produce, but its more pervasive effect is what I would call *affirmative* history, a kind of writing that constitutes a discrete theatre spatial practice as a coherent historical object, and constructs a developmental narrative that justifies it. The historioscenographic parallax can be seen in the way Arnold Aronson writes the history of environmental scenography, for example, as a practice that explicitly rejects the norms of theatre design that Izenour exalts. Environmental scenography, popularized in the late 1960s by Richard Schechner, undoes the frontal placement of stage action with respect to a stationary spectator and, in extreme forms, altogether eliminates the divide between spaces of performance and observation.[45] In his authoritative history of this movement, Aronson withholds his own judgment of its aesthetic and political merits, preferring to soberly describe its manifestations and situate it, with great erudition, in the long span of theatre history. There are other signs of affirmative history in Aronson's work. He shares Schechner's contempt for the proscenium, which in later work he has called "without doubt, the most awkward and irrational stage space ever conceived," and sees environmental theatre as opposed to the spatial protocols of the Wagnerian proscenium model.[46] In environmental theatre, he writes, "confrontation is replaced by integration."[47]

Aronson's aesthetic and intellectual positions regarding the proscenium tradition could not be more diametrically opposed to those of Izenour, but, in a way analogous to Izenour's exaltation of optical rationalism, the affirmative tones in Aronson's work reflect the absorbtion of conceptions of space and time that were synthesized and promulgated by the environmental tradition itself. This tendency pervades many histories of theatre space. If theatre produces conceptions of space, renders them comprehensible, and helps them propagate beyond the narrowly defined situation of theatrical performance, it follows that the premises of theatre historiography are partly produced by the object onto which they are later foisted, in the guise of naturalized categories. Insofar as historio-scenography pervades histories of theatre architecture, it explains not only affirmative histories of particular traditions, but also the blindness of many historians to historical theatre and performance spaces with qualities that deviate from the historians' assumptions about the nature of space itself. These assumptions explain the contempt historians have displayed for tennis court or *jeux-de-paume* theatre spaces, for instance, spaces that provided vital infrastructural support to French actors in the sixteenth through eighteenth centuries, only to be dismissed as barbaric by Enlightenment reformers.

Positivist theatre historiography grants unity to a theatre that synthesizes abstract space and progressive time, and inscribes it in a robust narrative, but all ideological postures are susceptible to similar inscription practices. In the remainder of this essay, I would like to propose a way that theatre historians might nullify its pervasive and subtly distorting effects by taking an evasive route suggested by Adorno's response to speculative identity in Hegel.[48] Hegel, in an effort to resolve what he saw as gulfs in Kant's attempt to construct an account of the relationship between objects and human knowledge of them, abandoned the application of logic to discrete sense experiences and pursued, instead, dialectical reasoning that concerned reality as a totality. In discussing totalizing speculative identity, Hegel wrote that everything depended upon the identity of identity and nonidentity. Adorno, writing after the ravages of the mid-twentieth century, concluded that Hegel's speculative identity amounted to an unacceptable violence against difference. "Identity," he writes, in *Negative Dialectics*, "is the primal form of ideology."[49] Adorno attempts to invert Hegelian dialectics, embracing the nonidentity of subject and object. In the terms of Adorno's critique, theatre historiography should embrace nonidentity in historical cognition by discovering diversity and contradictions in the space and time of its objects.

Such a move can be readily applied to Grobert, whose program for the theatre includes a single-minded quest to free it of error and absurd appearances, two of its greatest resources. Grobert adopts a rigid framework of first principles: the best theatre (stage) is that which produces the "greatest possible illusion" by the simplest means, and the best house is the one where spectators enjoy this illusion most completely and comfortably.[50] Grobert's fidelity to illusion is unrestrained and unexamined. Not only is it the central organizing aesthetic concept of his treatise, it is "the only goal of theatrical art."[51] His discussions of stage scenery make clear that illusion, which he never defines outright, is a delicate phenomenon generated by faithful imitations of nature. Improbable shadows, inaccurate ethnic costuming, and absurdities such as actors appearing to enter through solid walls all present a pervasive threat to faithful imitation, yet, he concedes, theatre unavoidably traffics in absurdity. Shadows remain immobile while whole revolutions of the planet are represented, and characters of far-flung origin converse with each other in French.

Grobert maneuvers himself into admitting the failure of his effort to minimize deviations from the appearance of nature on stage in part because he miscomprehends the organizing purpose of his program. While he weighs in on many aspects of theatre practice, his energy is devoted foremost to a polemic against "the infinite errors that are inseparable from perspective painting."[52] He foremost addresses a rift in representations of space that still tortured French theatre at the end of the eighteenth century, but, rather than campaigning for a unified and uniform spatial field on stage, he frames an antagonistic relationship between two terms, illusion and error, that is divided against itself. Grobert implies that illusion is just the effect produced by a meticulous copy of natural appearances and that error refers to any unforced deviation from an ideal copy.

This premise might be sustainable if Grobert did not indulge in an understanding of illusion that included error as a predicate. As Marian Hobson observes, the eighteenth century saw a shift in the meaning of artistic illusion, from a sense of dissimulation and disclosure—for which the illusory object was understood to hide its own nature and simultaneously point to something beyond itself—to a sense of adequate simulation and seeming—for which the object corresponds to something not really there. Art objects before this shift were understood to be both true and false, and thus false, in the terms of mature eighteenth-century aesthetics.[53] Grobert clearly adheres to the Platonic notion of illusion. He seeks appearances that correspond or accord (*s'accorder*) with natural effects, thus his program is committed to eradicating minor errors in the interest of a larger error. This paradox allows—or forces—Grobert, to militate against the infinite and "inseparable" error of theatrical perspective, while excusing perspective painting for those near the front of the stage, from whom errors "are almost hidden."[54]

The central contradiction in Grobert's project is announced in the epigram to *De l'Exécution dramatique*. Marcilio Ficino's prefatory synopsis to his translation of Plato's *Republic* provides the thought: "Socrates was accustomed to saying that science should accuse error, rather than teaching truth."[55] This injunction leads Grobert to assiduously expose the ways that theatre space and light deviate from the play of solar rays, and prompts him to reduce his critique to the ineradicable corruption of an artistic practice (perspective painting). It is a timeless lesson for theatre historiographers so concerned with the sun of truth that they cannot see the deviations of light that make visibilitypos sible.

Notes

1. Michel Foucault, "The Eye of Power: A Conversation with Jean-Pierre Barou and Michelle Perrot," *Power/Knowledge: Selected Interviews and Other Writings 1972–1977* (New York: Pantheon, 1980), 149; emphasis in the original.
2. George C. Izenour, for example, sees the triumph of a rational approach to theatre design, which followed the discovery of timeless physical principles, their relationship to the physiology of human perception, and advances in engineering. See Izenour's *Theatre Design*, 2nd ed. (New Haven and London: Yale University Press, 1977), 2–8, 131–61.
3. Oscar Brockett, *History of the Theatre*, 9th ed. (New York: Allyn and Bacon, 2003),171.
4. See, for instance, Richard Schechner, *Performance Theory* (London: Routledge, 1988),161–64.
5. Key studies in this area include Marvin Carlson, *Places of Performance* (Ithaca, NY: Cornell University Press, 1989); David Wiles, *A Short History of Western Performance Space* (Cambridge, UK: Cambridge University Press, 2003). See also Bert O. States, *Great Reckonings in Little Rooms: On the Phenomenology of Theater* (Berkeley: University of California Press, 1985), 25–29.
6. Henri Lefebvre, *The Production of Space*, trans. Donald Nicholson-Smith (Oxford, UK, and Malden, MA: Blackwell, 1991), 4, 11, 370–83.
7. See, for example, David Harvey, *The Urban Experience* (Baltimore, MD: The Johns Hopkins University Press, 1989); and Edward Soja, *Thirdspace: Journeys to Los Angeles and Other Real-and-Imagined Places* (Oxford, UK, and Cambridge, MA: Blackwell, 1996).

8. David Wiles invokes Lefebvre in his study of performance space, and Michal Kobialka observes that Lefebvre's notion that space is produced on distinct but interacting levels (conceived, perceived, and lived). See Michal Kobialka, "Historiography," *Journal of Dramatic Theory and Criticism* (Spring 2004): 119–22, and Wiles, *A Short History*, 9–13.
9. Henri Lefebvre, *The Critique of Everyday Life Vol. 1*, trans. John Moore (New York: Verso, 1991), 148.
10. Lefebvre, *Production*, 188.
11. Marvin Carlson, *Theories of the Theatre: A Historical and Critical Survey, from the Greeks to the Present*, exp. ed. (Ithaca, NY: Cornell University Press, 1993),92.
12. Alfred Sohn-Rethel, *Intellectual and Manual Labor: A Critique of Epistemology*, trans. Martin Sohn-Rethel (London: Macmillan, 1978), 56–57.
13. Edward S. Casey, *The Fate of Place: A Philosophical History* (Berkeley and Los Angeles: University of California Press, 1997), 130–93.
14. See, for instance, Izenour, *Theatre Design*, 2–8, 131–61.
15. See Michael Friedman, *Kant's Construction of Nature: A Reading of the Metaphysical Foundations of Natural Science* (Cambridge: Cambridge University Press, 2013), 11–17.
16. See, for instance, Thomas Postlewait, *The Cambridge Introduction to Theatre Historiography* (Cambridge: Cambridge University Press, 2009), 17.
17. Lefebvre, *Production*, 230.
18. Ibid.,285.
19. Ibid.,268 , 285–91.
20. See, for example, Sohn-Rethel's discussion of abstract time and space. *Intellectual and Manual Labor*, 48–49.
21. Jacques-François-Louis Grobert, *De l'Exécution dramatique, considérée dans ses rapports avec le matériel de la salle et de la scène* (Paris: Schoell, 1809).
22. Jacques-François-Louis Grobert, *Description des pyramides de Ghizé, de la ville du Kaire, et ses environs* (Paris: Rémont, 1801).
23. Military and theatre space overlapped in Grobert's career. Grobert fixes the conventional placement of light sources in perspective scenery and the maximum angle for artillery fire at the same 45-degree angle, "the eighth part of a circle." See Jacques-François-Louis Grobert, *Machine pour mesurer la vîtess initale des mobiles de différens calibres* (Paris: Bailleul, 1803); and *Observations sue le Mémoire du général Lloyd* (Paris: Pougens: Magimel, 1803).
24. Grobert, *De l'Exécution dramatique*, xvii—xix. See Pierre Patte, *Essai sur l'architecture théâtrale, ou de l'ordonnance la plus avantageuse à une Salle de Spectacles, relativement aux principes de l'Optique & de l'Acoustique* (Paris: Chez Moutard, 1782); Boullet, *Essai sur l'art de construire les théâtres, leurs machines et leurs mouvemens* (Paris: chez Ballard, 1801).
25. Grobert,122, 123n.
26. Ibid.,8.
27. Ibid.,46, 110–11.
28. Ibid.,88.
29. Ibid., 124. See also 114–15, 119.

30. Ibid.,99–100.
31. Ibid.,100.
32. Ibid.,88–89.
33. Ibid.,5, 270.
34. Ibid.,129–30.
35. Giorgio Agamben, "Time and History: Critique of the Instant and the Continuum," *Infancy and History: The Destruction of Experience*, trans. Liz Heron (New York and London: Verso, 1993), 97.
36. Jacques-Francois-Louis Grobert, *La Bataille des Pyramides* (Paris: Barba, 1803), 43, 47.
37. Ibid.,14.
38. Izenour, *Theater Design*, 1–6, 71, 597–99.
39. Ibid.,28.
40. Lefebvre, *Production*, 70.
41. Andrew Pickering, *The Mangle of Practice: Time, Agency, & Science* (Chicago: University of Chicago Press, 1995).
42. Lefebvre, *Production*, 268–69.
43. Sebastiano Serlio, *On Architecture*, vol. 1, trans. Vaughan Hart and Peter Hicks (New Haven: Yale University Press, 2005), 82–88.
44. Izenour, *Theater Design*, 75–76.
45. Arnold Aronson, *The History and Theory of Environmental Scenography* (Ann Arbor: UMI Research Press, 1981), 1–2, 13.
46. Arnold Aronson, *Looking into the Abyss: Essays on Scenography* (Ann Arbor: University of Michigan Press, 2005), 38, 49.
47. Ibid.,99.
48. Theodor W. Adorno, *Negative Dialectics* (New York and London: Continuum, 1973),135–61.
49. Ibid.,148.
50. Grobert, *Del'E xécution dramatique*, 14.
51. Ibid.,200.
52. Ibid.,271.
53. Marian Hobson, *The Object of Art: The Theory of Illusion in Eighteenth-Century France* (Cambridge, UK, and New York: Cambridge University Press, 1982),14–17.
54. Grobert, *Del'E xécution dramatique*, 141.
55. "*Socrate avoit coutume de dire que la science doit s'occuper plutôt d'accuser l'erreur, que, d'enseigner la vérité.*" I thank Roshan Abraham for his help locating the source of this epigram.

Bibliography

Adorno, Theodor W. *Negative Dialectics*. New York and London: Continuum, 1973.

Agamben, Giorgio. *Infancy and History: The Destruction of Experience*. Translated by Liz Heron. New York and London: Verso, 1993.

Aronson, Arnold. *The History and Theory of Environmental Scenography*. Ann Arbor: UMI Research Press, 1981.
———. *Looking into the Abyss: Essays on Scenography*. Ann Arbor: University of Michigan Press, 2005.
Boullet. M. *Essai sur l'art de construire les théâtres, leurs machines et leurs mouvemens*. Paris: chez Ballard, 1801.
Brockett, Oscar, and Franklin J. Hildy. *History of the Theatre*, 9th ed. New York: Allyn and Bacon, 2003.
Carlson, Marvin. *Places of Performance*. Ithaca: Cornell University Press, 1989.
———. *Theories of the Theatre: A Historical and Critical Survey, from the Greeks to the Present*, Expanded Ed. Ithaca, NY: Cornell University Press, 1993.
Casey, Edward S. *The Fate of Place: A Philosophical History*. Berkeley and Los Angeles: University of California Press, 1997.
Foucault, Michel. "The Eye of Power: A Conversation with Jean-Pierre Barou and Michelle Perrot." *Power/Knowledge: Selected Interviews and Other Writings 1972–1977*. New York: Pantheon, 1980, 146–65.
———. "Of Other Spaces." *Diacritics* 16, no. 1 (Spring 1986), 22–27.
Frantz, Pierre. *L'Esthétique du tableau dans le théâtre du xviiie siècle*. Paris: Presses Universitaires de France, 1998.
Friedman, Michael. *Kant's Construction of Nature: A Reading of the Metaphysical Foundations of Natural Science*. Cambridge: Cambridge University Press, 2013.
Grobert, Jacques-François-Louis. *De l'Exécution dramatique, considérée dans ses rapports avec le matériel de la salle et de la scène*. Paris: Schoell, 1809.
———. *Description des pyramides de Ghizé, de la ville du Kaire, et ses environs*. Paris: R émont, 1801.
———. *Machine pour mesurer la vîtess initale des mobiles de différens calibres*. Paris: Bailleul, 1803.
———. *Observations sur le Mémoire du général Lloyd*. Paris: Pougens: Magimel, 1803.
Harvey, David. *The Urban Experience*. Baltimore, MD: The Johns Hopkins University Press, 1989.
Hobson, Marian. *The Object of Art: The Theory of Illusion in Eighteenth-Century France*. Cambridge, UK: Cambridge University Press, 1982.
Izenour, George C. *Theatre Design*, 2nd ed. New Haven and London: Yale University Press, 1977.
Knowles, Ric. *Reading the Material Theatre*. Cambridge, UK: Cambridge University Press, 2004.
Lefebvre, Henri. *The Critique of Everyday Life Vol. 1*. Translated by John Moore. New York: Verso, 1991.
———. *The Production of Space*. Translated by Donald Nicholson-Smith. Oxford, UK, and Malden, MA: Blackwell, 1991.
Patte, Pierre. *Essai sur l'architecture théâtrale, ou de l'ordonnance la plus avantageuse à une Salle de Spectacles, relativement aux principes de l'Optique & de l'Acoustique*. Paris: Chez Moutard, 1782.
Pickering, Andrew. *The Mangle of Practice: Time, Agency, & Science*. Chicago: University of Chicago Press, 1995.

Postlewait, Thomas. *The Cambridge Introduction to Theatre Historiography*. Cambridge: Cambridge University Press, 2009.
Schechner, Richard. *Performance Theory*. London: Routledge, 1988.
Schivelbusch, Wolfgang. *Disenchanted Night: The Industrialization of Light in the Nineteenth Century*. Berkeley: University of California Press, 1988.
Sohn-Rethel, Alfred. *Intellectual and Manual Labor: A Critique of Epistemology*. Translated by Martin Sohn-Rethel. London: Macmillan, 1978.
Soja, Edward. *Thirdspace: Journeys to Los Angeles and Other Real-and-Imagined Places*. Oxford, UK, and Cambridge, MA: Blackwell, 1996.
States, Bert O. *Great Reckonings in Little Rooms: On the Phenomenology of Theater*. Berkeley: University of California Press, 1985.
Wiles, David. *A Short History of Western Performance Space*. Cambridge, UK: Cambridge University Press, 2003.

10

The Ground of (Im)Potential: Historiography and the Earthquake

Gwyneth Shanks

Form ygr andparents

Prologue

 Growing up, I would pull the binder off the bookcase in our living room. I spent hours flipping through the pages, skipping quickly through those listing obscure family members' birth and death dates. I rarely read the family stories either, but instead searched for the photos. All black and white, they show severe, stoic faces, bodies carefully still and poised. The people stand or sit in the photos, bodies seemingly inflated with a held breath, the intensity of their gaze the work of holding a breath in, fighting not to exhale, ensuring an absolute stillness. Instead, I exhale, my face close to the page, finishing their long held, frozen breaths. My father's mother created the thick black binder of family history for my sister and me. She died before I was born, when my older sister was still a toddler. Knowing she was dying, she spent the last years of her life documenting and compiling the family history. Only as I have gotten older have I gone back, returned to those oft-skippedpage s.[1]

 The binder begins with a letter to my older sister. "Dear Hannah," she writes, "and any who may follow her." I am the "any who may follow," the unknown, yet imagined child. She continues with an apology of sorts: "The [binder] isn't very well organized. I kept thinking of tales to tell after pages were completed, and in places I find I have repeated myself." At the bottom of the page, she adds a *postscriptum*. The ink is darker, as though newer; she writes, "I wrote the above as an introduction to the history almost two years ago. Since that time the book has grown enormously and much of it has been rewritten." The binder, as I reread these words, seems heavy with time, and not simply the past times of long dead family members, but also the time of my grandmother's labor. Yet, in a certain sense, my grandmother's labor fails in its recounting, fails to produce, with the thick black binder, a "proper" archive of our family history. A proper chronology of our family's history is replaced with a backtracking sort of history. Addendums to stories appear regularly. The binder jumps between my father's mother's side of the family and his father's side, backtracking tens of decades to begin a new history. The binder performs a sort of unsettledness, a twisting narrative of retraces, back steps, and add-ons. The different times shift against each other—of generations and decades past, of my grandmother's various pasts as she wrote and rewrote the binder over two years' time—each page a thin tectonic plate, pushing up against its following page. As I turn the page, a new story, a new decade emerges—children grow ten years, parents die, my grandmother's voice in the present of the 1980s reasserts itself. The pressure of history pushes up against each page, the pressure building until there is a shift, a quake, and a new story emerges. In those shifts, those mini quakes, stories, memories are lost, left blank, fall away, in the shaking ground of (re)constructed histories.

Stories fill the binder. There is the story of my great-great grandmother Christine taking the train across the country from St. Paul to San Francisco, and of my great-great grandfather Olaf mining for gold in the Yukon. Emerging as a manifestation of the earthquake-like unsettledness I read onto the binder is the story of Christine, Olaf, and their young daughter Ruth surviving the 1906 San Francisco earthquake, only a page of the binder; yet the earthquake, the fact that my father's family lived through it, has become an important part of the family archive. The story is one of those moments in which a rupture, a defining instant of American, of West Coast history becomes our particular history. My great-great grandfather was a cabinetmaker, and, so, the story of the earthquake is also a story of a family's economic security, born out of the destroyed city. It is a story that epitomizes an American mythos: we were there, the story whispers, there when this event that came to define the modern city of San Francisco occurred; we were there to feel the earth shake, to look down from our house on the hill and see the city crumbled and destroyed; we were there to see the fire turn the sky a glowing red; and we were there to survive, to look back on 1906 from now.

* * *

This is an essay about earthquakes, unsettled earth, and the tumbled worlds left in the wake of shaking ground. Caught always in the inhale between two quakes, the relationship between those who live on active fault lines and earthquakes is similar to scholar Sandra Richards's description of one's relationship to memory. Memory, she writes, "operates through the conflation of chronological time. [...] No matter how much we strive for a full recuperation of a past event [...] the meanings we make are determined by our location in the present."[2] One returns to memories of past quakes, memories determined by their location in the present, and, yet, to recall the memory of a quake is also to jump forward into an imagined future in which the next quake—perhaps the next "big one"—will come. A historiography read onto and within an earthquake is one that, like awaiting the next "big one," disrupts notions of chronological time and replaces them with an anticipatory logic of time that exists at the threshold of philosopher Giorgio Agamben's notion of (im)potentiality.[3] Im-potential, for Agamben, is the ability to do nothing, to become nothing, existing instead in a state of suspended inaction, much like the suspended stasis of still tectonic plates.[4] To assert im-potential is necessary to the assertion of potentiality—that the earth actually will shake. Within Agamben's theorization, im-potential, potential, and actuality become inextricably linked: potential necessarily requires im-potential to exist as a distinct effective mode, differentiated from actuality. Will the still, im-potential of the earth persist, or will the ground, with a jolt, tumble the parameters of a knowable world? Historiography-as-earthquake disrupts a notion of historical fixity. It grapples with a mode of reality-making that plays between times, between the space of potential and (im)potential, the still ground and the shaking earth. Historiography-as-earthquake is not only of the past, but is prescient about and beyond the now. It is a mode of thinking in which fixity is eschewed for the ever shifting—or about to shift—ground of the quake. Such a theorization is predicated upon the material conditions and environment of and after an earthquake. It is through the shaking of the earth, the shock waves rippling through the layers of crust, mantle, and ground soil, that one feels and knows the earthquake, and it is through the effects of the earthquake on the material environment that one verifies the existence of the quake.

In constructing a theory of historiography-as-earthquake, this essay turns first to a theorization of what time means in relationship to the quake. The first half of this essay reads the historiographic earthquake, predicated upon the instability of memory, alongside Agamben's notions of potential and its constituting other, im-potential. The second half of this essay turns from time to an exploration of matter in relationship to the quake. How does history-making affect the matter, the materiality of a space? How is the material environment of a place affected by an ever shifting, or about to shift, historiography? The word "matter" does not simply imply materiality; it also implies the phrase, "it matters." Within this dual meaning of the word, this essay seeks the link between the inherent material grounding of the earthquake and the *why* of its import, the why of the "historiographic quake." I ground this essay—for all that the ground is the liquefied, shaking ground of the earthquake—in the 1906 San Francisco quake and the resulting fire that swept the city. My great-great grandparents and great-grandmother survived the quake, and their stories spanned the twentieth century, reaching forward four generations to me.

In the late 1880s, Olaf Bengtson, my great-great grandfather, immigrated from Göteborg, Sweden, to the growing city of San Francisco, its population continually bolstered by the discovery of gold in 1849. My grandmother writes that he had a sister and brother in the city, and, perhaps, his siblings drew him to the States as a young man. (No other mention is made of these siblings in the binder.) Christine Dahlman, my great-great grandmother, emigrated from Östersund, Sweden, in the 1880s to St. Paul, Minnesota, before saving enough money to travel overland to Los Angeles, and then, by ship, up the coast of California to San Francisco. Both her journey across the Atlantic and then across a continent are forgotten stories, my grandmother explains: "She came by herself and we never knew what drew her to San Francisco. She didn't even remember why it was always her goal." The draw of the mythic city overwhelms the need for narrative details, for memories, and, thus, the journey and the goal are lost to history and only the result—coming to San Francisco—is remembered. In San Francisco, my great-great grandmother found employment as a "second girl," or maid, in the home of Mayor Edward Pond, who ran unsuccessfully for governor in 1890. How Olaf and Christine meet is not explained in the binder, but they married in 1892, and their only child, Ruth, was born almost exactly nine months later in 1893.

Olaf turned 50 exactly a week before April 18, 1906, the date of the great San Francisco earthquake. Christine was 46 and Ruth was two months past her thirteenth birthday. The earthquake struck at 5:12 in the morning.[5] The first tremor lasted approximately 40 seconds, and, then, for 10 seconds, there was nothing but silence and stillness. The second tremor lasted about 30 seconds and was stronger.[6] Later estimates calculate that the earthquake was a 7.9 on the yet-to-be-invented Richter scale. The pressure building up between the North American Plate and the Pacific Plate reached a critical point that April 18 and released, causing the two plates to lurch past each other by about 15 feet. The epicenter of the earthquake was offshore, a few miles south of where the Golden Gate Bridge now crosses the bay, and the quake itself affected communities along two hundred miles off the California coast, from Fort Bragg in the north to San Juan Bautista in the south. In San Francisco, witnesses reported seeing the ground undulate in waves of two–three feet. The quake tore up city streets as thought they had been ripped apart by some giant hand, and twisted streetcar cables and rails. Five hundred tombstones toppled over in the city's graveyards, all the marble slabs lying toward the east, the exactness of the destruction seeming to point toward some sign, the translation of which could not be known.

The earthquake toppled telephone and telegraph lines, though one telegram managed to make its way out, alerting the rest of the world to the city's destruction. The earthquake broke the water mains leading into the city and fires spread, as residents, unaware that the earthquake had broken their chimneys, lit their fireplaces and kitchen stoves. Gas escaping from ruptured gas lines also caught fire, and the city was soon engulfed in three large, fast spreading fires, which the fire department, unable to pump water, was hard pressed to contain. The fire burned itself out after three days, when easterly winds, which had fanned the blazes, shifted to the west and rain begin to fall.

The earthquake and resulting fire in San Francisco is still considered one of the worst disasters in the history of the United States. The original, official death toll was 500, a number considered inaccurate at the time, indeed, current estimates calculate that 3,000 people perished.[7] A quarter of a million people, some two-thirds of the city's residents, lost their homes. Huge tent cities sprang up, in the earthquake's aftermath, the largest of which was in Golden Gate Park. The Park, designed to give the city's urban residents a chance to enjoy the 'wild, untamed natural world' within the safe limits of the city, served as a home base for those left homeless, a surreal and ironic appropriation of the space. Twenty-eight thousand buildings were destroyed by the earthquake and fire, at an estimated loss of close to $500 million, the total United States federal budget for 1906.[8] The destruction that the earthquake wrought, however, did not end when the fires burned out: 15,000 horses died from exhaustion hauling rubble out of the city.[9] The wholesale destruction of San Francisco "created [an] international aftershock that contributed to [the] panic of 1907 and a 40% drop in US industrial output."[10]

The brief page about my great-great grandparents' and great grandmother's experiences in the binder replaces the effect the earthquake had on people with a sort of documenting of matter, of the material world of things. Things, such as houses, survived, or did not, china was broken, furniture moved. Olaf, Christine, and Ruth lived on Roosevelt Way. In 1906, their house was on the outskirts of San Francisco, overlooking the city. My grandmother writes,

> From their house on the hill they could watch the fire as it spread. As it continued to burn out of control, they realized that if it once jumped Dolores Street and got to the Swedish Lutheran Church there was nothing to stop it from burning right up 16th Street to them. It was then that they took the silver and other valuables and buried them, well hidden, in the back yard.

The entry ends on a rosy note, as my grandmother writes that Olaf "had plenty of work in the rebuilding of the city and everyone helped everyone else." Reading through various accounts of the earthquake and fire, my grandmother's rosy historical optimism does not seem out of place. A number of political and business interests quickly and strategically recast the catastrophic events of April 18 and the devastating photographic and film footage of rubble and fires not as an apocalypse for the modern era, but, rather, as a chance for the city to rebuild itself in its own self-styled image: the bright, white city on the hill, a symbol of manifest destiny for the twentieth century.

Pulsations:(Im)PotentialM emories

Joan Didion describes her relationship to earthquakes in her book *The Year of Magical Thinking*:

> After [...] failing to find meaning in the more commonly recommended venues I learned that I could find it in geology. [...] This [...] enabled me to find meaning in the Episcopal litany [...] *as it was in the beginning, is now and ever shall be, world without end*, which I interpreted

as a literal description of the constant changing of the earth. [...] I found earthquakes, even when I was in them, deeply satisfying, abruptly revealed evidence of the scheme in action.[11]

Her words capture the power of the earthquake, a power that, with a jolt, with a shake, recalls the Earth's molten core, its shifting plates, bumping up against one another, and reminds us that nothing, not even solid ground is settled.

"*As it was in the beginning, is now and ever shall be, world without end*" is a phrase that collapses chronological time, elongating a notion of past and present into a never-ending continuum. It is a litany that replicates the collapsed space between potential and im-potential that Agamben theorizes. It is a logic of time, of memory making, in which a body is forever poised in anticipation, searching for the firm footing of a certain future. It is a logic of waiting for the end, which, in the end, never comes but persists as a *world without end*. Agamben writes, "What do I mean when I say: 'I can, I cannot'?" It is a question invested in the limits of the possible, in the ability to obliterate a boundary separating the words can and cannot.[12] Im-potential is the "possibility of privation," the ability to do nothing, to become nothing, existing, instead, in a state of suspended inaction. Potentiality and im-potentiality entwine each other, like a Möbius Strip in which the two are merely the same edge of a single-sided surface. The turn to potential actualized, in relation to the stasis of the un-shaking earth, is a turn to the future, to the imagined moment, prescient in the knowledge of past earthquakes, when the next "big one" will come.

The static earth bears the memory of past quakes, a memory that promises that the earth will shake again. Didion writes of the days following numerous smaller quakes in southern California, "At odd moments during the next few days people would suddenly clutch at tables, or walls. 'Is it going,' they would say, or 'I think it's moving.' They almost always said 'it', and what they meant by 'it' was not just the ground but the world as they knew it."[13] The potentiality of the historiographic earthquake, thus, is the potentiality of imagination—the potency of waiting for the unknown. It is in this space, in which the im-potential of the still earth perpetually gives itself to itself via the anticipatory imagining of an unknown quake yet-to-come, that time ceases to function as a forward vector. The earthquake meshes times, forcing an understanding of historiography that can never simply be of the past, but must, instead, grapple with its positionality within the present, the now, and the future. The now, as it shifts between im-potential and potential, past and future, is destabilized, poised as if on the brink of an earthquake.

Jack London and his wife Charmian lived 40 miles from San Francisco in 1906. In the days following the earthquake, the two walked the streets of the destroyed, burning city. London's experience touring the ruins was published in *Collier's Weekly* magazine. "Not in history," his article begins, "has a modern imperial city been so completely destroyed. San Francisco is gone."[14] Numerous photos survive to document the destroyed city, hinting at the destruction Charmian and Jack must have encountered. Photos of the city, taken from atop one of the city's numerous hills, show a sky gray with hazy smoke. People fill the photos. Silhouetted against the burning city, the bystanders are reduced to dramatic, black outlines. Huge crowds clog the streets, watching the city burn just blocks away from where they gather in the photos. The people in the photos all seem calm; there is no blurring caused by running crowds. Rather, people in the photos stand around, as though observing a particularly interesting sporting event, the stillness of the frozen images exacerbating the eerie quality of calm they convey.[15]

"Nothing remains of [the city]," London writes, "but memories and a fringe of dwelling-houses on its outskirts."[16] The undestroyed houses on the fringes of the city, of which my great-great grandparents' home was one, gestured toward the future, toward lives still allowed to continue, the walls of those still-standing homes tense with the potential to accumulate memories. To examine the historiographical earthquake alongside a notion of im-potentiality is to be always already engaging a notion of actuality that exists at the margins of the possible and that which is becoming possible. It is an actuality that, like memory, is pregnant with the potential to change and shift. French theorist Pierre Nora writes, "Memory is life, borne by living societies founded in its name. It remains in permanent evolution, open to the dialectic of remembering and forgetting, unconscious of its successive deformations, vulnerable to manipulation and appropriation, susceptible to being long dormant and periodically revived."[17] The promise, the seduction of memory is the promise (or fear) of reliving, of conjuring a past, yet, to call upon a memory is not to enter the past, but rather to enter a present *pastness*. It is a false gift, in that a memory is only the trace of a past experience that lives in the present from the moment one calls it to memory.

Only in the stasis of im-potential will the earth remain solid, memories—un-recalled—remain fixed, history remain clear, and time remain progressive. The tectonic plates, however, are never still, but continually building in pressure, awaiting the moment when they will jolt past each other, awaiting the moment when the stasis of a forgotten memory is recalled and, with the jolt of recollection, becomes something new. The act of remembrance shifts, awaiting the act of gathering the recollections that will form the narrative of a past, of a history. The anticipatory logic of the quake fuses times, forcing an understanding of historiography that can never be clean. Historiography is never of the past, but shifts between past, present, and future, scrambling temporalities, scrambling clarity. As Nora articulates it, memory, like the anticipatory logic of the quake, is never clear, but, rather, "remains in permanent evolution [and is] open to [...] remembering and forgetting, [...] vulnerable to manipulation and appropriation."[18] Within the anticipatory logic of the quake, something called historical truth or ethics disentangles itself, and historiography—and the memories upon which it is predicated—becomes more and more distant from the actual event or experience.

The narratives created in the aftermath of the San Francisco earthquake and fire recast the destruction of the city in various politically and economically charged ways.[19] In her entry on the San Francisco earthquake for *A New Literary History of America*, Kathleen Moran describes Maynard Dixon's cover illustration of the city for the May 1906 edition of *Sunset Magazine*. At the bottom of the illustration, clouds of black smoke issue up from the burning city to engulf the rest of the black-and-white drawing. Emerging out of this conflagration is a beautiful woman whose naked torso fills almost the whole cover. Her hair swirls in the smoke cloud and her hands are propped on the roofs of the burning city, as though she has just recently hoisted herself out of the wreckage. The image is one of rebirth, the secular phoenix rising from the ashes of destruction, a reading that the text across the illustration supports: "New San Francisco," the cover proclaims. The image is not simply an illustrated promise that the city would survive the disaster and rebuild, but also that the earthquake and fire were, in some way, the best thing that could have happened to San Francisco. Only in its wholesale destruction, the illustration implies, could the modern city emerge.[20]

Dixon's vision of San Francisco fit within the larger official narrative of the city's destruction, disseminated by city and state governments and by prominent businessmen. The damage and devastation wrought by the disaster were downplayed. The death toll was officially underestimated, indeed, a book released by the city in 1907, entitled *Modern San Francisco*, makes no mention of the disaster. Rather, its articles and photos document the splendor of the city,[21] a vision fulfilled less than ten years later, when San Francisco hosted the Panama Pacific International Exposition, broadcasting to the world its newly rebuilt modern splendor.[22]

My grandmother's reflection on the earthquake mirrors the official narrative. She writes, "Eventually they [my great-great grandparents and great grandmother] got back to normal none the worse for the excitement." These narratives, whether they are or are not consciously aware of the liberties they take with the effects of the earthquake, point to the way in which historiography-as-earthquake never forwards a solidified "truth," rather, a world of scrambled temporalities, smoky clarity, migrating truths, and normalized memories. Dixon's new city illustrates not devastation, but, rather, a turning point, a city pushed off the cusp of the nineteenth century that is moving forward, bravely and beautifully, into modernity.

Matter:M aterial Archives

My grandmother writes, "We have a little survivor of the earthquake in our den." I imagine a tiny man, perched on my grandparents' bookcase. Dressed in a frock coat, he perhaps nurses a broken arm or leg, a casualty of the earthquake's destruction. The tiny survivor, though, is a small teacup, two and a half inches wide by a bit over two and a half inches high. Its small size and thin china walls seem to defy logic; a house is destroyed by the forces of tectonic shaking and raging fires, yet a teacup survives. The heat from the fire melted most of the paint off the cup, and it is now a grimy grey. Black soot, permanently burned into the cup, drips, in frozen rivulets, down its sides. It has become a part of the Shanks family, proudly displayed in my grandfather's office, though the teacup had little to do with our family. It was a gift from my great-great grandmother Christine to a friend whose house was destroyed in the earthquake and fire. How the teacup passed from my great-great grandmother's friend to my family is left out of the story.

In addition to the teacup, my parents inherited a thick, heavy slab of black marble scavenged from the interior of the San Francisco City Hall, infamously and almost completely destroyed in the earthquake and fire. I have no idea who took it—Olaf, perhaps, hired to help rebuild the structure. My father remembers his parents turning the marble into a coffee table when he was a child, and I remember it collecting dust under my sister's bed. The San Francisco City Hall is, perhaps, the best-known public building destroyed in 1906. In the days following the earthquake, the fire spread down Larkin Street until it reached the shoddily constructed building, which had toppled over in the earthquake and destroyed the city's archives.[23] Images abound of the crumbling City Hall, its large spire saved from collapse only by the frozen media of photography and pen and ink drawing, it seems, though they were images still warm enough in 1909 to fuel the trial of the mayor and other city officials over the building's easy destruction in the earthquake.[24]

Both cup and marble are keepsakes, heirlooms, souvenirs, each word signifying a different temporal relationship to the past, to memories. Susan Stewart writes of the souvenir that it "distinguishes experiences. [...] We need and desire souvenirs of events that are reportable, events whose materiality has escaped us, events that [...] exist only through the invention of narrative."[25] The teacup and the marble slip in between Stewart's definition. They are not my souvenirs; both were gathered and saved decades before I was born, yet the materiality of the 1906 earthquake and fire has most assuredly escaped me, the disaster existing now simply as memories, as a family narrative. As Stewart observes, "[The souvenir] will not function without the supplementary narrative discourse that both attaches it to its origins and creates a myth with regard to those origins."[26] Akin to Walter Benjamin's materialist theorization of the collector, an object is transformed into a collectable—or souvenir—in relationship to the narrative such an object weaves, in the temporal spaces between the collector's embodied presence/present and the object's history. It is not the object divorced from its context that holds potency, but, rather, the object most particularly placed in a historical context, a familial, a personal context.[27] As Stewart notes, "The souvenir moves history into private time."[28] The teacup and marble are filled with historical narratives, indeed, all that remains are stories to validate the two objects as items of worth, of value, worthy of being remembered, worthy of the archive.

More than simply the temporal move of shifting history into private time, the teacup and marble, as archived souvenirs of the disaster, shift our understanding of historiography and the archival material upon which narratives of the past are grounded. This shift, mirroring the shifts of the land during an earthquake, allows for a reexamination of the power behind historiography, as the material objects upon which narratives of the past are based tumble off their shelves, the walls of City Hall shaking loose from their foundations. The historiographic quake allows one to attend to the materiality of the surrounding world and the way in which it comes to matter. This attention to the mattering/material world arises paradoxically, however, in the moment of the quake's destruction. One notices the material world only to notice that it has shaken loose, has tumbled apart, and in that destruction has dramatically reconfigured one's knowledge of the structures of the surrounding, mattering world.

San Francisco, on that April day in 1906, was, suddenly and drastically, a radically different city than it had been merely a minute before the first quake hit. Buildings lay toppled, cable lines twisted, the once level streets a mass of jumbled cobblestones. The material city was largely destroyed. The two souvenirs of the earthquake that vividly attest to my ancestors' presence in the city during the quake oddly had nothing to do with their day-to-day worlds. Both objects were steps removed from the objects that filled their lives—a friend's china, marble from City Hall—yet these objects tell the story of the quake, help to weave the narrative of the days after the disaster. Historiography-as-earthquake conceives of history-making as predicated upon material uncertainty, upon a certain chaotic matter. The archives have been shaken and destroyed, their contents lie strewn across the streets for any to take. When the matter that records the history of a place is shaken, is scattered—City Hall has toppled, is burning—a way of thinking about history-making is revealed that is disjointed and predicated upon destruction and unmade truths. This notion, however, is two-edged. It allows what might have been, could have been, should have been to emerge, allows for a historiography of imagination. More dangerously, though, like the "official" death toll of the earthquake, some 2,500 victims short, it is not necessarily attached to an ethical imperative. Historiography-as-earthquake preserves a notion of the narrative born of displaced matter. While the earthquake highlights this scattering, this chaos, this material destruction—indeed, exaggerates it—such material displacement is a part of any sort of history making: archives disintegrate, objects disappear, memories fade. In the earthquake, though, the scattered matter of history, of historiography, is revealed: the schema in action.

Artifacts bespeak a type of archeology. Stumbling through the remains of the cracked city, one comes upon the small, burnt, grey teacup, and the thick slab of black marble. There are no carefully excavated trenches, no surveyor's kit to document the exact angle of each artifact uncovered, no camera to photograph each item's position. Rather, it is a gathering, a walk—perhaps a stumbling, picking sort of walk, as one negotiates cracked streets, and fallen, burnt beams—during which the walker periodically stops, attention caught by an item. She bends and picks up the grey teacup, sitting now on its special shelf in the well-kept living room, sitting now in 2015, within a history that began with the ash, that began with the fire, that began with the earthquake, that began with the San Andreas fault, that began with a tectonic pressure, that began with a molten core, a shifting center.

Derrida writes "that the meaning of 'archive' [...] comes to it from the Greek *arkheion*: initially a house, a domicile, an address, the residence of the superior magistrates, the *archons*, those who commanded."[29] The institutionalization of the archive, present from its linguistic origin, is a move from private to public, from common to authorized privilege, from disparate to consolidated, collected, and catalogued. I return to this archeological gathering, in which the *arkheions* of the magistrates have been laid bare, toppled by an earthquake, burnt by a fire, their archives spread and destroyed. It is not only the *arkheions*, though, that lie in rubble. The private collections of things, the objects of average lives, are also strewn across the path of the archeologist, who picks her way through this maze of tumbled-together things, seeking not to document the context of her finds, but simply to gather, overwhelmed by the newly wrought chaos of the world. It is an archeology that bridges times: collecting things from a recently destroyed past, there is no need to document that past (it is, within the mind of the archeologist after all, still the present). Yet, the collector within the scavenger's body knows that she is at a turning point in time. The marble of the City Hall, the mightiest of *arkheions*, lies strewn on the streets, and so the architectural *archons* of the city's grandest archive have been displaced, spurned, cast off. The uncommon archeologist welcomes the marble, collects it, unknowingly constructing a private narrative, a familial history, which will persist for decades to come. For all that the archeologist is uncommon in her methods, she is thoroughly, commonly, average.

Sitting under a child's bed so many decades later, collecting dust, the slab of marble nonetheless smiles to itself, in on the joke. For all that it no longer adorns the façade of City Hall, it still finds itself in an archive, still finds itself a part of a history, continuing to matter.

Ends

What does it mean for this essay's argument about *historiography-as-earthquake* to turn to family history, to reveal its narratives, its constructedness? It is a turn to family memories, long-known stories, an always-present nostalgia to know these ancestors. It is a turn that asserts the materiality, the matter, of history within the now of my own body, the now of my own memories. Pierre Nora argues that memory shifted from "the historical to the psychological, from the social to the individual. [...] Memory became a private affair."[30] In part, the 1906 earthquake is most particularly a private affair—my private, familial affair—and, yet, historiography-as-earthquake muddles the clear distinction between what "private" and "memory" might mean or signify. If my private, familial memories of the earthquake are grounded in an archive produced out of the crumbled remains of the San Francisco City Hall, then to speak of the private is to always already be speaking of the collective.

What does it mean to remember a past, to turn to the now of memory? "We speak so much of memory," Nora writes, "because there is so little of it left."[31] His assertion does not offer any sort of fixity as to what memory might be so much as it underscores an anxiety that seems to cling to it. For all that memories are constantly being created anew, they are half-creations, the pulsing bright trace of an object that remains when one closes one's eyes. The anxiety Nora notes speaks to my own urge to write this essay. The family artifacts and stories I seek to mine for theories almost seem to pulsate with their absent memories. There, the pulsation of my absent grandmother, who compiled and wrote the black binder, is strong. Her absence looms large, the fragments of her presence hinting at the fullness of herself.

Notes

1. My grandmother's binder is an unpaginated manuscript, which is owned by my family.
2. Sandra L. Richards, "What Is to be Remembered?: Tourism to Ghana's Slave Castle-Dungeons," *Critical Theory and Performance*, eds. Janelle G. Reinelt and Joseph R. Roach (Ann Arbor: University of Michigan Press, 2007), 85.
3. In *Metaphysics* Aristotle writes, "That, then, which is capable of being may either be or not be; the same thing, then, is capable both of being and of not being" (830). Agamben reads this as the founding ontology of potential, namely, that it rests first upon *not* being or doing. Agamben theorizes potentiality as not simply the precondition of actuality, but rather as its own sovereign modality of being (which, perhaps paradoxically, must be a modality of *un*-being). When im-potential becomes actualized, the moment embodies the giving of potentiality to itself. Agamben writes, "To set im-potentiality aside is not to destroy it but, on the contrary, to fulfill it, to turn potentiality

back upon itself in order to give itself to itself" (Giorgio Agamben, *Homo Sacer: Sovereign Power and Bare Life*, trans. Daniel Heller-Roazen [Stanford: Stanford University Press, 1998], 46). Agamben continues that "at the limit, pure potentiality and pure actuality are indistinguishable" from each other. Agamben's (im)potential offers circular mode of conceiving of time, the space between potential and im-potential obliterated in the move of giving a self to itself (47). Aristotle, "Metaphysics," *The Basic Works of Aristotle*, ed. Richard McKeon (New York: The Modern Library, 2001); Giorgio Agamben, "On Potentiality," *Potentialities: Collected Essays in Philosophy*, ed. Daniel Heller-Roazen (Stanford: Stanford University Press, 1999), 177–84.
4. Agamben, *Potentialities*, 181.
5. Robert S. Yeats, *Living with Earthquakes in California: A Survivor's Guide* (Corvallis: Oregon State University Press, 2001), 4.
6. See Rand Richards, *Historic San Francisco: A Concise History and Guide* (San Francisco: Heritage House Publishers, 2007), 171–89, for a complete account of the earthquake. My description is based on the materials provided byR ichards.
7. Yeats, *Living with Earthquakes*, 4.
8. Richards, *Historic*, 191.
9. Ibid.
10. Kathleen Moran, "The San Francisco Earthquake," *A New Literary History of America*, eds. Greil Marcus and Werner Sollors (Cambridge: Belknap Press of Harvard University Press, 2009), 504–505; Richards, *Historic*, 171–89.
11. Joan Didion, *The Year of Magical Thinking* (New York: Vintage Books, 2005), 189–90; emphases in the original.
12. Agamben, *Potentialities*, 177.
13. Joan Didion, "Excerpt from Los Angeles Days," *The L.A. Earthquake Source Book*, eds. Richard Koshalek and Mariana Amatullo (New York: Art Center College of Design, 2008).
14. Jack London, *Jack London and the April, 1906, San Francisco Earthquake*. http://projects.crustal.ucsb.edu/understanding/accounts/london.html (December2011).
15. See the photographs documenting the earthquake and fire in William Bronson, *The Earth Shook the Sky Burned* (Garden City, NY: Doubleday & Company Inc.,1959).
16. London, *Jack London and the April, 1906, San Francisco Earthquake*.
17. Pierre Nora, "Between Memory and History: Les Lieux de Mémoire," *Representations* 26 (1989): 7–24.
18. Ibid.,7–24.
19. While I do not address it in this essay, one of the ways the disaster was narrativized was as the wrath of God, a view countered in an ad of the time: "If, as some say, God spanked the town for being over-frisky, why did he knock the churches down and save Hotaling's Whiskey?" Moran, "The San Francisco Earthquake," 504–505.
20. Moran, "The San Francisco Earthquake," 506; Maynard Dixon, *New San Francisco Emergency Edition*, http://www.sfmuseum.org/sunset/cover.html (December2011).

21. *Modern San Francisco* (Western Press Association: San Francisco, 1906–1907).
22. Richards, *Historic*, 197.
23. Bronson, *Earth Shock*, 57.
24. Richards, *Historic*, 194–95.
25. Susan Stewart, "The Souvenirs," *On Longing: Narratives of the Miniatures, the Gigantic, the Souvenir, the Collection* (Durham: Duke University Press, 1993), 132–51, 135.
26. Stewart, *Longing*, 136.
27. Walter Benjamin, "Eduard Fuchs, Collector and Historian," *Selected Writings, Volume 3 1935–1938*, eds. Howard Eiland and Michael W. Jennings, trans. Edmund Jephcott, Howard Eiland et al. (Cambridge: Belknap Press of Harvard University Press, 2002), 260–302.
28. Stewart, *Longing*, 138.
29. Jacques Derrida, "Introduction," *Archive Fever*, trans. Eric Prenowitz (Chicago: University of Chicago Press, 1996), 2.
30. Pierre Nora, "General Introduction: Between Memory and History," *Rethinking the French Past: Of Memory, Volume I: Conflicts and Divisions*, trans. Arthur Goldhammer (Columbia University Press: New York, 1992), 11.
31. Nora, "Les Lieux de Mémoire," 7.

Bibliography

Agamben, Giorgio. *Homo Sacer: Sovereign Power and Bare Life*. Translated by Daniel Heller-Roazen. Stanford: Stanford University Press, 1998.

———. *Potentialities: Collected Essays in Philosophy*. Edited by Daniel Heller-Roazen. Stanford: Stanford University Press, 1999.

Aristotle. *The Basic Works of Aristotle*. Edited by Richard McKeon. New York: The Modern Library, 2001.

Benjamin, Walter. "Eduard Fuchs, Collector and Historian." In *Selected Writings, Volume 3 1935–1938*. Edited by Howard Eiland and Michael W. Jennings, translated by Edmund Jephcott, Howard Eiland et al. Cambridge: Belknap Press of Harvard University Press, 2002, 260–302.

Bronson, William. *The Earth Shook the Sky Burned*. Garden City, NY: Doubleday & Company Inc., 1959.

Derrida, Jacques. *Archive Fever*. Translated by Eric Prenowitz. Chicago: University of Chicago, 1996.

Didion, Joan. "Excerpt from Los Angeles Days." In *The L.A. Earthquake Source Book*. Edited by Richard Koshalek and Mariana Amatullo. New York: Art Center College of Design, 2008, 132–37.

———. *The Year of Magical Thinking*. New York: Vintage Books, 2005.

Dixon, Maynard. "New San Francisco Emergency Edition." *Virtual Museum of the City of San Francisco*. December 2011. http://www.sfmuseum.org/sunset/cover.html.

London, Jack. "Jack London and the April, 1906, San Francisco Earthquake." *Understanding Earthquakes*. December 2011. http://projects.crustal.ucsb.edu/understanding/accounts/london.html.

Modern San Francisco. San Francisco: Western Press Association, 1906–1907.

Moran, Kathleen. "The San Francisco Earthquake." In *A New Literary History of America*. Edited by Greil Marcus and Werner Sollors. Cambridge: Belknap Press of Harvard University Press, 2009, 503–507.

Nora, Pierre. "Between Memory and History: Les Lieux de Mémoire." *Representations* 26 (1989), 7–24.

———. *Rethinking the French Past: Of Memory, Volume I: Conflicts and Divisions*. Translated by Arthur Goldhammer. New York: Columbia University Press, 1992.

Richards, Rand. *Historic San Francisco: A Concise History and Guide*. San Francisco: Heritage House Publishers, 2007.

Richards, Sandra L. "What Is to be Remembered?: Tourism to Ghana's Slave Castle-Dungeons." In *Critical Theory and Performance*. Edited by Janelle G. Reinelt and Joseph R. Roach. Ann Arbor: University of Michigan Press, 2007, 85–107.

Stewart, Susan Stewart. *On Longing: Narratives of the Miniatures, the Gigantic, the Souvenir, the Collection*. Durham: Duke University Press, 1993.

Yeats, Robert S. *Living with Earthquakes in California: A Survivor's Guide*. Corvallis: Oregon State University Press, 2001.

11
Thinking the Space(s) of Historiography: Latina/oEt hnicity Theatre

Jon D. Rossini

As a theorist trying to do history, I want to engage with what I consider a fundamental problem within the thinking of theatre historiography: an inevitable, even desired, slip into the language of representation. While a critical gesture away from representation as an end point has emerged across a range of qualitative disciplines, for example, in projects such as non-representational theory in geography, the question of representation in the practice of performance historiography has particular poignancy because performance demands engagement with something other than representation as its product.[1] The notion that performances produce, indeed, ARE representations presents a problem because one of the ontological claims of performance as practice is its emphasis on process and experience, on a doing as much, or perhaps even more, than on a thing done. This shift is reflected in concepts like performative identity, in which identity is itself a doing. As the not quite debate between Jacques Derrida and J. L. Austin in Derrida's *Limited, Inc.* suggests, context is central to any working understanding of the performative, even as accounting for the fullness of context inevitably fails, resulting in a practice of representation that is necessarily incomplete.[2]

At some level, the crux of performance studies is an attempt to examine, embody, and experience the possibility of performance as epistemology or ontology, even as one acknowledges performance as a doing and a something done. For the purposes of this investigation, I want to explore a theoretical transubstantiation of matter into space, considering for a moment a way around the current thinking of identity, writ broadly in theatre studies. Even more specifically, I want to engage the concept of ethnicity, which is, ostensibly, and perhaps correctly, based on the material conditions of individuals currently marked by this term in contemporary discourse, a discourse that slips so quickly into issues of basic representation—visibility, political power, and the synechdochic transfer of power and understanding. I want to consider the possibility that thinking of ethnicity as fundamentally spatial might allow a shift away from current practices of scholarship and analysis in which, despite the nearly canonical status of identity as performance, ethnicity is nonetheless too quickly fixed by the critical and historical weight of the desire to chart manifestations of agency and to give voice to the marginalized. I suggest constructing performance historiography as something other than a movement toward representation and provisional fixity by imagining a process that is, perhaps, antithetical to the notion of historical narrative itself, a process that does not cohere sufficiently to allow an easy slippage into the partial (and in too many cases total) reification of historical representation as a practice.

The repetition of the ostensible is not incidental to the thinking of this essay, insofar as appearance as a practice is conceived as a fundamental signifying gesture, and, for some, "the" fundamental signifying gesture of theatre itself. This "pointing to" directs attention to a multiple object—the thing itself and the idea of the thing. This doubling functions as the first site in which the polysemous nature of theatre manifests itself as a deep structure of analysis for close readings of objects and bodies on the theatrical stage, and, in doing so, doubling suggests that representation-is-theatrical-activity-is-representation. This gesture, however, and capitulation to the claim that there is no outside to representation (or "discourse," as Ernesto Laclau and Chantal Mouffe have it[3]) both belie the doing of a performance by relying on what a performance has done. In many of the richer interventions in Performance and Theatre Studies, the doing includes gesture, experience, and embodied knowledge. While these elements are often represented (there is no question of that), not all gestures, experiences, and embodied knowledges are represented. The most obvious forms of absence or erasure occur in the context of marginalized or, tellingly, "under-represented" groups. In these cases, differences of experience and embodiment are elided or silenced, since, in a traditional argument, the hegemonic operations of dominant representation do not allow for their presence in a meaningfully interpretable way. This disparity fuels the social justice, community-based, and leftist-reparative narratives of identity politics in which the goal is representation of an "other" experience, even when the function of representation itself is recognized as a form of historical translation too easily shaped by operations of power. This familiar problem, never fully articulable but always haunting, of a necessary temporal/conceptual gap between the operations of perception and of interpretation, is actively explored in contemporary performance itself. In considering something other than representation as the endpoint of historiography, or even something other than an end point, I want to consider the possibility of a different geography, a thinking practice that structures equivalence as equivocation, a gesture that hints, through omission, at the presence of a conceptual space between possibilities.

This theoretical hairsplitting is necessary precisely because of the scholarly habit within practices of theatre historiography to understand itself as a "representation of the past." In their collection *Representing the Past: Essays in Performance Historiography*, organized around "the five categorical ideas of *archive, time, space, identity*, and *narrative*," Charlotte Canning and Thomas Postlewait argue that "all of us, as we carry out our historical inquiry, *think with*—not just about—each of these five modes of comprehension in our tasks of representing the past."[4] Despite their clear acknowledgment of historiography as practice, there is, nonetheless, a return to representation as the final product of history, as our "task," trapping performance in a presumptive representational function, rather than retaining representation as a partial account of a historical subject.

While historiography may be understood as the process of determining the value of various sedimentations on the conventions of a socially constructed reality, it is understood in Canning and Postlewait's collection as a problem of representation itself. In their invocation of two operative definitions of mimesis, Canning and Postlewait insist that "the representation makes a show—a deceptive performance—of the original, as if the reality of the thing itself is possessed by a disruptive *Doppelgänger*. The same thing is delivered as another thing."[5] Interesting here is the claim that representation's activity is that of a morally culpable performer, as if there were access to some kind of show that was not "deceptive." This figuration creates a second issue: insisting on the problem of representation as a problem of simple mimesis, the temporal, spatial, or material gap between an object or event and its representation (which points to the ways in which the practice of historiography is haunted by a desire for a reification) is constituted as a simple fact. Canning and Postlewait argue, "All representations, in the process of describing past events, require temporal and spatial coordinates."[6] These coordinates of representation, however, are too often plotted in a manner that presupposes both the axes and the planes on which time and space are located. I would like to suggest, as a means of thinking historiography otherwise, the possibility of an alternate topography or geography, one of vectors rather than coordinates, a different relation between temporal and spatial geography that does not so easily slip into the desire for fixity.

The problem of specificity and precision matters not just to an empiricist structuring of history, but also to a process-driven conceptual project; indeed, I take to heart Postlewait's insistence, in his *Cambridge Introduction to Theatre Historiography*, on the fundamental fuzziness of contextualization:

> The primary claim of a contextual approach is that social and political relations are not merely represented in plays and productions, but somehow located, situated, embodied, or embedded there in such a manner that the context becomes the primary source of meaning. [...] But in saying this, we must recognize that our vocabulary about being "located, situated, embodied, or embedded" is still a metaphorical rhetoric that remains vague and unexplained.[7]

The question of specificity that Postlewait calls to attention here, however, runs the risk of further solidifying the model of historical location he presents. What worries me, as a scholar of the theatre and performance of ethnicity, is that the operation of location in ethnicity is too often a process of fixing representation (in a simultaneously corrective and coercive gesture) in order to sustain the specificity of context, so that meaningful political action can occur.

Canning and Postlewait select "Identity" as one of the five categorical ideas they explore in the collection. "No wonder the concept of identity is so important," they observe. "It is the basic and pervasive idea that we discover and derive from the archive; it is the subject or subjects (both human subject and events as subject matter) that we attempt to designate and construct (or should we say reconstruct?) as we delve into any historical topic."[8] "It is impossible to understand the past," they further declare, "without the primary ideas of *identity*, *time*, and *space*."[9] This is an important parallel with the current collection, which privileges time, space, and matter, but the shift in terms, from identity to matter, is particularly crucial in offering a different vantage point from which to determine the historiographic operation that might occur prior to identity as representation, assuming (problematically, but potentially fruitfully) a transformation of matter as a transformation into a historiographic narrative.

To a large extent, the scholars writing about identity in *Representing the Past* understand the complexities of the problem. Xaoimei Chen, Catherine M. Cole, and Harry J. Elam, Jr., all insist on the importance of introducing identity as a concept into the practice of historiography. Chen insists that "as historians we need to proceed carefully and cunningly. [...] We should take seriously the identity politics that guide both the producers and audiences of the performance culture. We need to see the writing and performing subjects as historical agents who must negotiate their relations with both the present and the past."[10] In her conclusion, Cole asks, "Might not all historical writing enfold the historian in a web of complicity and responsibility? What would happen if all historians had to answer repeatedly the questions: 'Who are you? And why are you here?' How would our histories be different?"[11] Elam's version is:

> What I am suggesting, rather, is the need for sensitivity to and increased awareness of the materials at hand, enabling us to understand identity and its power within the historiographic scene. We must develop a progressive concept of history and history making that takes such matters of identity into account. With such a strategy we can and must observe more fully the battles over identity and identity politics that play out within the space and through the agency of dramatic text and performance.[12]

I am sympathetic to these claims, which stress the importance of identity to understanding the agency of historical actors within their context, and the need for a self-reflexive historiographic narrator, sensitive to and aware of the ways in which the history is reconstructed. In each of these claims, however, there is still a haunting sense of representation as necessary fixity. In telling the stories of the subjects and the actors in representation, we seem left with, on the one hand, paying more careful attention to the agency of the actors as a means of more accurately representing history, and, on the other hand, paying more careful attention to the operations of the historian. As such, these attempts at progressive historiography can be understood as well-intentioned attempts at a gradual shifting of power from historian/ethnographer to speaking subject. While this practice of retained and granted power is consistently questioned, a critique in which Chen, Cole, and Elam would, no doubt, participate, Cole nonetheless acknowledges the issue of a "web of responsibility and complicity." This web, itself, is underscrutinized. What matters is not so much who you are as where you are. I do not mean the simple articulation of a positionality that Elam describes as "an outmoded politics of location that would limit historiography by race," but, rather, an attempt to find an alternative conceptual space for the historian as thinker.[13] To begin this search, I want to call attention to a space in Elam's conclusion where this possibility is not realized.

Elam calls for "the need for sensitivity to and increased awareness of the materials at hand, enabling us to understand identity and its power within the historiographic scene." In this formulation, it is "the materials at hand," the historical materials already processed, not the matter itself, that demands our attention. This is a powerful call to arms and one I don't want to reject, but my concern is where Elam leaves us in realizing this strategy: "we can and must observe more fully the battles over identity and identity politics that play out within the space and through the agency of dramatic text and performance." The "more fully" seems of particular importance here, the details and tracing of lines of force, of connections and relations, but his figuration of the historiographer observing "battles over identity and identity politics that play out within the space" suggests that space itself is, to Elam, a fixed category (perhaps emerging from a "sensitivity to the materials"). This fixity of space leads to an ability to attend to "the battles," and this presumption of conflict, a predetermination of an aspect of the nature of the interaction itself, is what I would like to call into question. In a sense, Elam's formulation risks being reducible merely to more carefully observing negotiations (battles) over representation that "play out" in the scene. What is needed, instead, is a call to engage the structure and form of the scene itself and of the space it produces. Whether or not one can successfully add a layer of provisionality as an additional shifting variable and a continued deferral of representation seems at least in part predicated on a claim about historiography not as narrative and thus representational, but as a practice of thinking and thus potentially also practicing otherwise. A more complex spatial approach to identity provides a potential alternative practice.

While it is easy to argue for an alternative route, even in the face of careful scholarship, it is much more difficult to meaningfully articulate one. To do so, to think about space as a necessary starting point for the matter that is identity, I will examine the concept of ethnicity through the specific usage of the word "Latina/o" within theatre historiography. In a specific, United States context, there has been a fairly recent sea change in the conventional wisdom surrounding the concept of identity—a shift from ethnicity as a white identification of a specific region or national origin to a term reflecting increasing concern with marked bodies of color, following the changes in immigration legislation in the mid-1960s that increasingly enabled individuals from Asia and Latin America to enter the United States as legal immigrants. It is not merely the subjects constituted by the concept that have shifted, however, but the very ground on which the concept rests. One can argue, in fact, that the very idea of ethnicity as a marker of identity is under scrutiny. If we understand ethnicity not as a category of representation, but, rather, as a process or mode of thinking and creative activity, then we have to shift the very terms through which we take the idea of identity for granted. While the majority of theatre historians are not arguing for an essential concept of identity, there is, nonetheless, a sense that the historical operation fixes identity in place. There is an unspoken assumption about ethnicity's representational function beyond which a politics of identity is continuously moving, but which, nonetheless, retains a powerful influence as a supposedly receding event horizon.

Is "Latina/o" a micro-historical categorization that could not "mean" before it was broadly articulated in the 1990s by theatre critics, practitioners, and scholars, or can its conceptual contours be extrapolated to include, at least partially, cultural productions initially articulated as Puerto Rican, Nuyorican, Cuban, Cuban American, Mexican American, Chicana/o, Spanish American, or Hispanic? The answer is both yes and no, depending upon the values of the scholar/historian/cultural commentator and the mode of sedimenting what counts as Latina/o. This question is constantly elided in critical accounts that cross questions of language and geography, national origin, and aesthetic practice, but which implicitly include work that involves an exploration of identity, represents a community, questions mainstream representation, tells the story of a community or family presumed to be Latina/o (or has at least some characters marked by name and self-description), or offers a progressive left or liberal politics intended to foster the possibility of reimagining the status quo.

For Jorge Huerta, the articulation of a Chicana/o aesthetic is not possible, but a Chicana/o mythos is:

> What makes this vase "Chicano?" I will ask my students, having drawn a rudimentary flower vase on the board. It is only a chalk outline of a

basic vase, curvilinear, but with no true signifiers of its cultural origins. It could be a classic Greek vase, but there are no Greek figures dancing on this vase, nothing but an outline. The students cannot identify the vase's "ethnicity," until I ask them to imagine a Virgin of Guadalupe painted on it. Suddenly, what else could it be but a Mexican or Chicano vase? If not sculpted by a Mechicana/o, the vase was at least decorated by someone who was attempting to appeal to a Mexican Roman Catholicm ythos.[14]

Huerta's account takes for granted, as does most scholarship on "ethnic" theatre, the contours of social construction as history. While there is a level of provisional qualification, the desire for articulating coherence as a value (which is present precisely because of material concerns about representation as a necessary political practice) trumps any attempt to narrate the complex threads of the "vase's" emergence, generated by a presumed individual artist (actually Huerta, but possibly the "someone" is the production line of a Chinese factory, contracted over the Internet). Of course, there is a second concern here, insofar as the object is an example of a shared institutionalization of aesthetics and culture emerging from a (generally delineated) geopolitical and cultural location. The object is to be read, not to be engaged.

The traditional narrative of contemporary ethnic theatrical history is progressive. In it, an increasingly complex understanding of shifting processes and identities reflects an increasingly complex and inclusive practice of theatre-making, working toward inclusionary visibility. Ethnicity becomes a way of thinking through an organization of aesthetics and politics and its relation to space and time. In this sense, ethnicity functions as a shorthand for representational practice itself, primarily framed in terms of contesting relations (vide Elam). Contest figures theatre as a site for negotiating the articulation of culture with a storyteller, who tells more, but not all, of the story, or who provides (not the story itself but) a frame for interpretation constituted as ethnicity. The danger here is that while the deployment of ethnicity is understood to enable the invocation of shared experiences or perceptual possibilities, these experiences and possibilities are placed within an already organized perceptual field.

What does this mean for the practice of theatre historiography? Insofar as contemporary, disciplinary conceptions of ethnicity emerge in the multicultural 1980s, they are imbricated into a neoliberal, market-based ideology. To think about the Latina/o in terms of the market, we can turn to Arlene Dávila's work about the making and marketing of a people, of an ethnicity as a demographic. This sense of the marketplace of identity and its relationship to performance seems to be part of a larger consciousness of identity.[15] In *The Social Construction of Reality*, Peter L. Berger and Thomas Luckmann argue,

> A society in which discrepant worlds are generally available on a market basis entails specific constellations of subjective reality and identity. There will be an increasingly general consciousness of the relativity of *all* worlds...It follows that one's own institutionalized conduct may be apprehended as "a role" from which one may detach oneself in one's own consciousness, and which one may "act out" with manipulative control. [...] The situation, then, has a much more far-reaching consequence than the possibility of individuals playing at being what they are *not* supposed to be. They also play at being what they *are* supposed to be—a quite different matter. This situation is increasingly typical of contemporary industrial society [...]. What should be stressed is that such a situation cannot be understood unless it is ongoingly related to its social-structural context, which follows logically from the necessary relationship between the social division of labor (with its consequences for social structure) and the social distribution of knowledge (with its consequences for the social objectivation of reality).[16]

Concerned, at a base level, with those institutionalized reifications of the social that obfuscate the work of construction, the authors use the uncommon term "objectivation" to think about the action of transforming a concept into an object. What is crucial is the claim that individuals "play at being what they *are* supposed to be" in conjunction with a social-structural context that itself is provisional. Even in early, explicit articulations of social constructions, the historicized nature of identity construction is predicated on a particular relationship to social structure.

Like later sociological formations, such as Bruno Latour's actor-network-theory and Nigel Thrift's non-representational theory, there is a shared investment in engaging the material conditions and structures of knowledge that maintain constructions of the social. Importantly, Thrift's work on "*the geography of what happens*," which he sees as "the beginning of an outline of the art of producing a permanent supplement to the ordinary,"[17] interacts (in a way similar to performance studies) with an investigation of experiential and experimental embodiments and analyses of lived experience. Bruno Latour, in *Reassembling the Social*, does not specifically reference performance, but usefully argues for "redefining sociology...as the *tracings of associations*."[18]

Tracing requires starting "from the *under-determination of action*, from the uncertainties and controversies about who and what is acting when 'we' act—and there is of course no way to decide whether this source of uncertainty resides in the analyst or in the actor."[19]

Latour's uncertainty marks a crucial shift away from the careful and nuanced focus on representation and its function in history illustrated by W. B. Worthen. Writing in the late 1990s, Worthen articulates history within the world of Chicano/a theatre as both a trope and a practice, and delineates the contours of their logics by presenting a now familiar account of the doubled practice of historical recovery/ recuperation combined with a questioning of the possibilities and limits of history as a means of representation:

> The dialectical representation of history characteristic of Chicano/a history plays emblematizes this intricate dynamics of identity in the process of theatrical and cultural production. These plays use the recovery of an occluded history of oppression to ground an effective Chicana/o identity politics; at the same time they appear to stage the limits of "history" in constituting an "authentic" ethnic subject.[20]

Here, a gesture is made toward the limits of history, but it is precisely the possibility of recuperation that functions as the goal, even though this practice is inherently limited. In the twenty-first century, the gesture toward representation has become politically insufficient and dramaturgically self-conscious.

Kristoffer Diaz's play *Welcome to Arroyo's*, which premiered in 2010 and is set in 2004,[21] offers an example of a historiographical work that is not merely a narrative of negotiating representation, but which points to an alternative concept that thinks ethnicity as *other than* a condition or an identity formation within representation. Diaz's play, located in a specifically Puerto Rican space on New York's Lower East Side, concerns a brother and a sister working through their grief at the loss of their mother, but, more importantly for this essay, the play's content explores how cultural production and historical inquiry create the possibility for self-transformation. The play argues, in a pragmatically utopian way, for the possibility of a broader community than self and for the production of an alternate social space through the recuperation of history and the production of culture.

Welcome to Arroyo's begins on the one-month anniversary of the death of Alejandro and Amalia's (Molly's) mother. Alejandro has transformed her bodega into a bar, Arroyo's, in which he aspires to create a community of engagement through a willingness to listen—doing the job of bartending "right." His sister deals with grief differently, shifting from a private to a public practice of making art (graffiti). Officer Derek (Jeter) catches Molly tagging the police station with her name and falls in love with her artistry. Two Hip-Hop DJ's, Trip Goldstein and Nelson Cardenal, serve as narrator/commentators for the play, and Lelly Santiago, a Puerto Rican graduate student researching the history of hip-hop, is its historian. Condemned by Trip as "the worst worst worst of everything that I'm talking about: a Puerto Rican Girl who left this neighborhood when it sucked and only comes back to claim it when shit becomes convenient,"[22] Lelly is the most important historiographic impulse in this play. A cultural historian, Lelly is attempting to reconstruct the history of hip-hop, recuperating her place within the community in the process, while generating a feminist reconceptualization of the Puerto Rican presence in hip-hop. The subject of her recuperation is Elisabeth Reina Arroyo, whom she believes is Reina Rey, a Boricuan hip-hop artist who disappeared from the scene in 1979. This possibility becomes the catalyst for a series of personal transformations, but the play's conclusion suggests that the existence of (the) possibility is itself sufficient. It is this form of history, of selective choice, that Postlewait finds problematic for performance historiography (in that belief is privileged over concrete historical evidence, and the possibility of a good story is as important as a true one). What is important in *Welcome to Arroyo's* is not the truth of the history, but the thinking operation of the historian, the practice of historiography as a practice of "thinking about," of making connections.

On one level, the play is a negotiation of the terms of heterosexual pairing. While Lelly's self-perceived failure to connect to Alejandro may stem from her shyness, a clichéd social trope for the intellectually insular graduate student, it also emerges from her overeagerness to share what she knows about Reina Rey. Lelly's investment in the personal only resonates when it is situated in a broader network of connections—people, things, and places—paralleling Bruno Latour's claims about the social. Diaz is invested in the conditions that enable pairing, but his account of historiography is about enabling the conditions for historical narratives to emerge.

Even though Lelly articulates her project in relation to her anxiety about "authenticity" and her position within the community, a personal, subjective concern, Diaz drives past this to explore how space provides a productive alternate to the ways that the psychological and biographical flatten the complexity of the history that emerges from them. While recuperative historiography is the driving engine of the narrative movement toward intimacy in the play, it is the creation of a space, rather than the specifics of individual relationships, that is the play's real political work. The emergence of a potential familial connection to hip-hop's "origins" provides both the genesis for Alejandro to allow the performance of hip-hop in his lounge and a canvas for Molly's artwork, all in the service of Lelly's suggestion to create "a community center. For adults. With alcohol."[23]

While her attempt to prove the identity of Reina Rey is conducted in a self-interested but historically rigorous way, Lelly's discussion of sushi with Alejandro offers a different version of historical thinking. I suggest that this play, following the invocation of the title, is not about the Arroyos, but about Arroyo's—the lounge itself rather than the people in it. Their identities emerge from the possibilities of the space and its contents. In this sense, Diaz moves toward the production of space as the fundamental social relationship, and he carefully negotiates between an auditor's conventional desire for an individuated subjective narrative and a more systemic symbiosis between spaces and cultural production, engagements and objects. In the terms of this analysis, Diaz's work is closer to actor-network-theory and non-representational geography than to a recuperative representation of a newly inclusive and affiliative ethnicity, a reading of the play clearly illustrated in Lelly's attempt to engage Alejandro through sushi.

Sushi, as object, generates a practice of thinking relationally that is articulated and imagined through food. As Lelly puts it to Alejandro,

> I think about sushi, I think about Japan. It's an archipelago—I mean, it's a bunch of islands, so they fish. Fine, that makes sense. Then I think about the fact that they don't cook it. Then I think about crab roe. And seaweed. And wasabi and ginger. And yes, I know, I'm just exoticizing the other, I've read Edward Said, I'm familiar with orientalism. But wasabi and ginger? Where did that genius come from? I think about how what they eat affects their body types, and their body types affect the amount of energy they have, and their energy affects the way they live, and the way they live affects what they produce, and that affects what we produce, and that affects what I eat, whether I turn around and eat sushi or not.[24]

While this trajectory has its limits, Lelly's articulation of the implications of consuming and thinking about sushi puts it within a series of physiological and cultural networks, within thinking and consumptive practices that are marked by different experiential histories shaped, of course, by a United States–based articulation that echoes Nigel Thrift's interest in the geography of what happens. Importantly, the object (sushi, thought) exists in the play; it is not a representation of an object. The process is one of engagement with and through the object, a relation created by matter that exceeds the act of reading Huerta invokes with the Virgin of Guadalupe vase. This privileging of the practice of thinking, enabled by the practice of listening, enabled by the implicit and explicit space of Arroyo's lounge, is, for Diaz, central to the political work of history itself. Rather than representation, it is thinking itself that enables a different connectivity, an alternative sense of process and location. Diaz's play refigures concepts, rather than affixing them.

Diaz does not resolve the question of whether Elisabeth Arroyo is Reina Rey. The material facts are not as important to Diaz or to his characters as the possibilities engendered by the space of thinking.[25] The recuperation is only partly accomplished in the play because Arroyo's is a space for the possibility of thinking about connections. Even so, the absence of a final determination about Reina Rey shapes the historiography articulated in the play. The intersection of history and desire is both recognized and deferred, as Lelly, who reminds herself that "the act of historicization is not about being loved," at the same time acknowledges, "I'm not sure if I'm using the word 'historicization' correctly."[26] Historicization, even when in the service of something else, remains a practice of thinking that is fundamentally emergent, like ethnicity, within space itself.

Diaz's vision of historiography as making space for ethnicity seems to point toward the possibility that the matter of ethnicity is precisely an issue of space, but it is not the simple substitution of one variable for another in an algorithm-generating historical narrative, rather a fundamental shift in the thinking practice of history-making itself. While the evidentiary record is constituted as a fictional exercise in this essay, the practice of employing ethnicity as a shorthand for representation remains a crucial problem. It will continue problematic as long as we maintain the claim that performance—and its historiography—is fundamentally representational.

Notes

1. N. J. Thrift, *Non-Representational Theory: Space, Politics, Affect*, International Library of Sociology (New York, NY: Routledge, 2008).

2. J. Derrida, *Limited, Inc.* (Evanston: Northwestern University Press, 1988).
3. Ernesto Laclau and Chantal Mouffe, *Hegemony and Socialist Strategy: Towards a Radical Democratic Politics*, 2nd ed. (New York: Verso, 2001).
4. Charlotte Canning and Thomas Postlewait, "Representing the Past: An Introduction on Five Themes," *Representing the Past: Essays in Performance Historiography* (Iowa City: University of Iowa Press, 2010), 7, 9.
5. Ibid.,11.
6. Ibid.
7. Thomas Postlewait, *The Cambridge Introduction to Theatre Historiography* (New York: Cambridge University Press, 2009), 202.
8. Canning and Postlewait, 14–15.
9. Ibid., 17; emphases in the original.
10. Xaoimei Chen, "Fifty Years of Staging a Founding Father: Political Theatre, Dramatic History, and the Question of Representation in Modern China," *Representing the Past*, 328.
11. Catherine M. Cole, "History's Thresholds: Stories from Africa," *Representing the Past*,279.
12. Harry J. Elam, Jr., "The High Stakes of Identity: Lorraine Hansberry's *Follow the Drinking Gourd* and Suzan-Lori Parks's *Venus*," *Representing the Past*, 300.
13. Ibid.,299 –300.
14. Jorge A. Huerta, *Chicano Drama: Performance, Society, and Myth* (New York: Cambridge University Press, 2000), 184.
15. Arlene Dávila, *Latinos, Inc: The Marketing and Making of a People* (Berkeley: University of California Press, 2001).
16. Peter L. Berger and Thomas Luckmann, *The Social Construction of Reality: A Treatise in the Sociology of Knowledge* (London: Penguin Press, 1967), 172–73; emphases in the original.
17. Thrift, *Non-Representational Theory*, 2.
18. Bruno Latour, *Reassembling the Social: An Introduction to Actor-Network-Theory* (New York: Oxford University Press, 2005), 5; emphases in the original.
19. Ibid., 45; emphasis in the original.
20. W. B. Worthen, "Staging America: The Subject of History in Chicano/a Theatre," *Theatre Journal* 49:2 (1997): 103.
21. Diaz, of course, is not Chicano and in this I am making a partial gesture toward the problematic but necessary umbrella term "Latina/o," but I should also acknowledge that the term "Latino" emerges in Diaz's play only from the voice of a graduate student talking about cultural history. Otherwise the terms used are "Puerto Rican" and "Boricua."
22. Kristoffer Diaz, *Welcome to Arroyo's* (New York: Dramatists Play Service, Inc., 2011), 23.
23. Ibid.,48.
24. Ibid.,40.
25. It is not incidental that the verification of Reina Rey's identity is made possible through a photo of a woman being arrested. The policing of a subject is what brings her into history, and the practice of recuperation becomes complicit in the practice of policing, something Diaz recognizes through the pragmatism of his history. Molly's reading of this moment is that the expression on the

woman's face, her looking out in the photo, can itself be read as an assertion of the rightness of her action, framing the activity not as criminality but as a moment of social justice denied.

26. Diaz, *Welcome to Arroyo's*, 20.

Bibliography

Berger, Peter L., and Thomas Luckmann. *The Social Construction of Reality: A Treatise in the Sociology of Knowledge*. London: Penguin Press, 1967.

Canning, Charlotte, and Thomas Postlewait, eds. *Representing the Past: Essays in Performance Historiography*. Iowa City: University of Iowa Press, 2010.

Canning, Charlotte, and Thomas Postlewait. "Representing the Past: An Introduction on Five Themes." In *Representing the Past: Essays in Performance Historiography*. Edited by Charlotte Canning and Thomas Postlewait. Iowa City: University of Iowa Press, 2010.

Chen, Xaoimei. "Fifty Years of Staging a Founding Father: Political Theatre, Dramatic History, and the Question of Representation in Modern China." In *Representing the Past: Essays in Performance Historiography*. Edited by Charlotte Canning and Thomas Postlewait. Iowa City: University of Iowa Press, 2010.

Cole, Catherine M. "History's Thresholds: Stories from Africa." In *Representing the Past: Essays in Performance Historiography*. Edited by Charlotte Canning and Thomas Postlewait. Iowa City: University of Iowa Press, 2010.

Dávila, Arlene. *Latinos, Inc: The Marketing and Making of a People*. Berkeley: University of California Press, 2001.

Derrida, Jacques. *Limited, Inc*. Evanston: Northwestern University Press, 1988.

Diaz, Kristoffer. *Welcome to Arroyo's*. New York: Dramatists Play Service, Inc., 2011.

Elam, Harry J., Jr. "The High Stakes of Identity: Lorraine Hansberry's *Follow the Drinking Gourd* and Suzan-Lori Parks's *Venus*." In *Representing the Past: Essays in Performance Historiography*. Edited by Charlotte Canning and Thomas Postlewait. Iowa City: University of Iowa Press, 2010.

Huerta, Jorge A. *Chicano Drama: Performance, Society, and Myth*. New York: Cambridge University Press, 2000.

Laclau, Ernesto, and Chantal Mouffe. *Hegemony and Socialist Strategy: Towards a Radical Democratic Politics*, 2nd ed. New York: Verso, 2001.

Latour, Bruno. *Reassembling the Social: An Introduction to Actor-Network-Theory*. New York: Oxford University Press, 2005.

Postlewait, Thomas. *The Cambridge Introduction to Theatre Historiography*. New York: Cambridge University Press, 2009.

Thrift, Nigel T. *Non-Representational Theory: Space, Politics, Affect*. International Library of Sociology. New York, NY: Routledge, 2008.

Worthen, W. B. "Staging America: The Subject of History in Chicano/a Theatre." *Theatre Journal* 49, no. 2 (1997), 101–20.

Contributors

Kelly Aliano received her PhD from the City University of New York Graduate Center. Her dissertation was entitled "Ridiculous Geographies: Mapping the Theatre of the Ridiculous as Radical Aesthetic." She has taught at Hunter College and has stage-managed numerous productions throughout New York City.

Patricia Badir has published on public space in medieval and Reformation dramatic entertainment in the *Journal of Medieval and Early Modern Studies, Exemplaria*, and *Theatre Survey*. She also writes on religious iconography and postmedieval devotional writing. She is the author of *The Maudlin Impression: English Literary Images of Mary Magdalene, 1550–1700* (University of Notre Dame Press, 2009). She is currently working on playmaking and the perils of mimesis on Shakespeare's stage and on Canadian Shakespeare in the first two decades of the twentieth century. This recent research has been published in *Shakespeare Quarterly*.

Rosemarie K. Bank has published in *Theatre Journal, Nineteenth-Century Theatre, Theatre History Studies, Essays in Theatre, Theatre Research International, Modern Drama, Journal of Dramatic Theory and Criticism, Women in American Theatre, Feminist Rereadings of Modern American Drama, The American Stage, Critical Theory and Performance* (both editions), *Performing America, Interrogating America through Theatre and Performance*, and *Of Borders and Thresholds*. She is the author of *Theatre Culture in America, 1825–1860* (Cambridge University Press, 1997) and is currently preparing *Staging the Native, 1792–1892*. A member of the College of Fellows of the American Theatre, a past fellow of the American Philosophical Society, and several times a fellow of the National Endowment for the Humanities, she was the editor of *Theatre Survey* from 2000 to 2003 and currently serves on several editorial boards. She is past president of the American Theatre and Drama Society, past convener of the International Federation for Theatre Research's Working Group in Theatre Historiography, and has served several terms on the Executive Committee of the American Society for Theatre Research.

Pannill Camp is Assistant Professor of Drama at Washington University in St. Louis. His research examines points of intersection between theatre history and the history of philosophy, especially in eighteenth-century France. Before joining the faculty of Washington University, he was a postdoctoral fellow at the Humanities Center at Harvard University (now the Mahindra Humanities Center) and taught in Harvard's Department of the History Art and Architecture. His work has been published in journals including *Theatre Journal*, *Performance Research*, the *Journal for Eighteenth-Century Studies*, and the *Journal of Dramatic Theory and Criticism*.

Will Daddario is an active theatre historiographer and performance philosopher. His research on sixteenth-century Venetian theatre and performance has been published in *The Journal of Dramatic Theory and Criticism*, *Ecumenica*, and anthologies such as the forthcoming *Failure, Representation, and Negative Theatre* (Routledge Press, edited by Dan Watt and Eve Katsouraki) and *Culinary Theatres* (Routledge, edited by Dorothy Chansky and Ann Folino White). Additionally, his work in the emerging field of performance philosophy has led to the compilation of two coedited anthologies, *Manifesto Now! Instructions for Performance, Philosophy, Politics* (with Laura Cull for Intellect Press, 2013) and the forthcoming *Adorno and Performance* (with Karoline Gritnzer for Palgrave). Will is the chair of the Performance and Philosophy Working Group within Performance Studies international, a core convener of Performance Philosophy (http://performancephilosophy.ning.com), and currently teaches at Illinois State University.

Michal Kobialka is Professor of Theatre in the Department of Theatre Arts & Dance at the University of Minnesota. He has published over 75 articles on medieval, eighteenth-century, and contemporary European theatre and theatre historiography. He is the author of *A Journey Through Other Spaces: Essays and Manifestos, 1944–1990* (University of California Press, 1993); *Further on, Nothing: Tadeusz Kantor's Theatre* (University of Minnesota Press, 2009); and *This Is My Body: Representational Practices in the Early Middle Ages* (University of Michigan Press, 1999); the editor of *Of Borders and*

Thresholds: Theatre History, Practice, and Theory (University of Minnesota Press, 1999) and a coeditor (with Barbara Hanawalt) of *Medieval Practices of Space* (University of Minnesota Press, 2000).

Jan Lazardzig is Associate Professor of Theater Studies at the University of Amsterdam. Since 2003, he is coediting the book series *Theatrum Scientiarum* (Walter de Gruyter), a study on the intersection between the history of science and the history of theater in the seventeenth and early twentieth century, alongside Helmar Schramm and Ludger Schwarte. His dissertation was published under the title *Theatermaschine und Festungsbau. Paradoxien der Wissensproduktion im 17. Jahrhundert* (Berlin: Akademie Verlag, 2007). He coauthored *Theaterhistoriografie: Eine Einführung* (G. Narr, UTB, 2012) with Matthias Warstat and Viktoria Tkaczyk. Together with Claudia Blümle, Jan edited a book on postwar theater architecture in Germany (*Ruinierte Öffentlichkeit*, Berlin: Diaphanes, 2012). His current research project questions the manifold relationships between theater and the police in nineteenth-century Germany.

Scott Magelssen teaches Theatre History and Performance Studies at the University of Washington. He is the author of *Simming: Participatory Performance and the Making of Meaning* (University of Michigan Press, 2014) and *Living History Museums* (2007) and coeditor of *Enacting History* (2011), *Theatre Historiography: Critical Interventions* (2010), and *Querying Difference in Theatre History* (2007). Scott is the editor of Southern Illinois University Press's Theater in the Americas book series. He hosts the website theater-historiography.org with Henry Bial and serves on the editorial boards for *Theatre Topics, Journal of Dramatic Theory and Criticism, Theatre History Studies*, and *Theatre/Practice*.

Kaitlin M. Murphy is Assistant Professor in the Department of Spanish and Portuguese at the University of Arizona. She received her PhD in Performance Studies from New York University and holds a master's degree in Visual Culture from the same university. Her current research focuses on the production and uses of film, photography, theater, and performance in human rights advocacy and activism in Latin America, in the contexts of dictatorships, transitional justice and truth-seeking processes, memory politics, and the borderlands.

Jon D. Rossini is Associate Professor and Chair in the Department of Theatre and Dance at UC Davis. His first book, *Contemporary Latina/o Theater: Wrighting Ethnicity* (Southern Illinois University

Press, 2008), is part of the Theater in the Americas series from Southern Illinois University Press. He has published articles in *Radical History Review*, *Text and Presentation*, *Gestos*, *American Drama*, *Journal of American Drama and Theater*, *Paso de Gato*, *Latin American Theatre Review*, and in collections such as *Neoliberalism and Global Theatres*, *Routledge Companion to Latino/a Literature*, *Codifying the National Self*, *Mediating Chicana/o Culture*, and *Death in American Texts and Performance*.

Gwyneth Shanks is a doctoral candidate in Theatre and Performance Studies at UCLA. Her research theorizes still works, or performances of stillness, as/through urban site-specific performance. Her dissertation, "Still Works: Stillness, Site-specific performance, and a Politics of Resistance," will argue that still works critically link performers, spectators, and the performance site to question, what are the *politics of stillness*? Shanks received her MA in Performance Studies from New York University and her BA in Theatre from Macalester College. Her work has been published in the *Journal of Dramatic Theory and Criticism* and *Third Text*.

Angenette Spalink teaches script analysis, acting, and performance studies. She recently choreographed Sarah Ruhl's *Dead Man's Cellphone* and Charles L. Mee's *Summertime* and cochoreographed Naomi Iizuka's *Skin* at Bowling Green State University, where she received her PhD in the spring of 2014. Her dissertation, "Choreographing Dirt," explores how natural elements are used in contemporary performance. She examines how dirt functions as a trans-corporeal choreographic element, creating an ecologically complex *pas de deux* that evokes an intricate rethinking of conceptions of species in performance.

Patricia Ybarra is Associate Professor of Theatre Arts and Performance Studies at Brown University. She is the author of *Performing Conquest: Five Centuries of Theatre, History and Identity in Tlaxcala, Mexico* (Michigan, 2009) and coeditor with Lara Nielsen of *Neoliberalism and Global Theatres: Performance Permutations* (Palgrave Macmillan, 2012). Her next book project is tentatively titled *Latina/o Travelogues: Latina/o Theatre under Neoliberalism*. She has published articles and reviews in *Theatre Journal, TDR, Modern Language Quarterly, Aztlán, Radical History Review*, and the *Journal of Dramatic Theory and Criticism*. She is the president elect of the Association for Theatre in Higher Education. She is also a director and dramaturg.

Yael Zarhy-Levo teaches theatre history, theatre criticism, and modern British theatre in the Department of Literature at Tel-Aviv University, Israel. Her publications include: *The Theatrical Critic as Cultural Agent: Constructing Pinter, Orton and Stoppard as Absurdist Playwrights* (Peter Lang, 2001); *The Making of Theatrical Reputations: Studies from the Modern London Theatre* (*Studies in Theatre History and Culture*, ed. Thomas Postlewait, University of Iowa Press, 2008); articles in *Poetics, Theatre History Studies, Journal of Dramatic Theory and Criticism, Theatre Survey, Semiotica, Journal of British Cinema and Television,* and *Theatre Research International*; chapters in *The Cambridge Companion to Harold Pinter* (Cambridge, 2001, and 2nd ed, 2009), and, with Freddie Rokem, in *Writing & Rewriting National Theatre Histories* (University of Iowa Press, 2004).

Index

Page numbers in italic denote figures.

Abdoh, Reza
   Law of Remains, 77, 85, 89n7
Aben, Rob, 195n36
Abraham, Roshan, 215n55
abstract space, 203–6, 209, 211
actor-network-theory, 245–6, 248
actors
   and German theatre reform
      movement, 126, 128, 132, 137–8
   Mitchell on, 100–1, 104, 106–8
   social, 3, 97, 108
   theatre, 115–16, 137, 187, 207,
      211–12, 241
Adorno, Theodor W., 10–11, 178–83,
   192–3, 203
   "Actuality of Philosophy, The,"
      179–81, 194n6–9, 194n11–12,
      194n14, 195n46
   Aesthetic Theory, 178, 194n4–5
   Negative Dialectics, 182, 211,
      215n48–9
Agamben, Giorgio, 6–7, 14n12,
   34n4, 207, 215n35, 221–2, 225,
   233n4, 233n12
   im(potentiality), 10–11, 221,
      232–3n3
Agricola, Rudolph
   De inventione dialectica
      (*Of dialectical invention*), 181–2
AIDS, 76, 78–9, 81, 84, 87
Aliano, Kelly, 8

Allende, Salvador, 154–5, 159, 161,
   165–7
Answers in Genesis
   Ken Ham (founder), 21, 31–3,
      34n8–9, 35n17, 36n33
   website, 7–8, 21, 26–7, 30–3,
      34n1, 34n8
   See also Creation Museum
      (Petersburg, Kentucky)
Anzaldúa, Gloria, 82, 89n17
Aragay, Mireia, 70n16–17,
   71n19–29
architecture, 110–12, 200–3, 205,
   208–9, 211, 231
archives
   Adorno on, 181
   of Chester mystery play, 95–8,
      100–16
   Derrida on, 124–5, 231
   family history, 220, 229–32
   German police theatre
      (*Landesarchive*), 124–5, 140
   Ruzzante's use of, 192–3
Arens, Egmont H.
   *Nativity and Adoration Cycle of
      the Chester Mysteries*, 102, *103*,
      104
Aristotle, 145–6n53, 182, 184,
   232–3n1
Aronson, Arnold, 210–11,
   215n45–7

art
  critics/reviewers, 56–61, 97–8, 115–16, 118n25
  galleries, 50, 112–14
  Grobert on, 212–13
  as icon/relic, 113–14
  of invention, 182
  middlebrow, 47–8
  painting, 184–5, 191
  political, 19, 30–4, 49–50, 60–2, 79–88, 156–70, 179–93
  re-valuing of (Theatre of Ridiculous), 44–52
  of scenery/space, 203–8
  Schiller on, 134–6
  schools, 68
Arts and Crafts movement, 95, 113
audience
  and German theatre reform movement, 9, 126–40
  and In-Yer-Face Theatre, 59
  and Mitchell's *Chester Mysteries*, 98–101, 110–11, 115–16
  participation, 45, 47, 49, 205
  and recursive neoliberalism, 83, 86–7
  and Ruzzante, 185, 189–93
August Ottokar Reichardt, Heinrich *Essay on the Parterre*, 129–30, 144n34–5
Austin, J. L., 237
authenticity, 33, 88, 109–10, 177–81, 201, 246–8
Avellar, José Carlos, 170n6
Aylwin, Patricio, 157

Badir, Patricia, 9
Baldwin, James, 102
Bank, Rosemarie, 13n4, 141n1
Barnes, Djuna, 102
Baroque, 10, 179, 183–93
Baur-Heinhold, Margarete, 194
Bell, Hugh Poynter, 118n25
Bell, Josephine, 102, *103*
Bellin, George, 104, 118n29

Bender, Wolfgang S., 144n32
Benjamin, Walter, 2–3, 12–13n2, 13n3, 111, 119n51, 194n17, 229, 234n27
  Arcades Project, 180–1, 194n10
Benson, Frank, 117n2
Beolco, Angelo (aka Ruzzante), 10, 179, 183–93
Berger, John, 108–9, 119n45
Berger, Peter L.
  Social Construction of Reality (with Luckmann), 245, 250n16
Bernert, Günther, 143n20
Bielfeld, Jakob Friedrich von
  Doctrine of Statecraft, 129, 132, 144n29, 144n31, 145n46
Billington, Michael, 65
Blavatsky, Madame, 113
Boon, Richard, 71n46
borderlands, 77–8, 81–3, 89–90n17
Bottoms, Stephen J., 50, 53n30
Bourdieu, Pierre, 56, 69–70n4, 70n10
Bourriaud, Nicolas, 97–9, 108, 115, 118n7, 118n26, 119n40, 119n59
Brecht, Stefan, 44–7, 51, 53n7–9, 53n14–15
Brennan, Timothy, 12, 14n14
Brockett, Oscar, 213
Bröckling, Ulrich, 130, 144–5n38, 145–39n40
Bronson, William, 233n15, 234n23
Burton, Julianne, 170n2
Bush, George H. W., 33
Bushuven, Siegfried, 144n32
Butterworth, Jez, 65
Bynum, Caroline Walker, 119n58

Cameralism, 125, 127–8, 132
Camp, Pannill, 10–11
Canning, Charlotte, 2, 239–40, 250n4–6, 250n8–9
Čapek, Milič, 14n13
capitalism, 3, 61, 77, 79, 83, 86–8, 200, 204
Carlson, Marvin, 213n5, 214n11

Carmichael, Franklin, 119n56
Carroll, Linda, 195n45, 195n47
Cartesian/Hegelian understanding of time, 20–1, 27–8
Casey, Edward S., 203, 214n13
Cazares, Victor
  and eschatology, 9, 77, 85–8, 90n28
  Ramses Contra los Monstruos, 8–9, 75–88, 90n1–2
  See also Mexico
censorship, 123–5, 131–4, 137, 140, 141n5, 145n50–1
Certeau, Michel de, 12, 14n15, 178, 194n3
Chakrabarty, Dipash, 22, 35n14, 37n39
Chaudhuri, Una, 35n10
Chen, Xaoimei, 241–2, 250n10
Cheng, Patrick S., 90n32
Chester Mysteries, 9, 95–100, 114–16, 118n9
  first modern performance, 117n2
  first full editions, 117n3
  and image archives, 108–14
  and paper archives, 100–8
  See also Mitchell, Roy
Chicana/o, 250n21
  migration narratives, 76, 83
  mythos, 243–4
  theatre, 246
  See also Latina/o
Chile
  and Augusto, Pinochet, 154–9, 161
  Pinochet's coup d'état, 153–67, 171n17
  and Salvador Allende, 154–5, 159, 161, 165–7
  and truth commissions, 157–8, 163, 171n8, 171n10
  See also Patricio Guzmán
chorus, 135–6, 146n62, 146–7n63
Christianity
  and Chester mystery play, 113, 115
  eschatology, 9, 77, 85–8, 90n28
  See also Creation Museum (Petersburg, Kentucky)
Churchill, Caryl, 60, 62, 66
Cicero, 142n16
cities, 5, 44, 210
  Berlin, 9, 124, 130, 137, 140
  city planning, 181
  Ciudad Juarez, 76, 78, 81–5
  gentrification, 84
  London, 62–6, 177n2
  Mexico City, 84
  New York, 41, 43, 48, 95, 98–9, 102–3
  and *Policey*, 123–4, 128–9, 144n29
  San Francisco, 220–32
  tent cities, 223
  Vienna, 9, 124, 130, 132–3, 140
class, 1, 3, 41, 136, 155, 179, 185, 189–90
Clopper, Lawrence, 117n1, 117n4
Cocco, Enzo, 191, 195n44
Cole, Catherine M., 241–2, 250n11
Collingwood, R. G., 22, 177
commedia dell'arte, 131, 145n42
communication, 23–5, 30, 209
communion, 99–100
community, 127, 156, 239, 243, 247–8
  communities of memory, 161–70
  of engagement, 246–7
Conroy, Frank M., 95, 98–9, 102, 104, 117n2
Cozzi, Gaetano, 194n17
Creation Museum (Petersburg, Kentucky)
  "Adam and Eve in the Garden of Eden" display, 24, 24–5
  and distinction between animals and plants, 34n9
  "First sacrifice" display, 24–5, 25
  and language of intelligibility, 18, 30, 34
  Lucy exhibit, 17, *18*, 26, 26–8, *29*, 29

Creation Museum (Petersburg, Kentucky)—*Continued*
  "Man vs. Ape" display, 23, *23*, 30
  Walk through History exhibit, 22–4
  See also Answer in Genesis
Crimp, Martin, 60, 62, 65–6, 68
Cuadros, Gil
  "Conquering Immortality," 84, 90n23
culture
  of abstraction, 3
  in Cazares's *Ramses*, 76, 82–3, 86–8
  cultural memory, 10
  culture of abstraction, 3
  and ethnic aesthetics, 243–9
  and In-Yer-Face Theatre, 57, 61–4, 68–9
  and materiality, 2, 5–6
  and mediation, 55–6
  and memory, 158–64
  nature/culture divide, 7–8, 17–34
  performance, 241
  and space, 203–4
  and temporality, 96–7, 102, 106
  and Theatre of the Ridiculous, 46–52
Cummings, E. E., 102

Daddario, Will, 10, 195n41
Dasgupta, Gautam, 49, 53n26
Dávila, Arlene, 244–5, 250n15
Davis, Ann, 113, 119n57
De Alwis, Lisa, 145n52
Delany, Samuel, 90n23
Deleuze, Gilles, 8, 19–21, 28, 184, 194n17
  What Is Philosophy? (with Guattari), 20–1, 34n5–7
democracy, 153–7
Derrida, Jacques, 9, 237, 250n2
  on archives, 101, 118n19, 124–5, 141n7–8, 231, 234n29
Dersofi, Nancy, 195n43

Descartes, Rene
  Cartesian/Hegelian understanding of time, 20–1, 27–8
  Discourse on Method, 210
Diaz, Kristoffer, 250n21
  Welcome to Arroyo's, 11, 246–9, 250n22–4, 250–1n25–6, 251n26
Didion Joan
  The Year of Magical Thinking, 224–5, 233n11, 233n13
Diederich, Hunt, 102
Dixon, Maynard, 227
Donohue, Joseph, 2
Dramatic Censor, The (journal), 145n51

Earth Ministry, 36n32
earthquakes
  Mexico City (1985), 84
  San Francisco (1906), 11, 220–32, 233n6, 233n15, 233n19
Echard, Siân, 106, 119n33
Edgar, David, 65
Egyptian Book of the Dead, 77, 85
Egyptian Theatre, 83–4, 90n20
Eichelberger, Ethyl, 43, 45–6
  Minnie the Maid, 46
Einstein, Albert, 3, 7, 14n13
Elam, Harry J., Jr., 241, 250n12–13
Enlightenment theatre reform, 88, 125–6, 134, 139, 202, 205, 207, 211
environmental theatre, 210–11
environmentalism, 31–3, 36n30, 36n32–3
eschatology, 9, 77, 85–8, 89n7, 90n28
Esslin, Martin, 70n14–15
  The Theatre of the Absurd, 56–8, 69
ethics, 3, 6
  bioethics, 5, 79–80
  environmentalism, 31–3, 36n30, 36n32–3
  ethical imperative, 193, 230
  See also morality

Index   263

ethnicity
  costuming, 212
  ethnic aesthetics, 243–9
  ethnic theatre, 244–6
  and historiography, 237–49
  See also Chicana/o; Latina/o
Evangelical Climate Initiative (ECI), 36n32
Everyman (play), 117n2
evolutionary biology, 28–9, 35n22–4, 37n35
exhibitions
  Group of Seven, 113
  Lucy exhibit (Creation Museum), 17, *18*, 26, 26–8, 29, *29*
  queer-history, 48
  Walk through History exhibit (Creation Museum), 22–4

Faith Action Network (FAN), 36n32
Ferguson, Ronnie, 195n45
Ficino, Marcilio, 213
Fletcher, John
  Preaching to Convert, 19, 34n2
Forsee, A., 14n13
Forstreiter, Erich, 141n6
Foucault, Michel, 22
  on governmentality, 127, 143n24
  and heterotopic space, 8, 42–3, 46–51, 52n1, 52n3–4, 53n12–13, 53n16–17, 53n20, 53n22, 53n25, 53n27, 53n32, 53n34, 53n36
  on history of spaces, 199, 213n1
  and Vitor Westhalle, 90n28
Fox, Claire, 77, 89n8
Fraser, Matthew J., 141
Freeman, Elizabeth, 51, 76–7
  Time Binds: Queer Temporalities, Queer Histories, 53n37, 80, 89n4–5
French, Samuel, 107
Freund, Philip, 194n16
Friedman, Michael, 214n15
Frühwald, Wolfgang, 143n20

Gamper, Michael, 141n1
gate-keepers, 57–8, 60–1, 63, 69, 70–1n18
Genesis, book of, 18, 21, 22, 24, 27, 30–3, 35n11, 35n14, 35n17
Glossy, Carl, 145n52
Goethe, Johann Wolfgang von, 134–5, 146n54
Goldberg, Roselee, 45, 53n10
Goldstein, Robert Justin, 141n5
Gonzáles Rodríguez, Sergio, 89n9
Gordon, Avery, 162, 172n20–3
Gottsched, Johann Christoph, 125, 131–2
Grandin, Greg, 157, 170n1, 171n12
Greenwich Village, New York, 8, 41
Greenwich Village Theatre (New York), 95, 98, 102
Grobert, Joseph-François-Louis, 214n22–3
  La Bataille des Pyramids, 205, 208, 215n36–7
  De l'exécution dramatique, 10–11, 205–9, 212–13, 214n21, 214n25–9, 215n30–4, 215n50–2, 215n54
Group of Seven, 113, 119n56
Guattari, Felix, 8, 19–21, 28
  What Is Philosophy? (with Deleuze), 20–1, 34n5–7
Gutíerrez, Gustavo, 87
Gutiérrez-Jones, Carl, 89–90n17
Guzmán, Patricio, 170n2–4
  La Batalla de Chile (The Battle for Chile), 153, 155–61, 164, 167, 170n5
  Chile, Memoria Obstinada (Chile, Obstinate Memory), 10, 155, 158–65, 168–70
  in concentration camp, 155
  in exile, 155–6
  See also Chile

Hägelin, Carl Franz von, 133, 145n22

Haider-Pregler, Hilde, 142n10
Ham, Ken, 21, 31–3, 34n8–9,
    35n17, 36n29, 36n31, 36n33
Hamilton, John, 142n16
Hammett, Dashiell, 102
Harris, Jonathan Gil, 96–7, 117n4–5
Harris, Lawren, 119n56
Hart House Theatre (Toronto), 95,
    98, 108, *109*, 111–16, 118n25
Harvey, David, 213n7
Hattenhauer, Hans, 143n20
Hauser, Andreas, 143n22
Hayner, Priscilla B., 171n10, 171n13
Heßelmann, Peter, 142n15, 142n17,
    144n33, 144n36, 145n41,
    147n69
Hegel, Georg Wilhelm Friedrich, 2,
    13n3, 20, 27, 211
Heisenberg, Werner, 3
Hellman, Lillian, 102
Hendrickson, Leonard, 155
Herlinghaus, Hermann, 89n13
heterotopia, 8, 42–3, 46–52, 208
Higgs boson, 3, 13n6
Hirsch, Marianne, 160, 172n19
historiography, theatre
    and British Theatre (1990s), 55–69
    and Deluzio-Guattarian notion
        of "human-becoming-animal,"
        17–34
    and ethnicity, 237–49
    historiography-as-earthquake,
        220–32
    and materiality of history, 177–93
    and materiality of memory, 153–70
    of neoliberalism, 75–88
    and *Policey*, 123–40
    positivist, 178, 181, 199–200,
        203, 211
    and revivals of medieval plays,
        95–116
    scholarship, 1–3
    and space, time, and matter, 4–7
    of the Theatre of Ridiculous, 41–52
    use of the term, 1

history
    family, 219–32
    and historiography, 1, 6–7
    materiality of, 9–10, 177–93
    and memory, 158–64, 168–70,
        220–30
    of modern British theatre, 55–69
    natural, 20–34
    and neoliberalism, 9, 76–88
    and progress, 27–8
    social construction of, 244–5
    and temporality, 4, 20–34
    of theatre space, 199–213
    See also archives
History and Theory (journal), 4
Hobson, Marian, 212, 215n53
Hofstaetter, Birgit, 182, 194n15
Höyng, Peter, 142n13, 145n51
Huerta, Jorge, 243–4, 249, 250n14
Huesmann, Michael, 144n32
hygiene (purification), prevention
    regime of, 130–4

identity politics, 237–46
immunization, prevention regime of,
    131, 134–6, 146n54
income, 79, 131
Infancy and History (Agamben), 6–7
*Interpreting the Theatrical Past:
    Essays in the Historiography of
    Performance* (Postlewait and
    McConachie), 1–2
In-Yer-Face Theatre, 8, 56–69
    and Antony Neilson, 57, 59–60,
        65, 67
    and Mark Ravenhill, 57, 59–61,
        65, 67–8
    and Martin Crimp, 60, 62, 65–6, 68
    and Philip Ridley, 65–7
    and Sarah Kane, 57, 59–62, 65,
        67–8
    use of the term, 57, 59
    See also Sierz, Aleks
Isaac, Dan, 53n28
Iseli, Andrea, 141n2

Izenour, George C., 208, 210–11, 213n2, 214n14, 215n38, 215n44

Jackson, A. Y., 119n56
Jakob, Ludwig Heinrich, 144n26
Jammer, Max, 14n13
Jeffreys, Joe E., 45–6, 53n11
Johnston, Franz, 119n56
Jordheim, Helge, 8
Journal of Dramatic Theory and Criticism, 3
Justi, Johann Gottlieb von, 125–6, 145n44–5
  Basic Pillars of Power and Happiness of the States, 131–2
  Foundations of Policey-Wissenschaft, 127–8, 143–4n25, 144n27

Kane, Sarah, 57, 59–62, 67–8
  Blasted, 65, 67
Kant, Immanuel, 179, 203–4, 211
Karstens, Simon, 145n49
Kent, Rockwell, 102
Kern, Stephen, 14n13
Kittler, Friedrich, 101–2, 118n20, 118n23
Klein, Hildegard, 70n16–17, 71n19–29
Klubock, Thomas Miller, 171n16
Kobialka, Michal, 13n4, 141n1, 201, 214n8
Koselleck, Reinhart, 4, 14n8
Kritz, Neil, 171n7, 171n11
Kurz, Otto, 183–4, 192, 194n17–23

labor, 76–82, 128, 186, 190, 220, 245
  craftsmen, 110, 113–14
  factory, 77, 89n8, 154–5, 244
Lacey, Troy, 30–1, 36n27
Laclau, Ernesto, 238, 250n3
Landesarchive (German police theatre archives), 125, 140.
  See also *Policey* and Policey theory

Landsberg, Alison, 159, 171n18
Landwehr, Achim, 143n21
Latina/o
  categorization, 243–5, 250n21
  dramaturgy, 75–88
  See also Chicana/o
Latour, Bruno, 97, 117n5, 118n6, 245–7, 250n18–19
  Reassembling the Social, 245
Law, John, 184–5, 194n17, 194n24
Lawrence, D. H., 102
Lazardzig, Jan, 9–10
Lefebvre, Henri, 200–1, 204–6, 209, 213n6, 214n8–10, 214n17, 215n40, 215n42
Leibniz, Gottfried Wilhelm
  La Monadologie, 184–5, 192, 194n23
Leonhardt, Nic, 141–2n9
Lessing, Gotthold Ephraim, 125–6, 133
liberation theology, 87
Lismer, Arthur, 119n56
London, Jack, 226, 233n14, 233n16
Luckmann, Thomas
  Social Construction of Reality (with Berger), 245, 250n16
Lucy exhibit (Creation Museum), 17, *18*, 26, 26–8, *29*, 29
Ludlam, Charles, 42–6, 48–9, 52n2, 53n23–4
  Big Hotel, 48, 53n21
Lüdtke, Alf, 143n19, 143n21
Luke, Timothy W., 22, 35n15

MacDonald, J. E. H., 108, *112*, 112–13, 119n56
Mackintosh, Charles Rennie, 113
Magelssen, Scott, 7–8, 35n26
Magliabecchi, Antonio, 183
Maier, Hans, 141n3
manners, 125–34, 139
Marperger, Paul Jakob
  Description of Trade Fairs, 128–9, 144n30

Marranca, Bonnie, 49–50, 53n26
Martens, Wolfgang, 142n13, 145n43, 145n48
Marx, Karl, 3, 13n5
Marxism, 200–1, 204–5
Massey, Vincent, 98, 113
Mbembe, Achille, 89n3
McConachie, Bruce, 1–2
McLuhan, Mashall, 101
mediation, 55–9, 62–4, 69
medieval theatre. See Chester mystery play
melodrama, 137, 205, 208
memory
 communities of, 161–70
 and history, 158–64, 168–70, 220–30
 materiality of, 10, 153–70
 prosthetic, 159
 public memory sites, 163, 172n24
Menninghaus, Winfried, 147n70
Menton, David, 26–7, 30, 35n21, 35n25
Merleau-Ponty, Maurice, 165, 168, 172n27–8
Methuen Drama
 Modern British Playwriting, 63–9
Mexico, 8, 75–88, 89n8, 89n10
 Ciudad Juarez, 76, 78, 81–5
 and Lázaro Cardenas, 84
 Mexico City earthquake, 84
 and narcotrafficking, 75–81, 84–5, 89n10
 See also Cazares, Victor
Miller, William Ian
 The Anatomy of Disgust, 25, 35n19
Mills, David, 117n1–3, 118n29
Mills, Robert, 48, 53n19
Mitchell, Elizabeth, 26–7, 35n21
Mitchell, Roy
 career of, 98
 Chester Mysteries, The, 9, 95–116

Creative Theatre, 99, 101, 111, 118n8, 118n14–18, 118n21–2, 119n32, 119n34, 119n39, 119n41, 119n52–3
 early years and family of, 98
 writings on theatre, 98–108, 111
Mladek, Klaus, 143n19
Modern British Playwriting, 63–9
modernism, 9, 12, 63–9, 96–100, 104–6, 111, 113, 116
modernity, 4, 48, 77, 228
Monck, Nugent, 117n2
Monforte, Enric, 70n16–17, 71n19–29
Montez, Maria, 42, 44, 51
morality, 36n32, 80, 123–5, 128, 131–5, 139–40. See also ethics
Moran, Kathleen, 227, 233n10, 233n19–20
Morris, William, 113
Mouffe, Chantal, 238, 250n3
Moulian, Tomás, 158, 170n1, 171n15
mourning plays, 135–6, 145–6n53
Muñoz, José, 51, 53n35, 75, 77
Murphy, Kaitlin M., 10
myth, 63, 192, 220–2, 229, 243–4

natural disasters. See earthquakes
Neilson, Antony, 57, 59–60, 65, 67
neoliberalism, 7–9, 76–88, 154, 163, 244
New Theatre Quarterly, 63
Nielsen, Lara, 77, 89n8
Nitschke, Peter, 141n2
Nora, Pierre, 5, 226–7, 232, 233n17–18, 234n30–1

Oerter, Robert, 13n6
O'Keefe, Georgia, 102
Osborne, John
 Look Back in Anger, 56, 59

photography, 108–13, 154, 161, 164–9, 224, 229–30
physics, 5–6, 13n6

Pickering, Andrew, 215n41
Pietrogrande, Antonella, 195n27–8, 195n30, 195n37
Pinochet, Augusto, 154–9, 161
Pinter, Harold, 62, 66
Pitchfork Disney, The (Ridley), 65
Plato, 212–13, 215n55
Playboy: A Portfolio of Art and Satire, 102
playwrights, 56–69, 132, 138, 178. See also *individual playwrights*
Poel, William, 117n2
Policey and Policey theory
 and autonomy, 134–6
 and Cameralism, 125, 127–8, 132
 and censorship, 123–5, 131–4, 137, 140, 141n5, 145n50–1
 and Christian Wolff, 125
 definitions, 123–4, 141n3, 143n20
 and Johann Gottlieb von Justi, 125–7, 131–2
 and *Landesarchive* (German police theatre archives), 125, 140
 Policeywissenschaft, 125
 and precautionary principle, 137–40
 and *Prussian Civil Code*, 126–7, 143n20
 and regimes of prevention, 130–1
 and *Ruhe* (peace, calm), 10, 126–31, 133–40, 142n16, 143n22
 and theatre censorship, 124, 131–4
political coup d' é tat, 153–67, 171n17
Postlewait, Thomas, 12n1, 55, 247, 250
 Cambridge Introduction to Theatre Historiography, The, 2, 69n2, 177, 214n16, 193n1, 193n2, 240, 250n7
 Interpreting the Theatrical Past (with McConachie), 1–2

Representing the Past: Essays in Performance Historiography (with Canning), 2, 239–40, 250n4–6, 250n8–9
poverty, 81, 124
precautionary principle, prevention regime of, 131, 137–40
presence, space and, 4–5
progress, time and, 18, 21, 27–8
protests, 155, 170n3. See also riots
public sphere, 10, 163–4
puppet shows, 145n50

queer, 9
 temporalities, 51, 76–7, 81, 85–8
 and Theatre of the Ridiculous, 48, 51–2

race. See ethnicity
Rancière, Jacques, 169, 172n29
Randerson, Ian, 13n6
Randerson, James, 13n6
Ranke, Leopold von, 2, 13n3, 177
Ravenhill, Mark, 57, 59–61, 65, 67–8
 Shopping and Fucking, 71n30
Rees, Catherine, 67
Reid, Trish, 67
Rich, Motoko, 37n38
Richard, Nelly, 156, 158, 171n9, 171n14
Richards, Rand, 233n6, 233n8, 233n10, 234n22, 234n24
Richards, Sandra L., 221, 232n2
Ridge, Lola, 102
Ridiculous Theatre. See Theatre of the Ridiculous
Ridley, Philip, 65–7
 The Pitchfork Disney, 65
riots, 167–8. See also protests
Roberts, Philips, 71n46
Roosevelt, Eleanor, 102
Rossini, Jon D., 11
Rousseau, Jean-Jacques, 146n56
Royal Court Theatre, 59–60, 63

Ruhe (peace, calm), 10, 126–31, 133–40, 142n16, 143n22.
See also *Policey* and Policey theory
Runia, Eelco, 4–5, 14n9–11
Russell Taylor, John, 58, 69
Anger and After, 58, 70n14–15
Ruzzante (Angelo Beolco,), 10, 179, 183–93, 195n26, 195n35, 195n39–43

San Francisco earthquake of 1906, 11, 220–32, 233n6, 233n15, 233n19
Santa Maria, Cara, 37
Sanuto, Marin, 187, 195n31–4
Sarlós, Robert, 1
Saunders, Graham, 67
Savran, David, 47, 53n18
scenery. *See* theatre space
Schechner, Richard, 210, 213n4
Scherer, Stefan, 147n68
Schiller, Friedrich, 125, 133–6, 146n54, 146n56, 146n58–60
Bride of Messina or the Hostile Brothers, A Mourning Play with Choruses, 135–6, 146n61, 146–7n63, 147n65–6
Schlegel, Johann Elias, 125
Schneider, Rebecca, 165, 172n25–6
Schulz, Georg-Michael, 142–3n18, 146n60, 147n64
Serlio, Sebastiano, 210, 215n43
Serres, Michael, 97, 117n5
Shanks, Gwyneth, 11
family of (Bengstons), 222–8, 232n1
Siemann, Wolfram, 143n20
Sierz, Aleks, 8, 70n13–14, 71n30–44
contribution to *Modern British Playwriting*, 63–9, 71n47–57, 72n58–70
and critical reception, 58–63
as gate-keeper, 57–8, 60–1, 63, 69, 70–1n18

In-Yer-Face Theatre, 8, 56, 58, 60–4, 66, 68, 70n8, 70n11
See also In-Yer-Face Theatre
Silva, Jorge Muller, 156
Smith, Jack, 42–6
What's Underground about Marshmallows, 44
social construction, 239, 244–5
social control, 123–40
social interstice, 97–8, 101, 106, 116
Sohn-Rethel, Alfred, 3, 13n5, 202, 214n12, 214n20
Soja, Edward, 213n7
Sonnenfels, Joseph von
Principles of Police, Commercial, and Financial Science, 125, 133, 145n49–50
Sontag, Susan, 108, 119n43–4
Spalink, Angenette, 7–8
Spencer, Wayne, 32, 36n32
Spranzi, Marta, 194n13
Stark, Gary D., 141n5
Starr, Edd, 36n28
States, Bert O., 213n5
Stevenson, Jill
Sensational Devotion, 19, 33, 34n3
Stewart, Susan, 229, 234n25–6, 234n28
Stolleis, Michael, 142n11, 143n23
Stowe, Harriet Beecher
Uncle Tom's Cabin, 6
Sulzer, Johann Georg, 125, 133, 145–6n53

Tavel, Ronald, 44, 50, 52n5
telenovelas, 75–6
theatre, social aspects
actors, 115–16, 137, 187, 207, 211–12, 241
audience behavior, 125–34, 139
audience participation, 45, 47, 49, 205
exclusivity, 51
morality, 123–5, 128, 131–5, 139–40

politics, 76–80, 86–7, 209–10, 238–49
theatre workers, 103
See also *Policey* and policey theory
Theatre Arts Monthly, 110
theatre culture
  costume, 44, 108, 186, 207
  and In-Yer-Face Theatre, 57, 61–4, 68–9
  and space, 203–8
  and Theatre of the Ridiculous, 46–52
theatre historiography. See historiography, theatre
Theatre of the Ridiculous, 8
  and Charles Ludlam, 42–6, 48–9
  emphasis on cultural references, 50–1
  and Ethyl Eichelberger, 43, 45–6
  as heterotopia, 46–52
  history and definition, 41–4
  and Jack Smith, 42–6
  and Maria Montez, 42, 44, 51
  and queerness, 48, 51–2
  use of the term "ridiculous," 48–50
theatre space
  architecture, 110–12, 200–3, 205, 208–9, 211
  color, 110–14
  historio-scenography, 208–13
  history of, 199–208
  and military space, 205, 214n23
  painted scenery, 111, 205–8
  perspective, 191, 205–6, 212–13, 214n23
  rational design, 11, 200, 202, 206–8, 210–11, 213n2
  and Theatre of the Ridiculous, 44–52
theatre studies, 2, 238
Thrift, Nigel, 245, 249, 249n1, 250n17
Tieck, Ludwig, 147n67–8, 147n70
  Puss in Boots, 137–40
Tomlin, Liz, 70n12

transnational justice, 171n10
truth commissions, 157–8, 163, 171n8, 171n10
Tumfart, Barbara, 141n5, 141n9

Upchurch, John, 31–2

Vaccaro, John, 43, 50, 53n21
Varley, Frederick, 119n56
Vercelloni, Matteo and Virgilio
  The Invention of the Western Garden: The History of an Idea, 186–7, 194n25, 195n29
Vince, R. W., 1
violence, 61, 107
  and abstract space, 204
  of AIDS crisis (1980s), 76–9, 81
  in Chile, 159, 168
  murder, 68, 76, 78, 85, 89n11, 157
  narcoviolence, 76–9, 84
  transnational, 8–9, 76–88, 171n10

wages. *See* income, 79, 131
Wakefield, Andre, 145n44
Walach, Dagmar, 141n6
Washington Valdez, Diana, 89n11, 90n20
Westhalle, Vitor, 87, 90n28–9
White, Alan, 36n34
White, Lynn, Jr., 22, 35n12–13
Wild, Christopher, 141n1, 146n62
Wiles, David, 213n5, 214n8
Willebrand, Johann Peter
  True Notion of the Police, 128, 132, 144n28, 145n47
Wit, Saskia de, 188, 195n36
Wölfel, Kurt, 146n55
Wolff, Christian, 125, 142n12
women
  murders of, 78, 89n11, 90n20
  playwrights, 60, 62
work. *See* labor
Worthen, W. B., 246, 250n20
Wright, Thomas, 104

Ybarra, Patricia, 8–9
Yeats, Robert S., 233n4, 233n6

Zarhy-Levo, Yael, 8, 69n3, 70n5–9, 71n45
Zedd, Nick, 51–2
Zelle, Carsten, 146n57
Zerdy, Joanne, 195n41
Zola, Émile, 6
Zozaya, Pilar, 70n16–17, 71n19–29
Zumbusch, Cornelia, 146n54

The manufacturer's authorised representative in the EU is Springer Nature Customer Service Centre GmbH, Europaplatz 3, 69115 Heidelberg, Germany. If you have any concerns regarding our products, please contact ProductSafety@springernature.com

Printed and bound by CPI Group (UK) Ltd, Croydon, CR0 4YY

23/03/2026

02076662-0015